THE ELIZABETHANS AND AMERICA

Ætatis suæ 21. A. 1616.

Matoaks als Rebecka daughter to the mighty Prince Powhatan Emperour of Attanoughkomouck als Virginia converted and baptized in the Christian faith, and Wife to the Worll Mr Tho. Rolff.

POCAHONTAS

THE ELIZABETHANS AND AMERICA

BY

A. L. ROWSE

HARPER & BROTHERS
PUBLISHERS * NEW YORK

Library of Congress Catalog Card Number: 59-10592

To

NANCY ASTOR
THIS TRIBUTE TO HER LOVE
FOR PLYMOUTH AND
VIRGINIA

PREFACE

IT is the greatest honour that has befallen me, and one for which I am deeply grateful, to have been asked by the University of Cambridge to give the first Trevelyan Lectures on their foundation. First and foremost, this gives me the opportunity to acknowledge the debt I owe, in common with other scholars, to a great historian for the inspiration of his work. In a time of confusion of standards, when so many do not know how to judge or what to think, G. M. Trevelyan's work stands out, a beacon for all of us, a model of integrity in scholarship and of accomplishment in art. These qualities in union alone give permanence to historical writing. In particular, I may here record, what I can never repay, the constant encouragement he has given me in my own work, the warmth of interest, the incitement to achieve.

A visit to America in 1957 gave me my subject — an appropriate one, I hope, in view of the family interest and Sir George Otto Trevelyan's masterly work on the American Revolution.

Here in this book is the beginning of the story. It has enabled me to expand the inevitably contracted treatment of the subject in a single chapter of my *Expansion of Elizabethan England*. My aim has been to make clear what the Elizabethans contributed to the making of the greatest of modern nations. Though the story of the Roanoke efforts and the Jamestown colony may be familiar, I have more that is new to offer. For example, though we know that Queen Elizabeth I was interested in everything that concerned America, no-one has hitherto put together the evidence and told us precisely what she did in the matter. The signal services of Sir Ferdinando Gorges towards the cause of New England colonisation have been largely overlooked. We may be too familiar with the story of the Pilgrim Fathers and the founding of Massachusetts — I do not tell it again; but I do not know that anyone has disentangled and brought out the Elizabethan element in all that, or the varied and striking reflection — much richer than is generally realised — of America in the literature of Shakespeare's age.

The nineteenth century was apt to think of the American story as beginning with the *Mayflower*. After the celebrations of the 350th anniversary of Jamestown in 1957, Americans appreciate better that their history goes back to at least the generation before. It is the purpose of this book to bring home that the story really goes back to the generation before Jamestown — to the high-water mark of the Elizabethan age, the 1580's, when everything began together, the madrigals and the war with Spain, the Shakespearean drama and the English colonisation of America, which was to receive in the fulness of time an unimaginable extension. If this book helps to push back the frontier of the Americans' consciousness of their beginnings by a generation to the heart of the Elizabethan age, I shall be content to have made my contribution to American historiography.

Never have I incurred with a book so many obligations in friendly hospitality and help, on both sides of the Atlantic. The idea of the book was first sounded out with the sage advice and encouragement of Mr. Cass Canfield in the congenial surroundings of the Century Club in New York. There, too, Mr. Orville Prescott and Mr. Francis Brown of the *New York Times* made valuable suggestions, from which I have profited. Professor Henry Steele Commager, most generous of friends, settled my title for me on a hospitable visit to Amherst. A chapter of the book was delivered as one of three public lectures at the University of Nebraska, under the kindly guidance of Professor Lane W. Lancaster. I owe my acquaintance with Jamestown to an invitation from Mr. Lawrence W. Towner and the active group of younger historians working at delightful Williamsburg. It is evident how much I owe to the work — as I deeply appreciate the encouragement — of Samuel Eliot Morison, greatest of living American historians, true successor of Prescott and Parkman : opposite number of our own George Macaulay Trevelyan.

At Cambridge it is a pleasure to record the hospitality and conversation of Dr. Trevelyan himself, the Master of Peterhouse, Professor David Knowles, Mr. Kitson Clark and Dr. J. H. Plumb. A number of people showed me fascinating treasures — the Master of St. John's the splendid portraits in his Lodge, Professor Nicholas Mansergh and Mr. Frank Thistlewaite college portraits of the Elizabethan period. The Master of Jesus, Dr. E. M. W. Tillyard, kindly got out a rarity from the Library — John Eliot's presentation copy of his Indian Bible to his old college.

At Oxford the Warden of All Souls generously lent me a rare Donne item; Miss Jean Robertson (Mrs. John Bromley) and Mr. John Buxton made valuable suggestions for my reading. Most of all, I am in the debt of Professor Jack Simmons of the University of Leicester for his unfailing critical sense and scholarship, the generous care with which he has scrutinised the text of this book. For my acquaintance with Suffolk I am obliged to Mr. Norman Scarfe, who took me round the fields and pastures of John Winthrop's Groton.

A. L. ROWSE

Madison, Wisconsin
Lent, 1959

CONTENTS

ILLUSTRATIONS

CHAPTER I

THE CONFLICT FOR THE NEW WORLD: SPANIARDS, PORTUGUESE, FRENCH, ENGLISH

THE discovery of the New World, it has been said, is much the greatest event in the history of the Old. Certainly as that discovery went further and gathered momentum it marked a vast difference between the modern world and the Middle Ages — which, in contemplation, have a certain static, enclosed quality in contrast with the ceaseless dynamism, the expansiveness characteristic of our world. In the title of these lectures I use the word America in the sense popular in England — not so popular in all parts of that Continent — to mean North America, English-speaking America. I am not dealing with Central and South America, though the Elizabethans concerned themselves very considerably with both: another field of the same subject. In this connotation — it is the heart of the subject — the discovery of America ultimately made the fortune of this island, transformed our situation in the world. In Trevelyan's phrase, here was a very taut, efficient little society within an island lying athwart the main seaways from America to North-Western Europe, a situation from which this country profited more and more. As America prospered and became more important, so did we.

We live in the midst of another profound transformation. In the dangers of our time the separateness of our history may be thought of as merging in the general history of the English-speaking peoples, who are drawn closer together by them. Within that community there is a natural shift of power and emphasis to the western side of the Atlantic. But already twice in our lifetime our country's

I

existence has been assured by the preponderant partner. What sort of a future could our small island expect looking out on a world riven between East and West, in the conflicts of giant land-masses, without that assurance? We may indeed think that calling in the New World to redress the balance of the Old takes on a more urgent, a more ominous, meaning today.

We owe this factor in our safety, the very condition of our lives, to the ambition and foresight, the enterprise and persistence, of our common ancestors, the Elizabethans. Their struggle to establish an English foothold on the other side of the Atlantic, their part in extending our language and institutions across the seas, the essential first steps that have led to an English world-community — history can hardly offer us a more significant theme.

But our ancestors arrived on the scene rather belatedly: the Portuguese, the Spaniards, the French were all there before us. It is a striking thought that more than a century elapsed between the time when the Spaniards made their first permanent settlement in America in 1493, and the English made theirs at Jamestown in 1607. The Elizabethan effort, which did not really get going until the second half of the Queen's reign, is all the more impressive: it shows what can be done by a small people, in the right circumstances, with a will.

The Portuguese had already shown what can be done. Theirs was an astounding achievement: a people of a million and a quarter discovered half the world in less than a century. It was amid the excitement of Lisbon, where the riches of the East were unloaded down there by the quays at Belem, that Columbus was caught up by the movement of oceanic discovery going back already half a century to Prince Henry the Navigator. (Henry, on his mother's side of the Lancastrian royal house, had English blood flowing in his veins; so also, by the way, had Vasco da Gama.) The next half-century saw the full flood-tide of Spanish conquest in America: one of the two or three movements of population of decisive importance in the

2

configuration of the modern world. By the middle of the
sixteenth century the Spanish Empire had about achieved
the historic form it retained for so long. And still the
English were nowhere — or rather, they remained at home.

They had, under the first Tudors, with the backing
mainly of the Bristol merchants and the inspiration of the
Cabots, made various sporadic, inadequate, baffled efforts
into and across the Atlantic. The significance of the discovery of the New World was grasped in the circle of Sir
Thomas More, whose brother-in-law John Rastell attempted
such a voyage and in his *Interlude of the Four Elements* wrote
the first English description of America. If only

> they that be Englishmen
> Might have been the first of all
> That there should have taken possession
> And made first building and habitation
> A memory perpetual!

More's *Utopia* offers the first reverberation of genius
out of the New World in the literature of the Old. But
Henrician merchants and voyagers like Thorne and Barlow
were reduced to hoping for an all-English route to the
riches of the East by the seas due north across the Pole.
Some hopes! We may well think that Henry VIII would
have done better to put some of the energy that went into
matrimonial, into Atlantic, enterprises. However, he did
much to create an English navy, the prime condition of
later maritime achievement, and he did procreate Elizabeth :
he could not have done much better.

The Cabot voyages were more important for their
consequences than for what they achieved. In 1497, while
the West Country was convulsed by two Cornish rebellions,
John Cabot set out from Bristol, crossed the Atlantic, made
a landfall near Cape Breton, coasted Nova Scotia and
sighted Newfoundland.[1] On his voyage next year he sailed
southward down the American coast, possibly as far as the
Chesapeake, and then was lost. He left a son, Sebastian,

[1] It is thought now that he made a preliminary reconnaissance in 1496:
see below, p. 159.

3

who had been born at Bristol: a somewhat mysterious and fascinating figure, about whom we know a good deal more — though we should like to know much more still. Going to and fro between the courts of England and Spain, he carried with him a secret: he thought that he had found the North-West Passage that led from the Atlantic into the Pacific and thus to the riches of the Far East. It is possible that on a voyage of 1508–9 he had entered Hudson's Strait and thought that was the opening which tantalised the minds, inspired the efforts and the sacrifices, of generations of Englishmen.[1] Discouraged he went into Spanish service, became pilot-major at Seville, the first school of navigation in the world. Years later the governing circle round the young Edward VI brought him back to this country to organise the efforts to find a passage through by the North-East — efforts which did eventuate in our first opening up trade with Russia through the White Sea and gaining the monopoly of it. The Elizabethan enterprises were continuous with those of the Edwardian circle, in more ways than one; and Sebastian Cabot, now an ancient mariner, was the link between the Mediterranean world of Columbuses and Cabots, Lisbon, Genoa and Venice — the maritime Renaissance — and the Elizabethan seamen.

The importance of John Cabot's voyage of 1497 was that he was the first to discover the mainland of America, while Columbus and the Spaniards were still occupied with the West Indies. When conflict over entry into and possession of territory in the New World became acute, the Elizabethans pounced upon this and made full use of it. Since the Spaniards based their claim to monopoly of the New World upon the right of prior discovery, the Elizabethans rejoined that Cabot had got to the mainland first: the one argument was as good as the other. International law has had to lend a learned ear to such considerations, may be said to have in part risen upon such constructions. One after the other, again and again as the conflict with Spain over the New World grows, the claim is urged, by

[1] *The Voyages of the Cabots*, ed. J. A. Williamson, 228.

John Dee, Hakluyt, Humphrey Gilbert, the government itself: the argument becomes a corner-stone in the Elizabethans' fabric of resistance to Spain's claim to monopoly, in the English demand for the open door to territory not previously occupied by other powers.

It is fairly certain that we should have taken this line and refused to recognise the Papal distribution of the outside world between Spain and Portugal — amended and confirmed by the treaty of Tordesillas (1494) — even if, *per impossibile*, this country had remained Catholic. When, after Cabot's voyage, the Spanish ambassador protested that the new continent belonged to his sovereign, Henry VII disregarded the Papal division of the world. All the same it was a great advantage to it that this country went Protestant, as we see from the reign of Mary and from the example of France. Under Mary, upon the insistence of Philip, English seamen were prohibited from voyages to Guinea, the Portuguese sphere — though they did not recognise the prohibition; [1] and Sebastian Cabot's pension was docked by one-half — it is said at Philip's instance. Voyages to the Arctic and to the North Pole — that was all right with Spain. Where would England have been if it had accepted this prohibition, or even if it had not fought it unitedly, undeviatingly throughout the Elizabethan age? It was unthinkable that England should sit down under this sentence of exclusion: the whole future of the country and of its place in the world was at stake. But on the Spanish side that was the settled determination, to keep everybody else out. Here was one of the two main causes of the long struggle the Elizabethans fought with Spain. The moment Elizabeth came to the throne the government reversed Mary's prohibition upon trading to Guinea; it was something after all to have the government on one's side. At one of Cecil's early interviews with the Spanish ambassador he informed him that the English government did not accept the Pope's claim to make territorial awards. The ambassador observed: 'nothing will

[1] *The Cambridge History of the British Empire*, I. 44.

bring these people to their senses. They claim to have a right to go to all lands or provinces belonging to friendly states without exception.' One sees that conflict was inevitable. As Elizabeth's position grew stronger we observe her coming out more openly on the side of her seamen, fighting their battle politically and diplomatically, as she well knew how. On that issue, with all that was at stake, we may say that the Victorians, Froude and Kingsley, were roughly, if somewhat crudely, right.

And what would have happened if we had not conducted the struggle unitedly, consistently, with Elizabeth's firm grasp of power, we may observe from the case of France. The French were active in America, North, Central and South, before we were and more aggressively.[1] Breton and Norman fishermen were off the coast of Newfoundland as early as 1504, though our own West Country fisherfolk were not far behind. The French were in South America as early, frequenting the coast of Brazil: a whole generation before the voyages of 'old' William Hawkins, founder of the dynasty, from Plymouth in the 1530's, who was merely following in their wake. So, too, with the West Indies: French interlopers were active there a generation before the English, who were quiescent and apt to respect, not the Spanish claim to prior discovery but the fact of effective occupation.

The French kings, however, lacked the will to overseas expansion of Portugal and Spain: they remained faithful to the traditional Mediterranean policy verted towards the Levant, disinterested in North-Western expeditions. The merchants and seamen of the Norman and Breton ports were left to their own devices, and they did remarkably well. They organised from Dieppe the expedition under Verrazano which in 1524 first traversed the Atlantic coast of America, linking the Spanish explorations in Florida with those of the Portuguese brothers Corte-Real (1500–2)

---

[1] In the following paragraphs I am indebted to the standard work of C. A. Julien, *Les Voyages de découverte et les premiers établissements (XVe-XVIe siècles)*, from which I have translated the quotations cited.

around Newfoundland and the coast of Labrador. From the 1520's the Portuguese began to put into practice their determination to destroy the French navigation to Brazil, massacring French sailors caught on expedition there. There was great indignation in Brittany, but Francis I accepted the veto on the navigation.

The 1530's and 1540's witnessed Jacques Cartier of St.-Malo's brilliant expeditions to and explorations of the St. Lawrence — by which route, of course, he hoped to find the expected outlet into the Pacific and the Far East. Francis I was at last interested, and from 1540 pressed in his diplomacy the doctrine of permanent and effective occupation as the only title to possession. He replied to the protests of the Spanish ambassador against Cartier's expeditions: 'the Popes hold spiritual jurisdiction, but it does not lie with them to distribute lands among kings, and the kings of France and other Christians were not summoned when the partition took place'.[1] This line was, however, not backed up by his successors, nor did he maintain it consistently himself. Cartier's third voyage of 1541 was reinforced by the Huguenot Roberval, who pushed on up the rivers as far as Ottawa. But Francis I, involved in renewed war with the Emperor, recalled Roberval, who three years later was killed by Catholics when coming out of a Protestant meeting.

In the 1550's French interlopers were increasingly active in the West Indies. But by the truce of 1556 France accepted Philip II's demand for prohibition of the trade, except by special licence from him — which was not readily forthcoming, we may suppose. The French sea-captains refused to accept this, but they were without the support of their government. Contrast England under Elizabeth: the fact that England went Protestant was an inestimable advantage, it gave us a free hand, we were no longer hampered and held back as the French were. By the definitive treaty of Câteau-Cambrésis (1559), Henri II, in the interests of

---

[1] q. E. G. R. Taylor, 'The Northern Passages', in *The Great Age of Discovery*, ed. A. P. Newton, 215.

7

Catholic unity, renounced all French enterprise in South America. From this time forward Mem de Sá was able to gain effective possession of Brazil for Portugal. The natives supported the French, but were gradually forced to submit. Till the end of the century France maintained a shadowy hold on the coast through the sympathy of the natives, by their own efforts, without any support from the home government. What France lost by the miserable (and orthodox) Valois! The torch passed to the hands of Admiral Coligny, the Huguenot leader, the true and far-seeing exponent of the interests of France. Testu and Thevet, returning from Brazil, dedicated to him their splendid coloured atlas of America. Checkmated in South, he turned his attention to North, America.

Ponce de Leon had given Florida its name in 1513: it was the Spaniards' name for North America, moving upwards from the base of their power in the centre. The years 1539–43 witnessed the expeditions of de Soto and Coronado, in the course of which they explored large areas of what is now the southern part of the United States. But for two decades after Spain did nothing to make her claim to these parts effective. In the years 1562–5 under the inspiration of Coligny as Admiral of France, three colonial expeditions were sent to Florida, the first headed by Jean Ribault and the Breton Protestant Laudonnière. On their return France was in the throes of religious war, with the English intervening on the Huguenot side. Ribault came over to London, where in 1563 he published *The Whole and True Discovery of Terra Florida*. The French settlers, like the English later, failed to cultivate the soil and suffered acute privations. In 1565 John Hawkins on his second voyage visited Fort Caroline and revictualled the French there — one sees the regular pattern of Anglo-French, or at any rate Anglo-Huguenot, co-operation against the monolithic power of Spain. The French, disheartened, were ready to return when a powerful reinforcement under Ribault arrived, sent out by Coligny.

Ribault made a settlement at Saint Augustine, then,

with most of his forces was caught and wrecked in a hurricane. Pedro de Menéndez had been commissioned by Philip to destroy them: here was a divine opportunity. He got the wrecked men to surrender in expectation of terms, and then in three successive massacres wiped them out. Some few French took refuge among the Indians, very few ever got away. Among these was Laudonnière, who not unnaturally took to a life of privateering against the Spaniards, like Drake after a similar experience at the hands of the Spaniards at San Juan de Ulúa a couple of years later. Spanish exultation was characteristic: 'men killed them rather by divine inspiration than by suggestion of any human intelligence'. In that one sees the loathsome spirit of Spanish fanaticism.

M. Julien comments, 'one would seek in vain in the Catholic writings of the time for a single page of protest. By contrast, Protestant polemic raised the debate to another plane and placed before European opinion the problem of the methods and the rights of Spain in America.' All this added fuel to the growing Protestant detestation of Spain, to the campaign against the treachery and ruthlessness of her methods, and the humanitarian propaganda — based on the revelations of her own Bishop Las Casas — against the barbarity of her settlers' treatment of the natives. The shock of these events was felt most acutely in England, still on terms of amity and alliance with Spain. This situation Hawkins was trying to take advantage of, with the official backing of the Queen, to try out a licensed trade with the Spanish colonies in the Caribbean, if possible with Philip's approval — for the colonists certainly needed and wanted the trade.[1]

There is a popular idea that Hawkins began the slave-trade to America. This is, of course, a delusion; I may as well correct it here. The Spaniards brought a few

---

[1] 'The whole of the Indies was an eager market for cloth, weapons, tools and hardware of all sorts, books, paper, wine, oil and slaves. Except for oil and wine, Spanish merchants could not export these goods in sufficient quantities or at competitive prices.' J. H. Parry, 'The New World, 1521–1580', in *The New Cambridge Modern History*, II. 585.

negroes as slaves into Hispaniola as early as 1502.[1] As the
aborigines proved hopeless for labour, a steady stream of
negroes began to flow across the Atlantic. The slave-trade
was no innovation : slaves had been imported into Spain
from West Africa regularly for the past half-century. In
1518 the Spanish Crown granted a sole licence for the
transport of 4000 negroes a year direct from Africa to the
West Indies, and these were supplied by Portuguese merchants who had the monopoly of the African coast-trade.
In 1538 the Emperor Charles V sold the privilege to two
German merchants of Seville for four years. In the second
half of the sixteenth century most of the contractors who
purchased the right were German, Flemish or Italian subjects of the Emperor or of his son. But the supply of slaves
was never enough for the demand, and Portuguese interlopers were the most persistent of those who sought to serve
the market outside the Crown's licence. It was into this
well-established trade that Hawkins sought to insert himself, and, if possible, to gain Philip's licence — since he had
been, in some sense, a servant of Philip's in England. This
may have been too much to expect, and on his third venture
he narrowly escaped destruction. But he was in no sense
an initiator in a trade of which, in any case, the dominant
ethical standards of the sixteenth century did not disapprove.
So let us hear no more of that.

This, then, is the significance of Hawkins's three famous
voyages, on the last of which the young Drake served as
captain of the bark *Judith*. King Philip's answer was the
piece of black treachery in the harbour of San Juan (now
Vera Cruz), when the Spanish Viceroy Don Martín de
Enriques broke his pledged word, Hawkins's ships were
suddenly attacked, his voyage overthrown, over a hundred
of his men lost to imprisonment, the lash, death at the
hands of the Inquisition ; himself returning across the
Atlantic, unspeakable sufferings on board his ship, only a
handful of men left to bring her into Mount's Bay. This

---

[1] Cf. A. P. Newton, *The European Nations in the West Indies, 1493–1688*,
19 foll. ; Sir Alan Burns, *History of the British West Indies*, 123 foll.

experience was never forgotten or forgiven by the English seamen. Drake said that Hawkins lost 70,000 ducats — no reason to disbelieve it. Drake himself followed Laudonnière's example and embarked on his own private war of .reprisals, and certainly made the Spaniards pay for it. It would be absurd to call this piracy, as it is absurd to call Drake a pirate. Of course he was a 'pirate', a *corsario*, to the Spaniards; but there is no reason why we should adopt their point of view. Hakluyt gives us the Elizabethan judgment on that subject: 'whoever is conversant with the Portugal and Spanish writers shall find that they account all other nations for pirates, rovers and thieves which visit any heathen coast that they have sailed by or looked on'.[1]

All this had a powerful effect in swinging this country away from the Spanish alliance. It stored up hatred of the Spaniards among the most nationalistic of peoples. The Queen took her own revenge most effectively, with her arrest of the Spanish treasure-ships that took refuge in her West Country ports in 1569. She 'borrowed' the money from its Genoese bankers — and paid it back later; but for want of it Alba's troops in the Netherlands mutinied, and the process of losing the Low Countries for Philip was well begun. The diplomatic revolution of the sixteenth century, the transformation of the traditional Anglo-Spanish alliance into hostility, was set in train. The struggle over entry to the New World was one of the two main factors; but this in turn was a pre-condition of our gaining a share in the New World.

The French were driven out. They did send a reprisal expedition under Dominic de Gourgues, which surprised three small Spanish forts. The Spaniards had massacred their victims, they declared, 'not as Frenchmen, but as heretics'. The French now hanged their prisoners, 'not as Spaniards, but as murderers'. But they did not dare to attack San Agustín, henceforth the base guarding Spain's outlet from the Caribbean, keystone of the Florida Channel. Catharine de Medici would willingly have taken advantage

[1] q. Burns, 163.

11

of a *fait accompli* that gave France a strategic position in Florida, athwart Philip's treasure-route. What *he* wanted was the destruction of Coligny, and in the Massacre of St. Bartholomew she procured it for him. The confusion of French policy, the inner conflicts of the religious wars, made it impossible to follow any consistent course and lost France her opportunities in America.

Julien sums up, 'with Coligny there disappeared the only Frenchman of the century who fully understood the importance of the policy of expansion and of the struggle against the Spanish and Portuguese empires'. France experienced a double defeat in Brazil and Florida, where she had 'every chance of success. . . . In the event France retained none of the territories she had explored or occupied.' And the Treaty of Vervins at the end of the century (1598) came back to the position of Câteau-Cambrésis midway through : Spain made not the slightest concession on trade with America.

We shall see how the English fared by contrast : how national unity and consistent political leadership enabled them to succeed where France failed — except for Canada, after peace was secured at the turn of the century, and where the Bourbon Henri IV inherited the Huguenot enthusiasm for colonisation.

But we must draw attention to what the English learned from the French in these matters, from their experience and example, the knowledge they had gathered about the New World, alluring, exciting, dangerous. It seems that the idea of American colonisation came to us out of that Huguenot circle. Serving together at Le Havre in 1562 were Richard Eden, Thomas Stukeley, Humphrey Gilbert.[1] Eden, a Cambridge man, was one of our first important geographers. Secretary to Cecil, he was one of the Northumberland circle active in forwarding English expansion. In Mary's reign, a member of Philip's household, he translated the sections of Peter Martyr's famous *Decades* dealing with the New

[1] Cf. *The Voyages and Colonising Enterprises of Sir Humphrey Gilbert*, ed. D. B. Quinn (Hakluyt Soc.), I. 5.

World, and then was deprived of his post for heresy. In 1562 he took service with the Huguenot leader, the Vidame de Chartres, and spent the next ten years in France, greatly extending his geographical knowledge in those circles. Brought back to England by the Massacre of St. Bartholomew, he continued his work of translation, passing on his knowledge : a factor in the spate of geographical publication that poured forth in the 1570's and 1580's.[1]

Jean Ribault, as we have seen, came over to England in 1563, where he was already well known, for he, too, had been in service in the Northumberland circle. He was well received by the Queen, who encouraged the project of an Anglo-French expedition under Ribault and Stukeley to occupy the site of the first French colony that had been abandoned. When Ribault returned to France the Queen gave Stukeley licence to plant a colony, but he — a light-headed adventurer whose adventures ultimately carried him beyond the boundaries of coherence and sense — preferred a marauding expedition at sea. Next year, 1564, the proposal was for Hawkins, a very different kind of man, who 'desired the name of an orderly person and had always hated folly', to establish a colony. In this he was anticipated by Laudonnière — as we have seen, Hawkins came to the help of the French there in 1565. After the disaster to Ribault and his colonists, the English interest was at once reflected in an account of it published in 1566. But the Spaniards had settled the issue in blood down there on the Florida coast.

The fact is that in these middle decades of the century there was something like an Anglo-French Channel community, particularly in evidence at the western end of the Channel, between Protestants on both sides of it. When one was in trouble, in opposition or beyond the law, the other came to the rescue. In Mary's reign Killigrews, Tremaynes, Carews, coming out in open defiance of Mary's Catholicism and the Spanish marriage, took refuge in France. In Elizabeth's reign they all provided intimate

[1] Cf. E. G. R. Taylor, *Tudor Geography, 1485–1583*, 20-3, 37.

members of her Court-circle. One of the Champernownes, cousins of the Gilberts and Raleghs, made a Huguenot marriage, to a Montgoméry. The young Walter Ralegh got his military apprenticeship serving under Huguenot command for several years in France : he, too, seems to have been brought back by St. Bartholomew. To the end of his life he retained French associations. When he came into the bright sunlight, and the cash, of high favour with the Queen he maintained the Huguenot artist Le Moyne while he did his drawings of Florida.[1] Hakluyt, one of whose motives in becoming chaplain to the ambassador in Paris was to learn all he could from French geographical circles, translated Laudonnière's account of the French enterprises in Florida and dedicated it to Ralegh. When the English got going, with their first colonial attempt in Virginia, the compliment was returned : Charles de l'Écluse, the eminent botanist and friend of Philip Sidney, translated Hariot's account of Virginia for the famous European publication on America of De Bry, which Hakluyt inspired.

Similarly Hawkins and Drake had close French associations, naturally enough from Plymouth, which had its Protestant opposite-number in La Rochelle, with which it was closely connected. When Drake, quite young, returned to the West Indies to recoup himself and Hawkins for their losses at San Juan de Ulúa by robbing the treasure-train outside Nombre de Dios, he did so in association with a French captain and crew. On a not dissimilar plane we find a community of ideas between the distinguished Huguenot leader Duplessis-Mornay and Philip Sidney, whom he wanted for his son-in-law. In 1581 Duplessis-Mornay urged a *coup* against the Isthmus of Darien, thus capturing a route to the East — the idea that haunted the minds of Drake and John Oxenham, who died in pursuit of it. These belonged to the stock of strategic ideas common to the western Protestants in their struggle with the Catholic colossus which would impose a complete embargo on their entry into, or share in, the New World. With the struggle

[1] Cf. *The Roanoke Voyages, 1584–90*, ed. D. B. Quinn, 546, 548.

becoming more intense, and France counted out by civil war for the rest of the century — maintained of course by Philip and necessitating our intervention for our own safety — in the hazards of that dangerous age not unlike our own, with a world riven in two by the struggle between Reformation and Counter-Reformation, Protestant and Catholic, the chances in North America fell to England. But it was certain they would have to be fought for.

CHAPTER II

QUEEN ELIZABETH I AND AMERICA

ELIZABETH I was the inheritrix and the continuer of the impulses and new leads coming from the Edwardian circle. She had been educated along with her brother by Cambridge tutors, of the second generation of the Renaissance impulse in England, Protestant Reformers; where her sister Mary had been brought up by Oxford tutors, of the first generation of humanists, Catholic Reformers. Elizabeth's mind was not enclosed within a dream of medieval faith; hers was an extrovert intelligence in touch with everything of interest happening in the real world of events and affairs. And not least in the New World. She was interested in everything that concerned America — its newness and strangeness, its occupants and products, its vast potential riches (she had a very Tudor nose for that aspect of things: not for nothing was she a granddaughter of that canny Welshman, Henry VII). She was interested, in several senses of the word, in the voyages and the voyagers, in the geography of America and the geographers, in the capital question of English colonisation, above all, in the political struggle with Spain for a place in that New World.

But — I hope I may be pardoned for saying — no-one has yet disentangled her share in these activities, made out precisely what her contribution was to making North America English. It was a major one. Strangely enough the historian of the age, Froude, did her a grave injustice in his famous History. Right enough about the seamen, he was vastly wrong about the Queen. Quite simply, they were not in disjunction, they were complementary to each other; the Queen always gave them her support, sometimes her instigation — in the cardinal instance of Drake's

Voyage round the World, against the wishes of her minister Lord Burghley, by then a sated power, gone rather conservative. It will be a good thing to rectify an historic injustice: I shall try to estimate her contribution politically and diplomatically, her financial interest in the voyages, her support for the idea of colonisation and of its exponents.

Let us look, first, at her contacts with the new cosmographers, so much involved in these enterprises, and with the seamen.

An idiosyncratic figure in this circle was John Dee, mathematician, cosmographer, astrologer.[1] A Fellow of St. John's, Cambridge, he became one of the original Fellows of Trinity, whence he went over to Louvain and made the acquaintance of the foremost Flemish geographers of the day, Gemma Frisius, Mercator, Ortelius. He went on to Paris where his lectures on Euclid, he said, made a striking impression. Dee was a Welshman: no-one ever possessed more recognisably Celtic characteristics, the touchiness and suspicion, the acuteness and imagination, the originality along with a certain haphazardness, the tendency to go over the borderline. He belonged by birth to that cousinage from the Welsh Border that surrounded the Queen — Parrys and Cecils, Aubreys and Lewises. The Queen knew him well and would stop at his door at Mortlake when passing by; she always treated him with favour, and sometimes cash. He cast the horoscope for her coronation day: no-one can say that it did not turn out well.

All his life Dee was concerned — among many other things, mathematics, the problems of navigation, spirits good and evil — with the over-riding problem of a route to the riches of the East. Could the English discover a route of their own, free of the Spaniards and Portuguese, by North-East or North-West? Over a period of thirty years he was connected with every voyage from England searching for a North-East Passage — a by-product of which

---

[1] The best account of his work is in E. G. R. Taylor, *Tudor Geography, 1485–1583*, cc. v, vi, vii. Cf. also C. F. Smith, *John Dee, 1527–1608*.

was the very profitable trade with Russia. (He thought that, once past the Vaigatz Islands, the Siberian coast sloped away south and all would be easy! He was apt to take insufficient account of obstacles.) But he was equally interested in the North-West Passage, its problems and outlets and, that brought him up against the American Continent.

He was, perhaps, the first to write about these problems in a series of what he called 'Atlantical Discourses', which remained, like a lot of his work, unfinished and unpublished. (He was one of those . . .) He thought that the term in general use then for America, 'West Indies', was misleading; if he could have had his way America would have become known as Atlantis.

John Dee inhabited an exciting, and sometimes tortured, world of fact and dream, as so many earlier and later scientists have done — we have only to think of Newton himself. He dreamed of a British Empire based on the sea: he was the originator of the phrase — a Welshman, the word with him is always Britain, not England. Thalassokratia Britanniké — his writings are full of such megalomaniac phrases. He planned a work in several volumes on this British Empire, only the first of which was published, the *Pety Navy Royall*, dedicated to Sir Christopher Hatton, the frontispiece proudly displaying the Queen seated in state in the ship of empire. Strange to say — and everything about Dee is strange — the megalomaniac proved prophetically right: perhaps he was not a clairvoyant for nothing after all.

In the discussions that resulted in granting Sir Humphrey Gilbert the patent under which the first English colonies in America were planted, Dee was drawn in to advise about the Queen's title to North America. A Celt, he was not content to go back to Cabot, he went back to King Arthur. (He named his son, by the way, Arthur.) John Dee held that the Friseland of the medieval Zeni brothers — apparently a deformation of Iceland — Greenland and Estotiland to the west of it, perhaps Newfoundland, had been colonised by King Arthur and hence were rightful appanages of the British Monarchy.[1] These features are prominently displayed on the map he drew to accompany his summary of the Queen's title. At the end of his manuscript *Great and Rich Discoveries* he transcribes Mercator's story of the westerners arriving in Norway, towards the end of the middle ages, from the colonies planted in the west by King Arthur. This may well be a reflection of the fact that in the fourteenth century the settlements in western Greenland were abandoned. To this Dee added the Welsh tradition of the discoveries of the Atlantic coast by Prince Madoc in the twelfth century; and this he imparted to Hakluyt, who duly incorporated it in his work, on the Elizabethan principle — never throw away an argument.

We read in Dee's Diary that he spoke with the Queen herself as to her title in two audiences he had with her at Windsor in the last week of November 1577.[2] He also spoke with Secretary Walsingham and Hatton, two leaders of the expansionist school in her Council, patrons of the seamen and colonisers. Dee had further conference with the Queen at Richmond for two hours in October 1578. Two years later he was dealing with Gilbert for a share in his grant of American discovery, and 'September 10th, Sir Humphrey Gilbert granted me my request to him, for the royalties to the North above the parallel of the 50th degree of latitude'.[3] This, as so often in Dee's life, was a purely notional acquisition, a chimerical gain. However, there were the consolations of the Queen's favour. A week later we have a vivid close-up of her: 'September 17th, the Queen came from Richmond in her coach, the higher way of Mortlake field, and when she came right against the church she turned down toward my house. And when she was against my garden in the field she stood there a good while, and then came into the street at the great gate of the field, where she espied me at my door making obeisance

---

[1] Cf. *The Private Diary of Dr. John Dee*, ed. J. O. Halliwell (Camden Soc.), 4; and cf. E. G. R. Taylor, 'The Northern Passages', in *The Great Age of Discovery*, ed. A. P. Newton, 199 foll.

[2] *Ibid.* On 15 August, he writes, 'I went toward Norwich with my work of *Imperium Britannicum*'.   [3] *Ibid.* 8-10.

to her Majesty. She beckoned her hand for me; I came to her coach-side, she very speedily pulled off her glove and gave me her hand to kiss; and, to be short, asked me to resort to her Court, and to give her to weet [know] when I came there.'

A fortnight later, October 3, 'at eleven of the clock before noon, I delivered my two rolls of the Queen's Majesty's title unto herself in the garden at Richmond, who appointed after dinner to hear further of the matter. Therefore between one and two afternoon, I was sent for into her Highness' Privy Chamber, where the Lord Treasurer also was, who did seem to doubt much that I had or could make the argument probable for her Highness's title so as I pretended.' Then, 'Oct. 7th, on Friday I came to my Lord Treasurer, and he being told of my being without, and also I standing before him at his coming forth, did not or would not speak to me, I doubt not of some new grief conceived.' Lord Burghley's disapproval gave Dee bad dreams, which he noted, full of persecution-mania.

It is fairly clear that Burghley regarded Dr. Dee much as Hotspur regarded that other Welshman, Glendower, who claimed

> all the courses of my life do show
> I am not in the roll of common men.
> Where is he living, clipped in with the sea
> That chides the banks of England, Scotland, Wales,
> Which calls me pupil, or hath read to me?
> And bring him out that is but woman's son
> Can trace me in the tedious ways of art
> And hold me pace in deep experiments . . .
> I can call spirits from the vasty deep.

> *Hotspur.* Why, so can I, or so can any man;
> But will they come when you do call for them?

(The interesting thing is that they would not come at Dr. Dee's bidding, without the aid of his medium, Edward Kelly.) It is funny, however, to see patient old Lord Burghley, who was actually more like a Polonius, in the impatient rôle of a Hotspur. It took all the Queen's graciousness to console the Doctor for his treatment at Lord Burghley's hands. She came over to Mortlake to comfort him, called on horseback at his door, 'and withall told me that the Lord Treasurer had greatly commended my doings for her title, which he had to examine, which title in two rolls he had brought home two hours before'. And so on, all very consoling to the wounded pride of a Welshman. More to the point, on All Souls' Day, the Lord Treasurer sent him a haunch of venison. However, even astrologers can hardly live by venison alone.

No terrestrial preferment, nothing to live by, came Dee's way, though the Queen was willing enough and made various suggestions : it seems the Lord Treasurer stood in the way. Once, when she was leaving Richmond on horseback, Walter Ralegh put her in mind of the old man; 'she said, "quod defertur non aufertur", and gave me her right hand to kiss'.[1] Once and again, she sent him a gift, forty angels or twenty from her own purse. At last, Dee accepted better prospects from the Continent and went off to raise the spirits with Edward Kelly in Prague. When he returned, the Queen did find a berth for him after all : she made him Warden of Manchester College, so that he spent his last years in security, if not exactly in the odour of sanctity.

These discussions and consultations in the 1570's had their practical issue in Frobisher's three voyages to the North-West in 1576, 1577 and 1578. As is well known, their promise of further geographical discovery in that region was deflected into the search for gold-bearing ore. These voyages were set forth by a combination of the forward school in the Court-circle with a body of merchants in the City. The leading figures among the Queen's intimates in these activities were Leicester and Walsingham — followed by young Philip Sidney, nephew of one, son-in-law of the other, and his friend Sir Edward Dyer.[2]

Dyer, courtier and poet, a favourite with the Queen

---

[1] *The Private Diary of Dr. John Dee*, ed. J. O. Halliwell (Camden Soc.), 20, 21.
[2] Cf. *Cal. S.P. Col., East Indies, 1513–1616*, 11, 23, 25, 37, 43, 46.

and evidently a charming man, is a characteristic and a sympathetic figure in these concerns. A Somerset man by origin, his father, steward in Henry VIII's household, got considerable grants of monastic lands there when the going was good.[1] The father built up a large estate, which the son spent on Court life. Edward Dyer was a good friend to Dee, whom he visited at his house along with Leicester and Philip Sidney. Dyer helped to circulate the appeal at Court for funds to back Frobisher's first voyage in quest of the North-West Passage. (Dee also tells us that he was introduced by Dyer to Humphrey Gilbert's *Discourse* on this subject.) Among the courtiers who subscribed were Leicester, Warwick, Walsingham and Sidney; among the merchants, Sir Thomas Gresham, Anthony Jenkinson, Michael Lok, Alderman Bond. Frobisher made a promising reconnoitre of the channel between Greenland and the coast of Labrador, and came back with specimens of supposedly auriferous ore.

The second voyage was then a larger and more enthusiastic affair, the Queen herself becoming much the largest shareholder, with a venture of £1000 — no doubt mainly represented by a ship of hers. Lord Admiral Clinton, Sir William Winter of the Navy Board, Walsingham and Pembroke made large investments (from £175 to £100); the Queen's cousin, her Lord Chamberlain Hunsdon, Dyer, Sir Humphrey Gilbert, Philip Sidney and his sister the Countess of Pembroke made smaller investments (of £50 and £25). On the return of the ships laden with ore, of which there were optimistic reports, the Court circle very much increased its stake for the third voyage set forth in 1578. We gather from Hubert Languet's correspondence that Philip Sidney would have liked to accompany Frobisher, how much he was excited by the 'marvellous story' of the second voyage, exploring 'that sea which he supposes to wash the north part of America'.[2] Interested in the cargoes

---

[1] R. M. Sargent, *At the Court of Queen Elizabeth : The Life and Lyrics of Sir Edward Dyer*, 40 foll.

[2] M. W. Wallace, *The Life of Sir Philip Sidney*, 195-6.

JOHN DEE

of ore brought back, Sidney asked Languet for any information he had regarding the reduction of ores. That severe Protestant, however, much disapproved of the craze for gold. Sidney continued to be interested in American projects, though behindhand with his subscription for the last voyage. The Queen increased her venture to £1350 — and was anxious that the voyage should be pressed forward.[1] Pembroke increased his stake; so did Walsingham and Philip Sidney — which neither of them could well afford. Others came forward — the gambling young Earl of Oxford for a large sum, all of which he lost; Hatton, Cumberland, Ralph Lane, even John Dee subscribed for a £25 share. The sage Lord Burghley put himself down for £100, but he was careful not to pay up.

The cold eyes of King Philip, who watched from that small study in the Escorial so much of what was going on all over the world, were upon the venture. He was much concerned at this incursion into his New World. He urged his ambassador in London, Mendoza, to make every effort to obtain a chart of Frobisher's voyage, though his own opinion was 'it is difficult to believe that in so cold a region there can be any richness of metal'.[2] Mendoza replied that he was hopeful of obtaining a chart through his spies. After several long talks with 'these people' at Court, he found that 'the only way for me to keep my temper is to bear in mind that I am one of the school of the Duke [Alba] and a soldier of his'. At an audience of the Queen, she adroitly raised the issue of Philip's denial of toleration in the Netherlands as the cause of his troubles there, and asked sensibly, 'what did it matter to your Majesty if they went to the Devil in their own way?' Mendoza's reply was the shocked reaction of stupid Spanish orthodoxy: these things were ordained of God, it was not in the power of princes to restrict religion, that is, Catholicism, etc. (On that sort of argument, perhaps it was ordained of God that England should be Protestant?) However, in September

[1] *Cal. S.P. Dom., 1547–1580,* 586.
[2] *Cal. S.P. Spanish, 1568–1579,* 594, 599, 601, 614, 664.

he was able to send on a chart of the voyage, which came safely to Philip's hand, along with some of the ore. After prolonged assays, it all turned out to be of no value, the voyages a dead loss. Philip could well afford to laugh — except that he was never known to laugh openly. Baffled in that direction, the English were not now going to give up : they turned to others.

The fact was that the conflict with Spain for a share in America was coming into the open and, joined with that over the Netherlands, the freedom of which was indispensable to our security, brought on the war. Drake's Voyage round the World announced the arrival of a new power on the world-scene ; it immensely raised the prestige of England on the threshold of the conflict, and helped to produce it — as the Queen knew it might, and took the risk.

The more one knows about that wonderful voyage the more wonderful it becomes, not less. What Bartholomew Diaz had done in rounding the Cape, Vasco da Gama in crossing the Indian Ocean, Magellan in spanning the Pacific — Drake accomplished in one voyage and came safe home to Plymouth Sound. The first English circumnavigator of the globe, he became the most celebrated Englishman of the day, with an aura about him for friend and foe alike. The *Golden Hind*, the ship of perhaps some 150 tons in which he accomplished it, was laid up at Deptford, one of the regular sights of London, until her timbers fell apart. It is pleasant to think that out of those timbers were made a chair that now reposes in the Bodleian Library, a table that stands in Middle Temple Hall. In addition to the riches she brought back in her hold for the Queen — nearly half a million in specie — Drake came back with an immense amount of new information about the wonders of the world, about America, the Pacific, the possibilities opening up for this country in the Far East. No wonder the Queen was closeted with him for hours alone, day after day, on his return. He presented to her the log-book of the *Golden Hind*, the daily record of that marvellous journey during the three years 1577–80. What would we not give to possess it today — treasure-trove of the age we should value more than anything, except, say, the letters of Shakespeare? This precious book disappeared, along with many other treasures of the Crown, either in the deplorable Civil War, or the fire at Whitehall in 1694 — along with the maps and charts of the New World, Cabot's among others, that used to hang, suggestive to the imagination, in the Queen's Privy Gallery.

What we do know now is that to the Queen alone belongs the decision to set forth that voyage — against the wishes of her Lord Treasurer, Lord Burghley. That is the significance of Drake's first question on coming into Plymouth Sound: 'Is the Queen alive?' It would have been the worse for him if she had died in the interval. The voyage worked out far more successfully than anyone could have expected — except perhaps Drake himself, always a sanguine, confident man; but in some respects it worked out differently. I do not think we need take so seriously the loss of the draft for the Voyage, for I suspect that a good deal of room was left for variation and flexibility, in the English manner. And certainly several objectives came together in it. It might very easily have been overthrown: that was the significance of Drake's execution of Thomas Doughty. He was Burghley's man in the expedition, placed there to hamper its operations: he might have succeeded, had it not been for Drake's determination, with the Queen's backing. He sailed with her commission: nothing vexed him more than to be referred to as a pirate: he was the Queen of England's officer, he insisted, and showed one of his Spanish prisoners off the coast of Peru his commission.[1]

One purpose of the Voyage stems from Richard Grenville's project of a few years before for an expedition into the South Seas, to seek the southern continent they imagined to be there, Terra Australis.[2] Grenville had pointed out, perhaps

---

[1] H. R. Wagner, *Sir Francis Drake's Voyage around the World* (San Francisco, 1926), is wrong on this point, p. 25, as in others of his interpretations.
[2] Cf. my *Sir Richard Grenville of the* Revenge, c. v.

disingenuously, that it would merely pass by those countries already in the occupation of Christian princes. Anyhow, under the influence of a temporary lull in relations with Spain, the Queen countermanded his voyage. What she would not permit to Grenville as a private venture, she permitted three years later to Drake as a quasi-official one, with herself as the dominant partner. Sir Christopher Hatton preferred Drake's suit to her and procured him an audience.[1] On emerging from the Straits of Magellan into the Pacific, Drake christened his ship the *Pelican* anew as the *Golden Hind*: it was Hatton's crest. Drake afterwards said that on parting the Queen addressed him these words: 'Drake! so it is that I would gladly be revenged on the King of Spain for divers injuries that I have received'. I see no reason to disbelieve this: it has the authentic ring. He added, 'her Majesty gave me special commandment that of all men my Lord Treasurer should not know it'. This sounds by no means improbable. In fact, what we know now from English and Spanish sources all hangs together.

There was indeed some secret between the Queen and Drake which has never transpired: some think it relates to the idea of a descent on the Isthmus of Darien and cutting the pipe-line of Spanish treasure there. Like enough: it was an idea that came to the fore in these years. In the preliminary discussions that were kept very secret — on the voyage out, no-one knew where they were bound for — the objectives were greatly extended, and its destination to the Moluccas. There was included an idea of looking for the Pacific end of the North-West Passage, the supposed Strait of Anian which should debouch somewhere about the coast of British Columbia — and perhaps of returning by that.

From very early it had been resolved that 'her Majesty be made privy to the truth of the voyage'.[2] With all the implications of a first incursion into the Spanish-Portuguese preserve of the Pacific, and with the intention of reprisals

---

[1] J. S. Corbett, *Drake and the Tudor Navy*, I. 205, 208.

[2] Cf. E. G. R. Taylor, 'The Missing Draft Project of Drake's Voyage of 1577–1580', in *Geographical Journal*, January 1930, 46 foll.; and 'More Light on Drake 1577–1580', in *Mariner's Mirror*, 1930, 134 foll.

against Philip, it was decided that the voyage could not be
left to a private syndicate. It became an official affair,
sponsored by the Queen and the forward party in her
Council, Lord Burghley sitting back and absenting himself,
well aware what it boded. As such its intentions could be
kept secret — as to some extent they have remained ever
since. The Queen contributed her ship, the *Swallow*, which
represented her investment. Among other investors were
her Lord Admiral Lincoln and Sir William Winter of the
Navy Board; Leicester, Walsingham and Hatton; Drake
whose investment represented his confidence in himself and
was as much as £1000, and John Hawkins £500: those
two were still out to recoup themselves for what they had
lost at San Juan. And so Drake left Plymouth Sound one
December day in 1577, bound for the other side of the
world; his mariners thought they were bound for Alexandria.

His colleague John Winter in the *Elizabeth* was beaten
back in the Straits of Magellan, and forced by his crew to
turn home again. While there he did take possession of
Tierra del Fuego in the name of Queen Elizabeth: I leave
that consideration to the international lawyers in the dispute that is still maintained over the Falkland Islands.
Drake was left to go forward on his own. He made a feint
to the west to look out for the coast of Terra Australis; then
went up the coast of South America, off which he captured
the treasure-ship the *Cacafuego*, then sailed north to California, where he landed and took possession in the name
of the Queen. The various accounts all agree about what
happened.[1] The native Indians were exceedingly friendly:
'they are a people of a tractable, free and loving nature,
without guile or treachery' — evidently inhabitants of a
golden age: we see how the myth of the noble savage, the
state of nature and other concepts of literature and political
theory grew up. To Drake's embarrassment — for he was
a firm Protestant, who always travelled with Foxe's *Book
of Martyrs* on board — the native Californians took to
worshipping the English as gods. The braves sought among

---

[1] *The World Encompassed*, ed. Sir Richard Temple, 51 foll.

the seamen till they found a god whose face pleased them, 'which commonly were the youngest of us'. It was all very understandable: the Elizabethans were not instructed in anthropology.

As a sign of good-will and a peace-offering the Indians came down bringing baskets 'filled with an herb which they called Tabah'. And they offering their obedience, Drake took 'the sceptre, crown and dignity of the said country into his hand, wishing nothing more than that it had lain more fitly for her Majesty to enjoy, and that the riches and treasures thereof (wherewith in the upland countries it abounds) might with as great conveniency be transported to the enriching of her kingdom here at home as it is in plenty to be attained there. . . . Before we went from thence our General caused to be set up a monument of our being there, as also of her Majesty's and successors' right and title to that kingdom: namely, a plate of brass, fast nailed to a great and firm post; whereon is engraven her Grace's name and the day and year of our arrival there, and of the free giving up of the province and kingdom, both by the king and people, into her Majesty's hands; together with her Highness' picture and arms, in a piece of sixpence current English money, showing itself by a hole made of purpose through the plate, underneath was likewise en-graven the name of our General. . . . This country our General named Albion and that for two causes; the one in respect of the white banks and cliffs which lie toward the sea; the other that it might have some affinity in name also with our own country, which was sometime so called.' It is nice to think of California as New Albion.

Drake proceeded north along the coast of Oregon until he came abreast of British Columbia, looking for the outlet of a North-West Passage. But, his chaplain Francis Fletcher wrote, 'we conjecture that either there is no passage at all through these northern coasts (which is most likely) or, if there be, that yet it is unnavigable. . . . Though we searched the coast diligently even unto the 48th degree, yet found we not the land to trend so much as one point in any place towards the east, but running on continually north-west, as if it went directly to meet with Asia.' They concluded, correctly, that 'the large spreading of the Asian and American continent which (somewhat northward of these parts), if they be not fully joined, yet seem they to come very near one to the other'.

So Drake returned to a harbourage just north of present San Francisco, thought to be the present Drake's Bay, for careening his ship before the long haul across the Pacific, upon which he disappeared.

Meanwhile the Queen at home had to face the music. Drake's depredations on the coast of Peru had made a great noise in the world and caused much indignation in Spain. When Winter came back in the summer of 1578 he was received with favour by the Queen, and was closeted alone with her to give her an account of the voyage.[1] In August next year Philip sent Mendoza reports of the events on their coast from the Viceroys of Peru and New Spain, 'which certainly disclose a very strange affair'. The impassive Philip was a master of understatement. Drake was expected home after two years — he was a year overdue before he eventually returned, and the Queen was growing anxious for news. She also wanted to know the purpose of the preparations in Spanish ports: Philip was on the eve of his conquest of Portugal, by which he gained an ocean-going fleet and added a second empire to his own. The situation was growing very dangerous: England was coming face to face with a world-empire, the balance of power in Europe quite thrown out with France paralysed by civil war.

Elizabeth wanted to find out where she stood. In January 1580 she invited Mendoza to a bear-baiting that had been laid on for her.[2] He wanted to know her attitude to Drake's piracies. She countered by asking the purpose of Philip's preparations at sea. At last she demanded with emphasis, 'Ut quid tot sumptus?' — the discussion being

[1] *Cal. S.P. Spanish, 1568–1579*, 602, 683.
[2] *Cal. S.P. Spanish, 1580–1586*, 3, 7, 10.

carried on, of course, in extemporary Latin.[1] Several times
Mendoza demanded another audience. At last the Queen
granted him one on 20 February, going out of her way to
be gracious by descending from her dais and coming forward six paces to meet him, Mendoza reported to Philip,
she was 'so much alarmed about the fleet, no doubt accused
by her own evil conscience'. Before he could say a word
she asked whether he had come as a herald to declare war
upon her. Mendoza replied that it was she apparently who
was going to war with all the world. Elizabeth returned
that she 'would never make war upon your Majesty unless
you began it first'. She pointed out that he already had
a war with the Moslems on his hands in the Mediterranean,
besides the rebellion of his subjects in the Netherlands to
deal with. She had always done her best for the tranquillity
of the Netherlands and to prevent France getting a footing
there. Mendoza complained of the plundering of Spanish
ships, especially on the American treasure-route. The
Queen immediately seized on this to ask if there were news
of any such ships returned. Mendoza was only able to
inform her, No — but he was sure they were being dealt
with as they deserved, by being sent to the bottom. The
Queen kept him in conversation for three hours, trying to
get out of him the extent of Philip's preparations, their
purpose and direction. Mendoza was satisfied that he had
increased her alarm by saying that he could guess the purpose of so great an enterprise: 'this frightened her more
than before and she was very amiable'. Mendoza was a
simple sort of man, who believed in frightening women.
He never understood that here was one who, the more
amiable, was the more dangerous and was not to be
frightened.

Mendoza had his spies in the West Country ports waiting for Drake's return, and one day in September Drake
was suddenly there with his cargo of treasure intact. His
return presented a very awkward problem for the government; but the spontaneous reaction in the country to his

[1] 'To what purpose such great charges?'

astonishing exploit, the pride in his achievement, his nation-
wide popularity, and behind all this the support of the
Queen, settled the matter. She received him in high
favour, saw him much alone, walked with him often in the
palace-garden, always noticed him in public. It was expected that she would knight him when she went down
to Deptford to visit the *Golden Hind*. And so she did,
contriving to lose a purple garter in the proceedings to
heighten good spirits, and handing the French ambassador
the sword to do it with, by way of associating France a
little in the event. The popular idea is that Drake got all
the treasure. On the contrary, the bullion all came to the
Queen, who put it safely in the Tower : she used it judi-
ciously to keep going resistance to Philip in the Netherlands,
so that he could never concentrate all his resources against
us. She graciously accepted Drake's presents of jewels, and
allowed him £10,000 reward, out of half a million, for his
eminent services. She decreed that the other shareholders
should receive as much again as they had invested : a
good 100 per cent. The respectable Lord Treasurer,
Mendoza said, refused ten bars of fine gold with 300 crowns
to each of them.[1] Whether this was true or no, Lord
Burghley was a virtuous man.

Out of this juncture, the protests and discussions it
provoked, there came a classic statement of the English
government's position in regard to America — in which no
doubt that wise intellect had a powerful share. Camden
had access to his official papers and reports it thus. 'The
Spaniards have brought these evils on themselves by their
injustice towards the English, whom, *contra ius gentium*, they
have excluded from commerce with the West Indies [that
is America]. The Queen does not acknowledge that her
subjects and those of other nations may be excluded from
the Indies on the claim that these have been donated to
the King of Spain by the Pope, whose authority to invest
the King of Spain with the New World she does not recognise. . . . This donation of what does not belong to the

[1] *Cal. S.P. Spanish, 1580–1586*, 75.

donor and this imaginary right of property ought not to prevent other princes from carrying on commerce in those regions or establishing colonies there in places not inhabited by the Spaniards. Prescription without possession is not valid. Moreover all are at liberty to navigate that vast ocean [the Pacific], since the use of the sea and air are common to all. No nation or private person can have a right to the ocean, for neither the course of nature nor public usage permits any occupation of it.'[1] It is the most succinct statement of the English position for which the struggle was now engaged.

The purpose of the struggle was to gain a footing in America : the idea of colonisation comes to the fore. Here we can only briefly indicate the Queen's part in all that; though we must remember that most of it went in discussions in Council, with her ministers and members of her Court-circle, audiences granted to private persons, interest, encouragement, inspiration. Of all this there would be only slight traces in written documents.

The person who undertook to carry out the idea of colonisation in America, as to which there had been so much discussion and so many abortive gestures in the direction of it, was Humphrey Gilbert. And from the Crown's patent he was granted in 1578 sprang the ultimate achievement. That patent gave him licence for six years 'to search, find out and view such remote, heathen and barbarous lands, countries and territories not actually possessed of any Christian prince or people'.[2] That was the regular formula, in pursuance of the government's consistent stand on American settlement. 'And the same to have, hold, occupy and enjoy to him, his heirs and assigns for ever.'

Humphrey Gilbert had been from the days of his youth a personal servant of the Queen, from the time when, as

---

[1] E. P. Cheyney, 'International Law under Queen Elizabeth', *Eng. Hist. Review*, 1905, 660 foll.
[2] *The Voyages and Colonising Enterprises of Sir Humphrey Gilbert*, ed. D. B. Quinn, I. 35.

Princess, she was in disgrace with her sister Mary.[1] We know little of Gilbert's expedition of 1578, which was secret, very mixed in its make-up — to which some genuinely piratical elements were attached and turned out a complete failure.[2] It is thought that he was aiming at settlement in Florida — in accordance with those ideas in the early 1560's. The Queen contributed a ship of her own, the *Falcon*: captain, Walter Ralegh. (I cannot help thinking she must have known him, certainly have known of him, long before the traditionally romantic account of her sudden falling for him — to which we have all subscribed.)

Gilbert's failure and, no doubt, her intimate knowledge of his defects of temperament, made her reluctant to support his last and most elaborate project, which has been described as branching out into 'a maze of individual and corporate enterprises for the conquest and settlement of North America, and, although Gilbert lost his life in attempting to carry out his part in it, led to the first plantation of Virginia less than a year after his death'.[3] She held Gilbert to be 'a man noted of not good hap by sea'; however, against her better judgment, she relented and gave him permission to go. Before he left, with characteristic graciousness, she sent him by Walter Ralegh — now in the first flush of favour — her good wishes, with a jewel for token, 'an anchor guided by a Lady'. She asked him to leave his portrait with Ralegh for her; she did not invest in the voyage. Gilbert went, took possession of Newfoundland, lost his flagship with all his stores for settlement, and was drowned in the bark *Squirrel* on the way home.

Ralegh was the heir to Gilbert's colonising projects, who carried them into execution. But it was entirely his favour with the Queen that gave him the resources to put his plans into operation: the prestige and opportunities of his position, the support and service he could now command,

---

[1] *Ibid.* 2-3. But note p. 1, that Modbury is in Devon, not Kent, and p. 46, Ockington should read Cockington (near Torquay).

[2] Mendoza had a spy on board from whom he hoped for an account of it on return. *Cal. S.P. Spanish, 1568–1579*, 607.

[3] D. B. Quinn, *op cit.* I. 55.

the gifts of lands and licences, the cash. Notice that the Queen's favour was not given for nothing: there was an implied contract of service. It was her way of attaching men of ability to the service of the state, and from the men she delighted to favour the state got good service. In all Ralegh's efforts for Virginia she was behind him: she backed him, she provided his resources. In addition, she made her own direct contribution.

In preparation for Ralegh's first Virginia colony Richard Hakluyt wrote his *Discourse of Western Planting*: 'Certain Reasons to induce her Majesty and the state to take in hand the western voyage and the planting therein'. It was an extremely able state paper, unique in that age in putting forth a complete argument for colonial expansion, on every ground — economic, political, strategic, religious — with a plan for its execution and a programme of settlement. Ralegh got Hakluyt an audience with the Queen, to whom he presented it on his knees. No doubt she read it: it was meant for her eyes, and was never printed until our own time.[1] But she was not persuaded.

The argument was that only the resources of the state could accomplish the colonisation of America. There was something in that: so many were to fail, fall by the wayside, having ventured everything and lost; the sacrifices in wealth and man-power, in suffering, privation and human life, were immense and terrible. But — a state enterprise? — in that age everyone plundered the government and every governmental undertaking. The Queen knew that better than anyone: had she not often had occasion to utter a *cri de cœur* against the 'insatiable cupidity of men'? Then, too, a state enterprise meant a head-on collision with Spain, a frontal challenge from which no retreat was possible. Failure would mean a total loss of prestige to the state. There can be no doubt that the Queen was right to put it aside, and there it remained unknown till our day.

[1] In *The Original Writings and Correspondence of the Two Richard Hakluyts*, ed. E. G. R. Taylor, II. 211 foll. The original is in the New York Public Library.

But this did not mean that she was not as anxious as anyone that colonisation should succeed. Ultimately, it did, under a characteristically mixed English form of enterprise, with private and public elements, and the Crown making a quasi-official contribution. To the first Virginia voyage led by Ralegh's cousin, Sir Richard Grenville — she could not in these first years of mutual fascination spare Ralegh from her side — she contributed a ship of her own, the flagship the *Tiger*, a well-armed ship of some 180 tons, and £400 worth of gunpowder from the Tower.[1] She had also intended to invest a small ship, the *Golden Royal*; but at the last moment this boat was switched to the attack on the Spanish and Portuguese fishing fleets off Newfoundland, which had been a favourite project of Gilbert's and which, now (1585) that the war was on, could be undertaken. It proved, of course, immensely profitable; but so did Grenville's first colonial voyage, by picking up a rich prize on the way back. The colonising Queen made a good profit on her investment. Grenville left his second in command, Ralph Lane, behind in charge of the colony: a cousin of Sir Edward Dyer, he was an equerry to the Queen, whose release from service in Ireland she had authorised to serve in Virginia.

Not least important, she contributed her name to Virginia. Everything with this politic woman meant something. The permission to use her name was not mere coquettishness, not only the suggestion of romance which, genuine enough in that day, it has come chiefly to signify for us. It was, like everything with her, an intensely personal act, calling attention to an aspect of her personality which, if not unique in a ruler, was an unforgettable element in her fame. But it was also politics: a characteristically ambivalent notice to the world that she personally was involved as well as the Crown of England, her good name pledged. It was therefore an unmistakable underlining of her claim, which could not chivalrously be disregarded, a warning to others to keep off. The name caught on at once — it

[1] *The Roanoke Voyages, 1584–1590*, ed. D. B. Quinn, 120, 148, 237.

evidently had life in it — with the poets no less than the seamen, the politicians and merchants. In these same eighties, while Ralph Lane was writing to her Secretary Walsingham from Virginia of the 'assurance of her Majesty's greatness hereby to grow by the addition of such a kingdom as this is to the rest of her dominions', Ralegh's friend Spenser was writing,

> Or fruitfullest Virginia who did ever view?

The name was to become in the fullness of time — with all its memories of Jamestown and Yorktown and Richmond, Washington and Jefferson, Robert E. Lee and Stonewall Jackson, Chancellorsville and Bull Run and Appomattox Court House — very famous and infinitely touching.

The great propagandist of English colonisation in America, the fugleman for Virginia, was Richard Hakluyt. No-one ever did more to keep the subject before the mind of the public : his services in this respect, and for English navigation and the seamen, were immeasurable. The Queen provided for him, and that enabled him to carry on his unique work. Though she was not persuaded by the argument of his *Discourse*, she gave him a prebend in Bristol Cathedral, where he was well placed for contacts with the West Country merchants and seamen. In 1594 he was given the benefice of Wetheringsett in Suffolk, where he was hardly less well placed for consultation with the East Anglian mercantile and maritime interests, in particular those of the Orwell, whence Thomas Cavendish, second English circumnavigator of the globe came ; Hakluyt married a connection. In 1602 he was made prebendary of Westminster — a better focus still for his work ; in 1604 chaplain of the Savoy. Altogether he was well provided for. Dying in 1616 he was buried in the Abbey : though that was usual enough for a prebendary, no-one ever deserved it more.

There he is not far from the Queen he served. For the rest of her life she was involved in the war that these events and conflicts had brought on. But though she longed for peace, she would never make it, except upon the condition of security for the Netherlands, their virtual independence, and the open door to settlement in North America. When she was dead, peace was made ; and, though nothing was said about either condition, in fact both were fulfilled. Within a couple of years the English set about their permanent settlement in Virginia. All that flowed from that, the manifold consequences that have been so decisive in modern history and that operate today, we owe to the long struggle waged under the leadership of the Queen.

CHAPTER III

RALEGH, HAKLUYT AND COLONISATION

THIS book cannot but have a West Country bias. For a notable consequence of the emergence of America was to bring the West Country very much to the fore, in the front-line of oceanic discovery and of the war with Spain. Bristol was the port from which the first American voyages set out, from those of the later fifteenth century in search of a fabled Atlantic island — the Bristol of William Cannings and of St. Mary Redcliffe, which so possessed the mind of the young Chatterton. But from the reign of Henry VIII and the rise of the remarkable Hawkins family there, Plymouth leaped ahead and becomes the centre of interest. The maritime activity of these ports provided grand opportunities for, and a focus for the energies of, the county families around them as well as of the merchants and seamen within them. Plymouth was as convenient for the operations of Gilberts, Raleghs, Grenvilles as it was for Hawkinses, Fowneses, Trelawnys within those walls of the old cramped town climbing up from Sutton Pool to the Hoe, with the splendid prospect opening out from there.

Walter Ralegh was no new man: he came from a very old family which had already made its place by the time of Henry II, who granted a member of it Nettlecombe in Somerset, which later became the home of the Trevelyans. (It is pleasant to think of the Trevelyans succeeding the Raleghs there.) But by Walter Ralegh's time the family had lost most of its property and become rather impoverished: a most humiliating and vexing situation, especially for an ambitious young man, to feel that you are somebody and haven't a bean. Something of this irritation may be seen all through Ralegh's career : he was always a man in a hurry, conscious of his gifts and abilities, yet always made to wait on circumstances — and maddened by frustration. And there was a yellow streak in Ralegh too — he was a great liar — a rift in him by which perhaps came the genius, for men have the qualities of their defects. There is no doubt of the genius : he bore all the stigmata of it.

The family were occupying Hayes Barton in the parish of East Budleigh, within sound of the sea at Budleigh Salterton, at the time of Ralegh's birth : go up the narrow Devon road west from the village and you come to the pleasant Elizabethan farm-house, still thatched, with its great chamber upstairs where he was born. The moment he came into clover with the Queen, somewhat conditionally, he wrote down to the West in his grand manner that he wanted to buy Hayes for he meant to seat himself there.[1] However, Mr. Duke would not sell and Ralegh never did seat himself there, or permanently anywhere.

Ralegh's mother was by birth a Champernowne, and widow of a Gilbert, so that these Gilberts — John, Humphrey, Adrian — were half-brothers of Walter and Carew Ralegh.[2] The Gilberts were brought up at Greenway on the Dart, the family seat being Compton Castle, that delightful rose-red H-shaped house of the fourteenth century, near Torquay, of which the roofless hall has been restored by Commander Walter Raleigh Gilbert, in the last few years. Humphrey Gilbert was some fifteen years older than Ralegh, and to him the young Walter owed his lead in sea enterprises and ideas of American colonisation. Where Gilbert led, at Oxford, in France and Ireland, at sea, over America, Ralegh followed. They had strong family characteristics in common : they were impulsive and intemperate, impatient of any opposition (they had all the more to put up with). They were not very nice men, but they had fascination and they were well-educated. They were men of ideas — indeed with them ideas went to their head

---

[1] E. Edwards, *The Life of Sir Walter Ralegh*, II. 26.
[2] J. L. Vivian, *The Visitations of the County of Devon*, 405-6, 638-9.

— and they had great imagination : they were projectors.

Gilbert, we have seen, was the leader in the efforts to put in hand English settlement in America, and from those efforts — in which he spent his own fortune and his wife's, in the end his life — all else stems. Gilbert's especial friend at Court was Walsingham, who had furthered the Frobisher voyages and took an active part in securing Gilbert's patent from the Queen.[1] Both Sir Henry Sidney and Philip supported Gilbert's project. Gilbert had licence to subinfeudate tenants in America in accordance with the normal English land-system, and Philip Sidney was assigned a mere three million acres, with power to inhabit and people them — an assignment which he passed over to the interested Sir George Peckham, who played with the idea of Catholic settlement.[2] But Sidney several times thought of going on an American voyage in these years, with Gilbert to Virginia or with Drake to the West Indies.[3]

For Gilbert's last enterprise Ralegh set forth in the *Bark Ralegh* of 200 tons, as vice-admiral. We remember Edward Hay's description of the voyage and of his taking possession of Newfoundland in St. John's harbour, investing 'the Queen's Majesty with the title and dignity thereof, and had delivered unto him (after the custom of England) a rod and a turf of the same soil, entering possession also for him, his heirs and assigns for ever'.[4] After the proclamation of laws, 'obedience was promised by general voice and consent of the multitude as well of Englishmen as strangers. . . . After this, the assembly was dismissed. And afterward were erected not far from that place the

[1] Conyers Read, *Mr. Secretary Walsingham*, III. 399.

[2] M. W. Wallace, *The Life of Sir Philip Sidney*, 286. It is interesting to observe the Catholic Peckham coming to Dee, 17 July 1582, 'to know the title for Norombega [*i.e.* North America] in respect of Spain and Portugal parting the whole world's discoveries'. *Diary, ed. cit.* 16.

[3] Cf. *The Roanoke Voyages*, ed. D. B. Quinn, 90. Sidney to Sir Edward Stafford, 'We are half persuaded to enter into the journey of Sir Humphrey Gilbert, very eagerly whereunto your Master Hakluyt hath served for a very good trumpet'. If the date, 21 July 1584, is correct this must refer to the Ralegh voyage and reveals the dominant impression Gilbert had made on Sidney's mind, for Gilbert was already dead; or perhaps the date should be 1583.

[4] R. Hakluyt, *Principal Navigations*, Everyman edn., VI. 18-19.

arms of England engraven in lead and enfixed upon a pillar of wood.' Among the fisher-folk who had long frequented the harbour Gilbert proceeded to parcel out land 'by the waterside, both in this harbour of St. John and elsewhere, which was to the owners a great commodity, being thereby assured (by their proper inheritance) of grounds convenient to dress and to dry their fish, whereof many times before they did fail, being prevented [*i.e.* forestalled] by them that came first into the harbour.'

One off-shoot of Gilbert's projects was the licence granted to his brother Adrian, John Dee and John Davis in 1583 to discover and plant in the north parts of Atlantis — observe the influence of Dee in the name.[1] Adrian Gilbert is the most mysterious of the three brothers, and perhaps not without reason for he was an alchemist. We find him in curious relationship with Dee, quarrelling and then making it up, with John Davis making a third in these amenities.[2] John Davis was one of the finest all-round navigators of the age. Born on the banks of the Dart, in the parish of Stoke Gabriel, he was a near neighbour of the Gilberts, of a class below them, coming from sound Devon yeoman stock. This licence to Adrian Gilbert led to the three memorable voyages of John Davis to north-western waters — to all of which Ralegh contributed — in which Davis penetrated further along the way to a North-Western passage than anyone hitherto.

But the real inheritor of Gilbert's schemes was Ralegh, who had the enthusiastic support of the Queen in these years, and that was important. Humphrey Gilbert at the end declared that he 'was now become a Northern man altogether'. Ralegh, however, decided to seek out more southerly territories for settlement, under the influence of Hakluyt with whom he was in correspondence and by whose advice he proceeded.

In these marvellous 1580's everything was beginning to ripen together in the heat of the tension with Spain. Poetry

[1] *Cal. S.P. Col.*, *East Indies, 1513–1616*, 93.
[2] John Dee, *Diary*, 6-7, 18-19, 32.

and the drama that had been so sparse and backward were coming to a head with Sidney and Spenser and Marlowe; the first Elizabethan madrigals appear in the very year the war begins. And this is the moment when the idea of American colonisation takes shape and wing — or, perhaps I should say, takes sail. In this activity the younger Hakluyt comes to the fore, makes himself the leading exponent of the idea, its most cogent and urgent advocate in his writings, a leading authority on America, adviser to all the voyages, collector and indefatigable publisher of all the information they brought back. We owe to Richard Hakluyt the preservation of all the early material we have relating to America. But this was only one side of his life's work. To the Elizabethan Age he was 'industrious' Hakluyt, and certainly his industry was prodigious. No less remarkable to us is his imagination: more than anyone else he glimpsed the vast potentialities of America.[1] Of the various people who made a cardinal contribution in the matter — the Queen, Gilbert, Ralegh, Sir Thomas Smythe and Gorges — no-one comes before Hakluyt.

There were two Richard Hakluyts and they were cousins, the elder a lawyer with connections in the City whose chief interest was as economic adviser to the various companies, from the Muscovy Company to Gilbert and Ralegh in regard to America. They too, like John Dee and the Cecils, came from the Welsh Border, from Herefordshire, and theirs was a Protestant family. At Oxford the younger Hakluyt was for a good many years supported by the Clothworkers' Company, on condition that he studied divinity. Known in that age as Preacher Hakluyt, his sermons won acceptance. As late as 1581 we find the Company lending him all eleven volumes of the works of St. Augustine, but he had already turned, more usefully, to geography where we may say his heart was.[2] He was the first to lecture at Oxford on the new geography, 'the

[1] It is all the more fitting that the authoritative work on Hakluyt is by an American scholar, G. B. Parks, *Richard Hakluyt and the English Voyages*.

[2] T. Girtin, 'Mr. Hakluyt, Scholar at Oxford', *Geographical Journal*, 1953, 208 foll.

new lately reformed maps, globes, spheres and other instruments of this art for demonstration in the common schools, to the singular pleasure and general contentment of my auditory'.[1] (We see, as with John Dee, that false modesty was not an Elizabethan vice.)

As early as 1580 Hakluyt got his Oxford friend John Florio to translate Cartier's voyages to Canada. Caught up in the excitement of Gilbert's projects, in 1582 Hakluyt published his first important collection, *Divers Voyages touching the Discovery of America*. This provided a storehouse of information, with narratives of all the voyages to the North American coast claimed for England; for, as in so many of his works, tirelessly, effectively, Hakluyt set out England's claim from the Cabots onwards. Next year he became chaplain to the ambassador going to Paris, with the intention of learning there all there was to be known from the French about America.

As we have seen, the French were much beforehand. Jacques Cartier had led three expeditions into the St. Lawrence and spent two winters there; Roberval had made another Canadian voyage in 1541. There had been the colonial enterprises in Brazil and in Florida. While in Paris for the five years, 1583–8, Hakluyt got hold of the documents that gave a complete account of French activity in America, somehow raised the money to publish them in French and then translated them into English *pour encourager les Anglais*. We know from him what was thought in Paris: 'the English of all others for their sluggish security and continued neglect of the like attempts . . . were either ignominiously reported or exceedingly contemned'. In Paris he inspired the publication of Laudonnière's *History of Florida* in French, helping to collect the materials himself, with a dedication to Ralegh celebrating his efforts now in full career, and later translating it into English. He got his French collaborator to translate the latest Spanish account of a voyage to New Mexico, by Espejo, and then published that in English.

[1] q. Parks, 59-60.

Meanwhile he himself was engaged in re-editing the complete text of Peter Martyr's *Decades of the New World* in Latin, with a long dedicatory letter to Ralegh in which he used his Latin to serve notice on Europe of England's claim, Cabot's priority on the mainland and all. He pointed to Ralegh's generous maintenance of the scientist Thomas Hariot to instruct him in navigational problems and brought out Peter Martyr's account of Spanish cruelties in the New World along with their pertinacity and achievements. All this while he was collecting the accounts and narrations of English voyages through the ages, to put the nation on the map, so to say. He returned in 1588 to work hard all through Armada year to produce in 1589 the first edition of his great classic, *The Principal Navigations, Voyages, Traffics and Discoveries of the English Nation*. In his dedication to Walsingham Hakluyt was able at last to say, 'in this most famous and peerless government of her most excellent Majesty, her subjects, through the special assistance and blessing of God, in searching the most opposite corners and quarters of the world and, to speak plainly, in compassing the vast globe of the earth more than once, have excelled all the nations and people of the earth'. What a decade of work on his part, and to what purpose in the end! But what a decade of inspiration! — bliss was it in *that* dawn to be alive: hence, in part, and in brief, the flowering of the Elizabethan age.

In April 1584 Ralegh dispatched two barks, under captains Amadas and Barlow, to reconnoitre a site for a colony in the southern section of the North American coast. They went out by the southern route via the Canaries and West Indies and then up to Cape Hatteras to the low-lying coast of what is now North Carolina, where among the shoals and lagoons they pitched on an island which they considered a promising site. The advantages of an island for purposes of defence are obvious, and the fact that it was situated among those sounds, with about the most difficult navigation in the world, afforded it some protection from Spanish attentions. Amadas and Barlow came back with a lyrical account of the country and its commodities. They explored a little about the island: 'when we first had sight of this country, some thought the first land we saw to be the continent. But after we entered into the haven we saw before us another mighty long sea; for there lieth along the coast a tract of islands, two hundred miles in length, adjoining to the ocean sea, and between the islands two or three entrances.' [1] They made contact with the Indians of the mainland, with their king, whose kingdom was called Wingandacoa 'and now by her Majesty Virginia'. They got the same impression of the Indians as Drake had had in California, if indeed this be not common form: 'we found the people most gentle, loving and faithful, void of all guile and treason, and such as live after the manner of the golden age'. They brought back with them two lusty young Indians of standing, Wanchese and Manteo, the first of whom was to belie these sanguine hopes, the second to remain ever faithful to the English. In that the pattern of so much in the subsequent story of relations between the races was foreshadowed thus early.

That summer, while Amadas and Barlow were away, Hakluyt wrote his *Discourse of Western Planting* at Ralegh's request to further the cause with the Queen. It is a most effective state paper: if there were no other evidence, this would be enough to show that Hakluyt was a man of a powerful and superior mind.[2] He summarises the reasons for undertaking American colonisation most cogently, and with a note of urgency, for fear of being forestalled. There were not only the Spaniards and the French, but Ortelius had told him that if it had not been for the war raging in their country the Netherlanders meant to take a hand in American settlement — as, in fact, after the peace with Spain they did. If Hakluyt places at the head of the advantages to be gained, the enlargement of the Reformed religion, that was an important consideration in that age

[1] R. Hakluyt, *Principal Navigations*, VI. 121 foll.
[2] Printed by E. G. R. Taylor, *The Writings and Correspondence of the Two Richard Hakluyts*, II. 211 foll.

of conflict between Reformation and Counter-Reformation, and, after all, hasn't it largely come about? It is interesting, from the internal point of view, that Hakluyt looked already to an emigration of Puritans to diminish strife at home. In time the former came about, without much sensible diminution of the latter.

With both Hakluyts economic considerations were in the forefront, though in the mind of the elder they were dominant, almost exclusive. They saw the importance America might have, especially the northern parts with their long cold winters, for the export of English woollens. The younger Hakluyt urges that the trade with Spain, now cut off by the war, may come in course of time to be more than replaced by that with America. Similarly with the newly opened Russian trade: Hakluyt expected the American soon to surpass it. He himself had seen the consignments of furs brought to Paris; of his own knowledge there was a great increase in the Newfoundland fisheries: furs and fisheries — in those two came to consist much of the early history of Canada. Hakluyt had all the up-to-date information about the interior of Canada from the French: the promise of red copper from Saguenay, the rumours of the Great Lakes. And, for his hope of a near passage to the sea on the other side of America, he refers to 'an old excellent globe in the Queen's Privy Gallery at Westminster which seemeth to be of Verrazano's making'.

By contrast with the depopulation of Spain, he draws attention to the increase of numbers in England. Here is an outlet for those without work or means of subsistence. And if he suggests that convicts for petty crimes should be transported, instead of being hanged or imprisoned, that was in fact an humane suggestion. The passage to America was easy and short and does not cut across other countries. At this moment, on the threshold of the twenty-year long war with Spain, Hakluyt's mind is filled with the strategy of the conflict and imbued with anti-Spanish feeling. American treasure was the foundation of Spain's intolerable ascendancy in Europe: it was felt to be intolerable, for it enabled Spain to intervene in everybody's internal affairs, not only Portugal and Italy, but France and the Low Countries, even in England.[1] Hakluyt did not forget the theme of Spanish cruelty, either in America or in Europe. He pointed to the devastation of the West Indies as they exploited them and then moved on to the mainland. Perhaps this was understandable in the circumstances of the conquest: all the same, it is generally recognised that the population of Hispaniola was reduced to one-third, from some three hundred thousand to one hundred thousand, while the Bahamas were left totally depopulated.[2] And there *was* the Inquisition: the seamen of other countries had a burning reason for hatred of Spain. We shall not understand the sixteenth century if we do not realise, what the Victorians well understood, that Protestant Europe loathed Spain — and with every good reason.[3] And by 1580, we must not forget, 'Philip II was the ruler of all the European settlements so far established in the New World'.[4]

Hakluyt's message, confronting the issue of war, is one with that of the seamen: there is no need to fear, or even to heed, Spain. He points to the wastage of Spanish manpower through the incessant wars, intervening over half Europe, the decreasing population, the internal decline that had already set in under Philip. So far as America is concerned, 'it is well known that the Spaniards, for want of people of their own country, have not been able now in the space of ninety-two years to inhabit a third or fourth part of those exceeding large and waste countries, which are as great as all Europe and Africa'. This was fair enough, and he proceeds to urge the Queen's claim by arguments with which we are already familiar. All things

---

[1] In the last two decades of the century the proportion of American revenue to Philip II's total receipts increased rapidly, and in the year 1585 reached 25 per cent. J. H. Parry, 'The New World, 1521–1580', in *The New Cambridge Modern History*, II. 589.

[2] Sir Alan Burns, *A History of the British West Indies*, 119-22.

[3] Cf. Francis Bacon, 'The policy of Spain hath trodden more bloody steps than any state of Christendom', in 'A Short View to be taken of Great Britain and Spain'. *Works*, ed. J. Spedding, VII. 26.

[4] J. H. Parry, *ibid.*, II. 588.

considered, Hakluyt's *Discourse* was well worth the prebend at Bristol with which she rewarded it. And so far as spread of imagination is concerned, it is a just reflection that Hakluyt's programme took about a century to achieve.[1]

Such was the background, and such the preparation, to Ralegh's first big colonial effort now taking shape. In December the Bill confirming his Letters Patent was before Parliament, and on second reading was handed over to a committee with an interesting membership.[2] There were the Queen's Vice-Chamberlain Hatton, her principal Secretary, Walsingham, Sir Philip Sidney, Drake, Grenville, Sir William Courtenay, Sir William Mohun and other West Country members specially interested in these matters. Upon third reading the Bill, 'after many arguments and a proviso added unto it, passed'. No-one has observed that this long proviso was directed against the expedition undertaking hostilities by sea or land; no doubt that was due to Burghley's influence and represented a concession to his point of view.[3] By the time the little fleet set sail, open war with Spain made the proviso out of date — and Grenville's privateering on the way home more than paid the expenses.

The Queen at this time not being able to part with Ralegh, the command was handed over to his cousin Grenville. John Hooker of Exeter, who knew them both, paid Grenville this tribute: 'a gentleman of very good estimation both for his parentage and sundry good virtues, who for love he bare unto Sir Walter Ralegh, together with a disposition that he had to attempt honourable actions worthy of honour', undertook the service.[4] And whatever may be said of Grenville — there are things to be said against him, all (and rather more than all) said by his second-in-command, Ralph Lane — he performed it. He made a successful cruise to the West Indies, where he took on board

[1] Cf. J. A. Williamson, 'Richard Hakluyt', in *Richard Hakluyt and his Successors*, ed. Edward Lynam, 34.
[2] Sir Simonds D'Ewes, *Journal of the Houses of Lords and Commons* (ed. 1693), 339, 341. [3] The proviso is given in Hakluyt, VI. 120.
[4] q. from Holinshed's Chronicle in *The Roanoke Voyages*, ed. D. B. Quinn, 174.

horses and kine to stock the colony and plants, including sugar, to plant. At the end of June he landed the colony on Roanoke Island. He remained there for a month exploring and prospecting, and then hovered off Cape Hatteras for another month — watching out for what he could find, I suppose — at the end of which he set sail for England. On 18 September 'the general came with the prize to Plymouth and was courteously received by divers of his worshipful friends'.[1]

That expedition to plant the first colony in America had an interesting membership. In addition to Grenville and Ralph Lane, there was the brilliant young navigator Thomas Cavendish from Suffolk, the second Englishman to make a successful voyage round the world. Also upon it were Thomas Harlot — the first scientist in the country — and John White, one of its best draughtsmen, cartographer to and illustrator of the expedition. Most of the leading spirits were West Country relations or neighbours of Grenville and Ralegh: one observes among the names an Arundell, a Stukeley, a Prideaux, a Bonython, a Kendall and, I am glad to say, Anthony Rouse, a friend of Drake. Left to himself in command, Lane responded with a violent outburst against Grenville, full of the usual Elizabethan persecution-mania and complaining of the unruliness of 'the wild men of mine own nation', let alone living among savages. It is clear that what they needed was a Grenville to keep them in order; it is also clear that the Queen's equerry was not the type, and indeed he does not appear again in colonial enterprises. To Philip Sidney he wrote of the strategic advantages of the situation for attacking the Spaniards in and from the West Indies — and that is one important aspect of these projects for settlement athwart the homeward route of the treasure-fleets through the Florida Channel.

Of the commodities and prospects of 'this her Majesty's new kingdom of Virginia', he wrote lyrically to Hakluyt.[2] 'We have discovered the main [land] to be the goodliest

[1] Hakluyt, VI. 138.   [2] *Ibid.* 140.

soil under the cope of heaven, so abounding with sweet trees that bring such sundry and pleasant gums, grapes of such greatness yet wild as France, Spain nor Italy have no greater, so many sorts of apothecary drugs, such several kinds of flax and one kind like silk, the same gathered of a grass as common there as grass is here.' It all sounds a bit tall: he knew to whom he was writing; Ralph Lane spent a good deal of his life in Ireland. He continues, 'besides that, it is the goodliest and most pleasing territory of the world: for the continent is of an huge and unknown greatness, and very well peopled and towned though savagely, and the climate so wholesome that we had not one sick since we touched the land here. To conclude, if Virginia had but horses and kine in some reasonable proportion, I dare assure myself, being inhabited with English, no realm in Christendom were comparable to it.' Well, I think we may say, that too has come to pass.

Ralegh went down to Plymouth to meet Grenville on his return, who reported in more objective vein to Walsingham, 'I have, God be thanked, performed the action whereunto I was directed as fully as the time wherein I have been absent from hence and all possibilities would permit me. I have possessed and peopled the same to her Majesty's use, and planted it with such cattle and beasts as are fit and necessary for manuring the country and in time to give relief with victual, as also with such fruits and plants as by my travail by the way thitherwards I might procure.'

It is not my purpose to tell once more the story of this first English colony in America, what happened to the hundred or so men — that became the usual number dispatched in these early efforts at settlement — upon Roanoke island during the year almost that they remained there. It is more to the point to enforce the cardinal importance of the 1585–6 colony in the whole story of those efforts. Its significance has been overlaid in the popular mind by the romantic appeal of the 'lost colony' of 1587. But in fact everything goes back to that first colony on Roanoke island, to the colonial experience they gathered there, the knowledge as to the physical conditions, the flora and fauna, the products of the soil — above all, what they learned about Indian life, native ways and food, the difficulties of relations with the Indians. Most of what we know about all this has come down to us through the observations made by Hariot and White, and some of it was made available to the European public at the time through the publications of Hariot and De Bry. We can see the influence of that first experience, as well as some lessons that should have been learned but were not, through all the subsequent attempts until at last permanent settlement was effected at Jamestown in 1607, and even beyond.

The fundamental lesson that early colonists failed to learn was the absolute necessity of getting down to cultivate the soil. But we must remember to what an extent they consisted of ragtag and bobtail who would not learn anything, idle and listless, recalcitrant to all discipline. (Here is where the grand advantage of the Puritans came in, when it came to their turn: in moral fibre and self-discipline.) The dependence of the early colonists on the Indians for food supplies naturally created acute troubles between them, for there was not enough to go round. Their relations, the characters of the Indian chiefs, the troubles between the natives and the newcomers, provide the chief interest of the story. The colonists were not yet discouraged, however, when in June 1586 Drake arrived off the coast with a powerful fleet from his West Indian expedition, on which he had wrought so much destruction. Coming up the Florida coast he had completely destroyed San Agustín, and the small outposts dependent upon it: the Spaniards ran off into the woods, to come back another day and repair the damage.

Ralegh's promised supply-ship was late in getting to sea; meanwhile Grenville was fitting out a larger expedition upon the North Devon coast. The Roanoke colonists were ready to remain and wait, when their nerve was suddenly broken by one of those tornadoes that that coast enjoys — and the prime defect of Roanoke was that it had

no satisfactory harbour. Drake offered to take the colonists
back with him and on a sudden impulse they decided to
accept. If Lane had been a stronger man, he would have
stuck it out. . . . And this provides one of the tantalising
'Ifs' of history; for immediately after they had gone,
Ralegh's supply-ship turned up, looked for the colonists
and, not finding them, returned with its provisions to
England. A fortnight after that Grenville arrived with
three ships well-provided. He himself travelled 'up into
divers places of the country' seeking for news of the colony
in vain.[1] Then, 'unwilling to lose the possession of the
country which Englishmen had so long held, after good
deliberation', he left a post of fifteen men on Roanoke
provisioned for two years to hold the fort. He has been
criticised for a wrong decision; but we do not know his
circumstances or his instructions: it looks clear to me that
he was expected to reinforce the existing colony, not plant
a new one, nor is it likely that his people would volunteer
to make a new settlement unprepared. The real point is
that Drake's unintended taking off the colonists completely
upset the planned synchronisation of Ralegh's efforts and
spoiled the best chance of settlement. After that everything
went wrong.

Ralegh was not yet discouraged, and Hakluyt did his
best to advertise his labours. In the dedication of his *Peter
Martyr* he spoke of a letter from the English Court 'in
which you freely swore that no terrors, no personal losses
or misfortunes could or ever would tear you from the sweet
embracements of your own Virginia, that fairest of nymphs
— though to many insufficiently well known — whom our
most generous sovereign has given you to be your bride.
If you persevere only a little longer in your constancy,
your bride will shortly bring forth new and most abundant
offspring . . . and cover with disgrace and shame those
who have so often dared rashly and impudently to charge
her with barrenness.'[2] Of course that is the way one had
to write in Latin: even so one sees that there were people

<hr/>

[1] Hakluyt, VI. 164.   [2] q. Taylor, II. 367.

ready to disparage and discourage. A more practical service was Hakluyt's insistence from now on that the best place to site the colony was on the Chesapeake, which had good harbourage and was not exposed: in that too he proved right.

In 1587 Ralegh sent out his second colony — actually it was the fourth voyage he had set forth — under John White. This had a somewhat different plan: it was not intended to supersede Roanoke but to supplement it with a settlement on the Chesapeake, and Ralegh gave White, as governor with twelve assistants, a charter to found the city of Ralegh in Virginia — a measure of self-government. Ralegh's directions were never carried out, for the sailors refused to carry the colonists to the Chesapeake but insisted on landing them on Roanoke. The colonists insisted on John White returning for further supplies, and that was the last that was ever heard of them. There were again just over a hundred in all, with seventeen women and half a dozen children. We know their names — including that of Ananias Dare, assistant to John White: they are those of simple English folk and not recognisably West Country.[1] Some think that they perished on their way through the forest to the Chesapeake, and that is likely enough: in their fate forerunners to how many countless pioneers who perished in the American wilderness.

In the spring of 1588 Ralegh sent out a couple of small pinnaces, which never got across the Atlantic in the disturbed conditions of that memorable summer. At Bideford Grenville was fitting out his strongest expedition yet, three tall ships and four barks. But with the Armada on the way he was not allowed to go: his Virginia voyage countermanded, he was ordered to take his ships around to Plymouth and serve under Drake. In 1589 everything in the West Country went into the big Lisbon expedition under Drake and Norris which was our riposte to the Armada. In that year for the first time Ralegh incurred a temporary disfavour with the Queen, and for the next two years he

[1] Cf. Hakluyt, VI. 209-11.

and Grenville, understandably discouraged, turned their attention to nearer colonising projects in Ireland.

In March 1589 Ralegh assigned his rights in the proposed city of Ralegh to Thomas Smythe, William Sanderson and other merchants of London, among whom Hakluyt's name was included. Sanderson was a connection by marriage who gave Ralegh constant financial support, so it looks as if the strain was telling on his resources. However, Ralegh's patent remained in force, his overall rights intact. In 1590 another syndicate of merchants set out a privateering expedition under (if that is the word) John White, who seems to have been able to exert no more control than before. White wrote that 'as I had sundry times afore been chargeable and troublesome unto him for the supplies and reliefs of the planters in Virginia' so he was indebted to Ralegh for procuring licence to go, on condition that the ships transported a number of colonists with further supplies.[1] But the crews, 'regarding very smally the good of their countrymen in Virginia, determined nothing less than to touch at those places': they went privateering until the end of the summer, when the weather turned too bad for that treacherous coast. White prevailed on them to call at Roanoke, where he saw the evidences of the spoil the Indians had made: 'we found five chests that had been carefully hidden of the planters, and of the same chests three were my own, and about the place many of my things spoiled and broken and my books torn from the covers, the frames of some of my pictures and maps rotten and spoiled with rain, and my armour almost eaten through with rust'. Upon a tree they found the letters CRO carved, which White understood to mean that the colonists had meant to make their way to Croatoan. The weather grew more foul; it was impossible to remain on the coast; he could not get the ships' crews to make the attempt. And that really was the end of the first cycle of Virginia enterprise.

The Armada years were full of work and activity for Ralegh and Grenville. As Lord-Lieutenant of Cornwall

[1] Cf. Hakluyt, VI. 211 foll.

Ralegh was responsible for the land-defences of the county most exposed to invasion. He was kept busy in the West, at Court and in Ireland. In 1591 Grenville was killed in the last fight of the *Revenge*, celebrated by Ralegh in unforgettable prose. Next year, with tension relaxed, Ralegh fell into utter disgrace with the Queen. Everything that he had so far been able to do was due to his favour with her: he had no independent position or footing, he was not a peer of the realm with estates and a feudal dependence, he had no fortune of his own. It all depended on his position with the Queen. A man like Ralegh had a difficult razor-edge to walk. The Queen liked very masculine types — though they also had to be intelligent. The language in which this maiden lady delighted was the language of love: a difficult situation for these high-spirited, highly-sexed men, supposed to be in love with her, though of course it was a platonic relationship, always at a certain distance. Nothing more exacting than to be admitted to so privileged an intimacy and at the same time to keep your distance and your head. For their vestal virgin who presided over it all was a jealous deity: they could neither have the Queen nor anybody else. It was more than flesh and blood could stand, particularly the hot flesh and blood of these Elizabethan courtiers. One after the other lost his balance, toppled over and fetched up for a spell in the Tower.

Ralegh was pretty free with women; at last he fell seriously in love with one and was caught: another Elizabeth, a Throckmorton and — what made it worse — a maid-of-honour to the Queen. It became evident, I think, that Ralegh had, in the technical sense, behaved badly: he compromised her, or they compromised each other. To the Queen, for psychological reasons that one can understand though perhaps not wholly sympathise with, the offence was unpardonable — after such protestations of love, a passion on an altogether higher plane, for her. Ralegh made it worse by denying that he had any intention of marrying the lady. The Queen clapped them both up in the Tower and had them ignominiously married, no-one knows when or how. She never admitted Lady Ralegh to her presence again: for her, poor lady, it was a prelude to a lifetime of trouble. I hope that Ralegh's fine phrase when condemned to death by James — 'I chose you, and I loved you, in my happiest times' — made up a little for it with her. They seem to have remained always in love; perhaps it was just as well, though Ralegh may have had some doubts when, for the next five years, the Queen kept him away from Court and all influence in the prime of his powers.

It was during these years that Ralegh developed his fixation — for it was no less — on Guiana. There was the urgent necessity to effect something striking to recapture the Queen's favour. It seemed clear enough now that Virginia was not going to do that; while Guiana was not yet occupied by the Spaniards and there was gold there.

> To seek new worlds for gold, for praise, for glory,
> To try desire, to try love severed far,
> When I was gone she sent her memory
> More strong than were ten thousand ships of war.

So he wrote in the long unfinished poem, *Book of the Ocean to Cynthia*, in which he recounted the experiences of his despair and with which he hoped to recapture her favour. Ralegh made his voyage, published his celebrated book on the *Discovery of the Large and Beautiful Empire of Guiana* and for the rest of his life was mesmerised by it. We are not concerned here with Ralegh's Guiana projects: out of bounds; but henceforth it took first place in his feverishly scheming mind.

In the last years of the Queen's reign Ralegh came back to his place at Court, though things were never quite the same between them again. In 1600 he was made Governor of Jersey, and local tradition there credits him with beginning the trade between the Channel Islands and Newfoundland.[1] Nor did he forget his interests in Virginia,

[1] A. J. Eagleston, *The Channel Islands under Tudor Government, 1485–1642*, 100.

the lost colonists there. Purchas tells us that in 1602 he sent out a bark under Samuel Mace of Weymouth: 'a very sufficient mariner, an honest sober man, who had been at Virginia twice before, was employed thither by Sir Walter Ralegh to find those people which were left there in the year 1587. To whose succour he hath sent five several times at his own charges. The parties by him set forth performed nothing; some of them following their own profit elsewhere; others returning with frivolous allegations.'[1] Ralegh's luck with Samuel Mace was no better: the ship's company refused, on grounds of weather and loss of tackle, to search the coast round Cape Hatteras to which they had been sent.

Ralegh was evidently preparing to renew his contacts when James came to the throne and Ralegh not long after was condemned for treason. He spent practically the rest of his life in the Tower: not a very good base from which to conduct colonial enterprises. However, he maintained his interest and his belief in the future of Virginia. 'I shall yet live to see it an English nation', he wrote grandly from imprisonment.

How to strike a balance in estimating Ralegh's colonial achievements, his services to America?

He was criticised in his own day, as he has been in ours, for not doing more. That splendid intellect but not very nice man, Francis Bacon, who was not above kicking a man when he was down, wrote in his essay 'Of Plantations', 'it is the sinfullest thing in the world to forsake or destitute a plantation once in forwardness, for besides the dishonour, it is the guiltiness of blood of many commiserable persons'. Everyone would know whom he had in mind. In our own time an American historian describes Ralegh as being 'difficult to acquit of the heartless abandonment of the Roanoke settlers to an unknown fate'.[2] Hakluyt, who knew all the facts and was in a better position to judge, says simply that Ralegh was disheartened by the great

---

[1] Samuel Purchas, *Purchas, his Pilgrimes* (MacLehose edn.), XVIII. 321.
[2] W. F. Craven, *The Southern Colonies in the Seventeenth Century*, 57.

expense and by the unfaithfulness of those he employed, 'after he had sent (as you may see by these five several times) colonies and supplies at his own charges and now at length both himself and his successors thus betrayed'.[1] Indeed, he made a fruitless attempt to go himself on a voyage to Virginia, if we may judge from a letter he wrote from the Tower to James I's Queen. 'I long since presumed to offer your Majesty my service in Virginia, with a short repetition of the commodity, honour and safety which the King's Majesty might reap by that plantation, if it were followed to effect. I do still humbly beseech your Majesty that I may rather die in serving the King and my country than to perish here.' [2]

We have seen something, not only of his difficulties and disappointments, the obstacles in the way, but the sheer impossibility of getting his orders executed on the other side of the Atlantic in his own enforced absence. Armchair critics of today often do not have the imagination to appreciate the physical and other conditions upon which achieving anything in the Elizabethan age depended, how much men were at the mercy of circumstances, of wind and weather, of personal caprice or royal favour, the undependability of agents, the perversity of things.

Yet Ralegh's efforts did bear fruit: a people's memory is more generous, and perhaps speaks more truly, than the professors. Ralegh put Virginia on the map. The first Roanoke colony was of prime formative significance: subsequent colonial enterprise in America built on that foundation. By his position at Elizabeth's Court he gave the most powerful impetus in practice to the idea of English settlement in America. Even his patronage of smoking tobacco, giving it social *cachet*, was not without its effect in helping Virginia's staple product, the crop by which she ultimately achieved economic viability.

There remained Hakluyt to carry on the continuity through the pause of the 1590's, when the country's energies

---

[1] q. C. C. Stopes, *The Life of Henry, third Earl of Southampton, 1573–1624*, 318. [2] E. Edwards, *Life of Sir Walter Ralegh*, II. 333.

were mainly absorbed in the war and mercantile interests moved strongly over to privateering. No shadow of un-respectability ever rested upon that reverend figure — though he had an odd experience one day in November 1605 when he found that, all unaware, he had been dining at the Mitre Tavern in company with the Gunpowder Plot conspirators.[1] He was, characteristically, on his way to peruse a rutter of Sir Francis Drake's navigations. In the last decades of his life his dominating concern with America spread to all four quarters of the globe. We find him inspiring the translation of works on the Far East and Africa : his motive becomes the universalised one of spread-ing geographical knowledge. All the time he went on collecting the narratives and accounts of the English voyages : at the end of the decade he was able to publish a very much enlarged edition of his great work. And after this he went on accumulating material, including five books on the Americas, down to the latest accounts of Virginia and North Virginia — to become New England. He had to take on a young man to aid him, John Pory, who later became Secretary to Virginia — though the materials Hakluyt left did not come to his hands unfortunately but to muddled-minded Purchas, described by Parks as 'the cringing, unctuous and indefatigable parson'.[2] As indus-trious as Hakluyt, intellectually he was of an altogether lower calibre.

Hakluyt continued, too, his practical contacts with American concerns. With the near approach of peace a new series of voyages began, the earlier efforts to be taken up again. Twenty years after Humphrey Gilbert had taken possession of Newfoundland, Hakluyt in 1603 persuaded the Bristol merchants to send out Martin Pring to prospect in Gilbert's northerly latitudes, and obtained Ralegh's per-mission for the voyage.[3] In 1606 he joined Bartholomew Gilbert in petitioning James for the first Virginia charter and was named one of the patentees. He was concerned in the councils preparatory to establishing the colony at

[1] T. Girtin, *loc. cit.*   [2] Parks, 226.   [3] Purchas, XVIII. 322.

Jamestown and in the propaganda on behalf of the Virginia Company. In 1609, the critical year for Jamestown, he translated and published de Soto's Travels, that it might 'yield much light to our enterprise now on foot'. Consultant to the East India magnate, Sir Thomas Smythe, now leader in the Virginia enterprise, Hakluyt appears along with him as a patentee of the North-West Passage Company. In 1616, the year of Shakespeare's death, he died. Each of them — it is not absurd to mention them together — in his spread of mind spanned the age, and the ages. Along the particular line of his prime interest, America, Hakluyt formed the true link between the strenuous fragmented efforts under Elizabeth, which yet have the cohesion and unity of a campaign, and their final fulfilment in Virginia.

CHAPTER IV

VIRGINIA

THE approaching end of the war with Spain, with the end of the century, made it certain that the English would now resume their efforts to settle in North America. After all, that was what they had fought Spain for — with success. The Queen would not make peace without guarantees for the Netherlands and the principle of the open door in America. On that negotiations had broken down in 1598 and 1599. When they were renewed, after her death, Spain was in a still weaker position to insist, and peace was made in London, the negotiations dominated by Cecil, who represented the continuity of Elizabethan policy.[1] The government obtained all that it wished in regard to the Netherlands. With regard to America there was no agreement. The Spaniards refused to accept the English position of freedom of trade with all parts not in effective occupation: hence the continuance of 'war beyond the line', that is the Pope's line, and the subsequent romantic and bloody history of the buccaneers.[2] On the subject of English colonisation, most important of all, nothing was said. The English were not going to admit that it was a

---

[1] Cf. S. R. Gardiner, *History of England, 1603–42*, (ed. 1900), I. 208 foll.

[2] The Venetian ambassador reported in December 1604, that the Spaniards had captured two English vessels. 'They cut off the hands, feet, noses and ears of the crews and smeared them with honey and tied them to trees to be tortured by flies and other beasts. The Spaniards here plead that they were pirates, not merchants, and did not know of the peace. But the barbarity makes people here cry out.' *Cal. S.P. Ven., 1603–7*, no. 307. The Venetian ambassador to Spain in 1596, referring to Spanish cruelty to English prisoners previously said that the English 'most certainly never approached anywhere near such cruel conduct towards the Spanish'. We may compare Drake's constant good treatment of the prisoners he took, or the humanity displayed at the capture of Cadiz, which astonished and impressed the Spaniards. However little people like to hear it — least of all some kinds of Englishmen — the truth is that the English record historically has been exceptionally humane.

subject for discussion: the only implication to be drawn
was that they would now go ahead.

Already exploratory voyages to the coast had been
resumed, and with a clear sense, expressed in the narratives, of the continuity with those of the 1580's. Notably
the voyage of Captains Gosnold and Bartholomew Gilbert
in 1602 to Sir Humphrey Gilbert's hunting grounds in the
north parts of Virginia — to become New England in a
couple of decades. They explored along the coast of Maine,
naming Martha's Vineyard and making contact with the
Indians; but they fell out and so failed to make a stay on
the coast. James Rosier made a report to Ralegh on the
country, its character and commodities, and on the Indians
with whom they trafficked for furs. We have seen that
Ralegh sent out Samuel Mace to the Roanoke coast in
1602, and in 1603 Bartholomew Gilbert took a small bark
to the Chesapeake, which he 'thirsted' to enter, 'to seek
out the people for Sir Walter Ralegh left near those parts
in the year 1587'.[1] And here he lost his life to the Indians,
who had had hostile exchanges with the Spaniards in the
Chesapeake years before.[2]

In 1605 the young Earl of Southampton and Lord
Arundell of Wardour set forth Captain George Weymouth
on a voyage to the northern part of the coast, where they
explored, finding a great river running up into the mountains: 'as we passed with a gentle wind up with our ship,
any man may conceive with what admiration we all consented in joy'.[3] Some of the mariners who had been with
Ralegh to the Orinoco, 'which echoed fame to the world's
ears', thought it was not to be compared with this. This
is the first appearance on the scene of a prominent actor
in these parts: Shakespeare's Southampton. As a young
man no better than he should be — or perhaps, rather
worse — in middle age he became, as sometimes happens,
an uncongenial Puritan. He had been next to Essex in

[1] Purchas, XVIII. 334.
[2] Cf. Clifford M. Lewis and Albert J. Loomie, *The Spanish Jesuit Mission
in Virginia, 1570–1572.*   [3] Purchas, XVIII. 351.

Engraved portrait with the surrounding inscription:

EQVITIS AVRATI ETC. VERA EFFIGIES PRÆCLARISS.^{MI} VIRI DOM: THOMÆ SMITH IN

The honourable Sr Thomas Smith Knight, late Embaß
:ador from his Ma.^{ths} to ye great Emperour
of Ruſſie Governour of ye Honble and famous
Societyes of Marcha tradinge to ye Eaſt
Indies Muſcovy the Freach and Sommer
Jlands Company. Treſure for Virginia &c.

Pub Mar 1.1709 by W. Richardſon. York Houſe 31 Strand

SIR THOMAS SMYTHE

Essex's conspiracy against the Queen, and narrowly escaped with his life. In the Tower he had plenty of time to study the new and much enlarged edition of Hakluyt; his interest may date from this profitable time for reflection. His family had been Catholic — he is said to have owed his conversion to Sir Edwin Sandys, who was still more important in Virginia concerns. Lord Arundell of Wardour lapsed back into Catholicism; anyone who knows much about him knows what a curious ass he was. The government definitely discouraged him from taking a hand in these enterprises.

The French, now released from civil war, and from war with Spain by the Treaty of Vervins (1598), took up once more their long suspended colonial ambitions — and with the active encouragement of Henri IV, who inherited the old Huguenot enthusiasm. In 1603 he granted M. de Monts, a gentleman of his bedchamber, licence to settle in lands between 40° and 46° N., and there followed the first settlement in Acadia, at Port-Royal. In these years the great Champlain was exploring these coasts and in 1608 clinched French power in the St. Lawrence with the founding of Quebec. Already the intrepid navigator Henry Hudson was scouring the Arctic ice from Greenland to Spitzbergen to find a way through to the East, and next year (1609) was exploring the Hudson and the Delaware on behalf of the Dutch. A new phase of international rivalry for North America was beginning.

In 1606 a body chiefly of West Countrymen came together to petition James I for licence to plant a colony — Ralegh's rights having lapsed by his condemnation for treason. These men were Sir Thomas Gates and Sir George Somers, from Devon and Dorset respectively, both of whom had seen much service on land and at sea in the late war; so had Edward Maria Wingfield, who had been taken prisoner in the Low Countries, with Ferdinando Gorges, in 1588. Wingfield came of a Catholic family, which kept the name Maria going in honour of Mary Tudor, who had been godmother to this man's father. In addition there were Ralegh Gilbert, Sir Humphrey's son, and Prebendary Hakluyt to give continuity. A new recruit was George Popham, kinsman of Lord Chief Justice Popham, who had vilified Ralegh at his trial. These were only the harbingers of those interested; for the Spanish ambassador Zuñiga, who watched the proceedings with a jealous eye and was suspiciously well-informed, regarded Sir John Popham, 'a great Puritan', as the ring-leader, and he was an associate, a Somerset neighbour, of Sir Ferdinando Gorges.

From this patent the subsequent colonisation sprang, in the northern part of Virginia, that is, New England, as well as the south. For it constituted two companies to carry out the twin projects envisaged. The southern company was to plant between 34° and 41° N., and was backed mainly from London. The northern colony was to plant between 38° and 45° N.; it was backed mainly from Bristol, Exeter and Plymouth, but came to be known as the Plymouth Company. The strength of the Plymouth Company, it was hoped, would lie in its fishing interests; London in finance: finance and fishing — there could be no doubt which would emerge the stronger. Though there was some interaction between the two, and more friction, I leave the Plymouth Company to my next chapter: from it sprang, if in various ways and in varying degrees, the colonisation of New England.

A paper at this time adduced 'Reasons to move the High Court of Parliament to raise a stock for the maintaining of a Colony in Virginia', pointing to the marvellous achievements of the Dutch East India Company in a few years, promising a gain of 2s. for every 1s. and urging that 'the whole state shall be interested in the benefit of it'.[1] Though the government rightly rejected the idea of a state enterprise — the money was to be raised by a public joint-stock and the public to take its chance — nevertheless the venture was given official backing from the first. The Crown was brought in, in a new and unprecedented manner,

---

[1] Alexander Brown, *The Genesis of the United States* (London, 1890), I. 36 foll. This is still the best collection of documents on the subject.

to give official warrant to the colonisation of Virginia. It also served to warn foreign powers that this was a national enterprise.[1] The Crown appointed a Council for Virginia in London, drawn from the leading members of both companies. We find the Privy Council constantly concerned to encourage, urge, awe with its authority, intervene, change the constitutional arrangements when necessary, until the day came when it was necessary for the Crown to take over the government of the established colony. That meant more independence for the colony, not less; and by then no-one was more anxious for the system of royal governors to continue, lest the Virginia Company should come back with its direct control, than the colonists in Virginia themselves.[2]

Money and management were to be supplied by the city of London; and here the merchants weighed in, above all the East India magnate Sir Thomas Smythe, to whom the establishment and survival of the colony at Jamestown is chiefly due. It is significant that where the independent and ill co-ordinated resources of courtiers, gentlemen and merchants had not answered earlier, the resources of the City merchants, made more manœuvrable by the mechanism of the joint-stock company, succeeded. One must pay tribute to the unfaltering leadership of these merchant magnates — both Smythe and his opponent Sir Edwin Sandys, with their supporters in the City — in all the discouragements and disasters that befell Virginia, for its ill-luck continued, on the Chesapeake as at Roanoke. Lesser men would have given up in despair, would have had to for want of resources. But these men had, no less important, resource, resilience, flexibility: they turned their hands to anything rather than see it fail. And this time they saw it through.

The little fleet of three ships, the *Susan Constant*, *Godspeed* and *Discovery*, with the usual complement of a hundred men,

---

[1] Cf. *Cambridge History of the British Empire*, I. 78.
[2] As against the old-fashioned prejudice against the Crown of Miss S. M. Kingsbury, ed. *The Records of the Virginia Company of London*, I. 11 foll.

sailed in December 1606 under the command of Captain Christopher Newport. Now a man of forty, who had been concerned in the capture of the *Madre de Dios*, richest of prizes in the war, he was one of the best-esteemed sea-captains of the day. From now until 1611 he made the Virginia voyage each year — five voyages in all. In 1612 he entered the East India service. Before his last journey he made his will, 'being to go with the next wind and weather, captain of the *Hope*, to sail into the East Indies, a long and dangerous voyage'.[1] On that voyage he died, at Bantam in 1617, leaving a good deal of property, £400 dowry to a daughter Elizabeth, but only £5 to Jane, 'in regard of many of her disobediences towards me, and other her just misdemeanours to my great heart's grief'. In that moment this long-dead sailor comes alive for us. Next year his son died, master's mate on board the *Hope*; making his will, sick in Table Bay, he leaves £10 to sister Jane on condition she has 'reformed her course of life'.[2] Somehow we feel that we know a good deal about Jane.

Christopher Newport brought his ships safe into the Chesapeake without let or hindrance. George Percy, brother of Ralegh's companion in the Tower, the 'Wizard' Earl of Northumberland, tells us of 'fair meadows and goodly tall trees, with such fresh waters running through the woods as I was almost ravished with the first sight thereof'.[3] They picked on the site of Jamestown, low and marshy as it was, unhealthy as it proved to be, because, being almost an island, it was defensible. There they constructed their fort. Opening their instructions, they found: 'if you happen to discover divers portable rivers, and amongst them any one that hath two main branches . . . make choice of that which bendeth most toward the North West, for that way you shall soonest find the other sea'.[4] In obedience to this they explored up the James River, till

---

[1] P.C.C., Meade 92.   [2] *Ibid.* 85.
[3] Purchas, XVIII. 407. Percy later excused himself to his brother for overspending himself at Jamestown on the ground that when governor he was 'bound to keep a continual and daily table for the gentlemen of fashion'.
[4] Brown, I. 80.

they were checked at the falls where now Richmond is.
Thus early they came upon the frontier between tide-water
and piedmont Virginia, so influential a factor in its later
history. We note the continuing stress upon finding a
passage through to the Pacific; they were continually led
to hope by stories of the Indians about a sea just beyond the
mountains, and hope was not entirely extinguished until
the end of the century. It is tribute to Captain John Smith's
sense that he describes the bounds of Virginia as on the east
'the great ocean; on the south lieth Florida; on the north
Nova Francia; as for the west thereof, the limits are unknown'.[1] To discover them constituted the epic of the
American people, and not until a couple of generations ago
was the process, set in being by the Elizabethans, complete.
In that sense, looking over the last prairie country to be
settled, going through Rockies or Cascades, we may feel
ourselves for a moment linked, in touch, with those first
Elizabethans who started it all.

Theirs were the sacrifices — and the cost in human life
in the first two decades of Virginia was terrible. No doubt
this first venture was experimental and exploratory;
Captain John Smith says that they had eaten up their provisions on too long a sea-voyage, had arrived too late to
plant and in any case were insufficiently provided. He
adds philosophically, 'such actions have ever since the
world's beginning been subject to such accidents, and
everything of worth is found full of difficulties, but nothing
so difficult as to establish a commonwealth so far remote
from men and means, and where men's minds are so unto-
ward as neither do well themselves nor suffer others'.[2] In
other words, there was what is called the human factor —
and it proved very human. There is no point in enter-
taining illusions about it — these voyages transported the
flotsam and jetsam of humanity, even the better average
proved selfish and listless and would not work to save themselves, let alone others. Famine and the marshes bred

---

[1] John Smith, *The Generall Historie of Virginia, New England and the Summer Isles* (MacLehose edn.), I. 43.   [2] *Ibid.* I. 93.

disease, and men began to die. Without any concentration of authority bickerings and quarrels increased; the council at Jamestown deposed Wingfield, its first president, making him the scapegoat, charging him, as a Catholic, with pro-Spanish sympathies. Kendall was executed for attempted mutiny. Robert Hunt, the Oxford man who had gone out as their chaplain — we hear of his books being consumed by fire; it must have been the first library in the colony [1] — did his best to reconcile quarrels and got Smith admitted to the council. By the end of the first winter, they were down to thirty-eight men left alive.

Then the first supply arrived just in time, for they might have given up. (The colony planted contemporaneously by the Plymouth Company in the North at Sagadahoc did give up and went home.) With two supplies sent out in 1608 things began to look up; buildings that had been burned down were repaired and the colonists began to plant a little. Faced with a second winter of privation, John Smith, 'whom no persuasions could persuade to starve', came to the fore and as President took matters forcefully in hand. 'If any would not work, neither should he eat': he threatened to drive those who would not work into the wilderness. And, 'since necessity hath not power to force you to gather for yourselves those fruits the earth doth yield, you shall not only gather for yourselves but those that are sick'.[2] He took what measures he could against the 'damnable and private trade' by which both planters and sailors traded away invaluable stocks and stores intended for the general use. He threatened to hang anyone attempting to steal away in the pinnace to Newfoundland.

By these means, and by his own energy and force of character, Smith carried the colony successfully through the second winter, with few losses. Among them, however, was the vicar of Jamestown, Robert Hunt: a sad loss for, like a good Oxford man, he was a man of the middle way

---

[1] Cf. M. P. Andrews, *Virginia: the Old Dominion*, 31.
[2] Smith, I. 182.

— according to Wingfield, 'not in any way to be touched with the rebellious humour of a papist spirit, nor blemished with the least suspicion of a factious schismatic'.[1] For more than a year the colony went without the ministrations of a clergyman, until the Rev. Richard Buck, another Oxford man, arrived to take Hunt's place.

That winter the colonists had enough novelties, excitements, dangers, consolations to last them a lifetime. They kept Christmas in bad weather 'among the savages, where we were never more merry, nor fed on more plenty of good oysters, fish, flesh, wild fowl and good bread, nor never had better fires in England than in the dry smoky houses of Kecoughtan'.[2] In spite of all difficulties, exploration of the vast bay and its rivers, the country round about, went on; Mr. Sicklemore, 'a very valiant, honest and a painful soldier' was sent out 'with two guides and directions how to seek for the lost company of Sir Walter Ralegh's'. He returned safely, 'but found little hope and less certainty of them'.[3] Relations with the Indians had all the complexity of contacts between races at very different levels of civilisation, by turns friendly and hostile — or rather, the same emotions in the same breast, so that a sharp look-out had to be kept all the time. The Company at home insisted on the coronation of Powhatan, the leading chief of the area, against Smith's better judgment: of 'subtle understanding and politic carriage', he was rendered all the more difficult to deal with. The most dangerous moment came when the small group of Germans in the colony conspired, characteristically, to betray it. They surreptitiously smuggled weapons to the natives and hoped to betray the colony to Spain. Equally characteristically, they got what was coming to them; a brace who got away to Powhatan had their brains beaten out for their treachery to the English. Then the Indians gave a masque or entertainment in the woods, after which their women pursued the

[1] q. H. C. Porter, 'Alexander Whitaker: Cambridge Apostle to Virginia', *William and Mary Quarterly* 1957, 333.
[2] Smith, I. 155.   [3] *Ibid.* I. 183.

embarrassed Smith with their pressing endearments. Or Powhatan's pretty daughter Pocahontas, not yet however nubile, would turn cart-wheels naked in the street of Jamestown to delight the hearts of the planters.

At home in England a wave of interest in Virginia was rising to the height of a national enterprise, a towering crest that broke into the big expedition of 1609 — upon the island of Bermuda as well as the Chesapeake — the second charter and all that followed. Already in 1607 large additions had been made to the membership of the joint Virginia Council in London. Impossible to enumerate them all here, some of the names are of special interest. For the London Company there were Sir Oliver Cromwell, uncle of the Protector and after whom he was named; Sir Fulke Greville, Philip Sidney's friend; Sir Maurice Berkeley, of the family to become important in the history of Virginia; Sir Edwin Sandys, who would wrest the control of the Company from Sir Thomas Smythe. For the Plymouth Company there were Sir John Gilbert, eldest son of Sir Humphrey, Sir Richard Hawkins, son of Sir John, Bernard Grenville, Sir Richard's son and heir. Elizabethans all — we note the strength of continuity with the efforts made under the Queen, in addition to that already represented on the Council.

The undertaking was gathering way and was launched in 1609 with the second Charter, the effective instrument in the creation of Virginia. For this incorporated the Virginia Company that governed the colony and saw it through its infancy to a permanent existence, and separated it from the Plymouth Company concerned now only with the North. The Virginia Company drew upon a most impressive array of support that can truly be said to represent the nation. It came to include 56 city companies and some 659 individuals — 21 peers, 96 knights, 28 esquires, 58 gentlemen, 110 merchants, 282 citizens and so on.[1] To read the names of the Adventurers is like hearing a roll-call of the most active elements in the society of the last years of

[1] Brown, I. 207.

Shakespeare.[1]   There they all are, from the Archbishop of Canterbury and Shakespeare's own patrons, the Earls of Southampton, Pembroke and Montgomery, through many names with more distant echoes, for there are Cecils and Cromwells and Chamberlains, Lord North along with the Spencer ancestor of the Churchills, while the Winston ancestor took shares later; Anglican bishops alongside of Puritans and Catholics, famous figures in the life of London down to an obscure Cornish squire like William Roscarrock, living on the Atlantic coast near Padstow, or Gabriel and John Beadle, two poor gentlemen who went out to Virginia in the first supply (1608).   Everybody who was anybody seems to have been in it, except the poets — and they as usual were short of cash.

However, the laureate Drayton wrote a poem, the splendid 'Ode to the Virginian Voyage'.

> You brave heroic minds,
> Worthy your country's name,
>   That honour still pursue,
>   Go and subdue,
> Whilst loitering hinds
> Lurk here at home with shame.
>
> Britons, you stay too long,
> Quickly aboard bestow you,
>   And with a merry gale
>   Swell your stretched sail,
> With vows as strong
> As the winds that blow you . . .
>
> And cheerfully at sea
> Success you still entice,
>   To get the pearl and gold
>   And ours to hold,
> Virginia,
> Earth's only paradise . . .

---

[1] I have adapted here some sentences from my Introduction to Ralph Hamor's *A True Discourse of the Present State of Virginia* (1615), reprinted by the Virginia State Library, Richmond, Va., 1957.

We miss the name of Shakespeare, though his friend and executor Sir Thomas Russell was there. And, as we shall see, the events of the voyage made an unforgettable impression upon that most sensitive of registers, his imagination. For, in the Atlantic, they ran into a great tempest.

The jealous attentions of the Spanish ambassador Zuñiga were aroused. Amazed at the response to Virginia in English society, he wrote home to Philip III that 'fourteen earls and barons have given 40,000 ducats, the merchants give much more, and there is no poor little man nor woman who is not willing to subscribe something. . . . Much as I have written to your Majesty of the determination they have formed here to go to Virginia, it seems to me that I still fall short of the reality.'[1] There was a spate of tracts, sermons, appeals, promotional literature of all kinds. The home-keeping Archbishop of York, Toby Mathew (who had not subscribed) reports, 'for of Virginia there be so many tractates, divine, human, historical, political, or call them as you please, as no further intelligence I do desire'.[2] Hakluyt inspired the publication of the *Nova Francia*, to show from the French experience that the southern regions were better for settlement. In April William Symonds preached at Whitechapel a sermon of twenty thousand words to the Adventurers and planters ready to go: 'this land was of old time offered to our kings. Our late sovereign Queen Elizabeth (whose story hath no peer among princes of her sex) being a pure virgin, found it, set foot in it and called it Virginia.'[3]

For Virginia itself the effective change made by the second Charter was the appointment of a governor with real power and authority, advised but not displaceable by the council there. The governor appointed, Lord De la Warr, was to follow. Meanwhile Sir Thomas Gates went as his deputy, with Sir George Somers as admiral of the fleet of eight ships that left Plymouth in May. This had some six hundred colonists on board, including a hundred women: the largest expedition for America until the mass

[1] q. Brown, I. 244.   [2] *Ibid.* I. 321.   [3] q. *ibid.* I. 285.

emigration to Massachusetts started in 1630. The sailing of Somers's little fleet has been described as 'the true beginning of one of the great folk movements of history. . . . The first planters of 1607 had served as scouts in advance of an unbroken migration which was directed between 1609 and 1612 to Jamestown, between 1612 and 1618 principally to Bermuda, from 1618 through 1623 once again and in mounting force to Virginia, after 1623 at an even more accelerated rate to the West Indies, and through the decade of the 1630's to New England, with a lesser stream to trace once more a reviving interest in the Chesapeake area. In this continuing though frequently redirected migration is found one of the major forces shaping the development of that Atlantic community of which so much is heard today.' [1]

Virginia's ill-luck held good. To avoid Spanish attentions and a long sea-voyage, Somers's fleet took a direct course across the Atlantic from the Canaries. They ran into a hurricane, and Somers's flagship was cast away upon the coast of Bermuda, though all the folk were saved. The 'still-vexed Bermoothes' were thought by the Elizabethans to be haunted by evil spirits. Out of the fusion of those two inspirations — for several accounts of it circulated at home — came *The Tempest*. The castaways found it pleasant and healthful, with plenty to eat; and there they passed an agreeable winter, while building a couple of pinnaces to take them to Virginia. The rest of the fleet, with four hundred of the people, had arrived there in a battered condition and went through a terrible winter. This was the real 'starving time' in Virginia history. By the time their leaders arrived from Bermuda in the spring, of all the four hundred and those there before, only some sixty remained alive. No doubt they brought disease with them, after so exhausting a journey, and added to that was the listlessness of despair undermining morale. But the main reason for the disaster — it was no less — was the absence of leadership, of all authority and discipline.

[1] W. F. Craven, *The Southern Colonies in the Seventeenth Century*, 96-7.

Elizabethans simply could not operate without it: with
their leaders wrecked in Bermuda — for all they knew,
drowned — the colony went to pieces. Provisions and live-
stock were all consumed; the Indians refused trade except
for the colonists' arms, implements and utensils, and then
turned on them, 'till there remained not past sixty men,
women and children, most miserable and poor creatures;
and those were preserved for the most part by roots, herbs,
acorns, walnuts, berries, now and then a little fish'.[1] There
was, in fact, an instance or two of cannibalism. 'Unto
such calamity', William Strachey, Secretary to the colony,
sums up, 'can sloth, riot and vanity bring the most settled
and plentiful estate.'[2] The Virginia Council at home sadly
admitted, on learning the facts: 'no man would acknowledge a superior nor could from this headless and unbridled
multitude be anything expected but disorder and riot'.[3]

When Gates arrived he set himself to restore order
sternly; but there was little he could do; men went on
dying and there were only four days' provisions left when
the colony gave up and set sail down the river. On their
way they met the incoming governor, Lord De la Warr, so
long delayed, and they were turned back to Jamestown.
Here, under proper authority, they were set to work once
more: 'every man endeavoureth to outstrip other in dili-
gence: the French preparing to plant the vines, the English
labouring in the woods and grounds; every man knoweth
his charge and dischargeth the same with alacrity.'[4] However, even during this period 150 men died, and De la Warr
himself fell ill and went home to die. In 1611 Sir Thomas
Dale was sent out with three ships, men and cattle and
provisions for a year. At Jamestown, according to Ralph
Hamor — one of the colonists of 1609 who survived all
through the founding period[5] — he found 'most of the
company at their daily and usual works, bowling in the
streets. These he employed about necessary works, as felling

[1] Smith, I. 204.
[2] W. Strachey, *The Historie of Travell into Virginia Britania* (1612), ed.
L. B. Wright and V. Freund, (Hakluyt Soc.), xxiv.
[3] q. Brown, I. 347.   [4] Smith, I. 208.   [5] He died in 1626.

of timber, repairing their houses ready to fall upon their heads.'[1]

One notices the mercurial ups and down of temperament among these Elizabethans, particularly exposed in those isolated conditions outside the firm framework of an authoritarian society. The fact was that the early Virginian voyages contained a large proportion of ne'er-do-wells and misfits, around the solid core of serious hard-working planters like Hamor. Here is a contrast with the Puritans in the North — and yet during their first winter at Plymouth one-half of the Pilgrims died. Gates and Dale brought over mainly artisans, and 'fewer gallants to escape evil destinies . . . lascivious sons, masters of bad servants and wives of ill husbands'.[2] There came over with Dale a promising young Cambridge clergyman, Alexander Whitaker, son of the well-known divine and Master of St. John's. Young Whitaker, who stepped out of a regular Puritan cousinage of Nowells, Chadertons and Culverwells, had experienced a genuine call to Virginia. Next year he published his *Good News from Virginia*, which attracted considerable attention. Whitaker became minister of Henrico, but the call was rendered null, the promise unfulfilled, by his drowning in the James River in 1617.[3]

With regard to the motives of the young men going over, a few traces are left in the records. Robert Evelyn writes in this year 1611, 'I am going to the sea, a long and dangerous voyage with other men, to make me to be able to pay my debts and to restore my decayed estate again.' A young Spelman describes himself, 'being in displeasure of my friends and desirous to see other countries'. The character of the remittance-man is to be seen in an unruly son of the Lady Finch who was sent to Virginia to be tamed, returned and within a week was killed in a drunken quarrel with the watch.[4] Not much chance of getting drunk in Virginia! Gradually consignments of women helped, let

---

[1] Hamor, *ed. cit.* 26.   [2] q. Brown, I. 355, 441, 484.
[3] For his career *v.* H. C. Porter, *loc. cit.*
[4] *The Letters of John Chamberlain*, ed. N. E. McClure, II. 502.

us hope, towards the stabilisation of society. In 1622, when everything else had lost money, the results of 'the joint stock for transporting a hundred maids to be made wives' gave the shareholders 'great contentment'.[1] Whether the colonists received equal contentment I do not know, for the girls arrived just in time for the great Indian Massacre, in which some three hundred and fifty colonists lost their lives.

Gates and Dale had been Netherlands campaigners, and they in turn imposed upon the colony the military laws that had governed the English army in the Netherlands. This answered: Hamor tells us that if these 'laws had not been so strictly executed, I see not how the utter subversion of the colony should have been prevented'.[2] Now they pressed on to found a new town, Henrico, fifty miles up the river in a more healthy situation than Jamestown. Hamor describes Jamestown for us as it was at this time with some pride: 'reduced into a handsome form, and hath in it two fair rows of houses, all of framed timber, two stories and an upper garret or corn-loft high, besides three large and substantial store-houses joined together in length some hundred and twenty foot and in breadth forty. And this town hath been, lately, newly and strongly impaled, and a fair platform for ordnance in the west bulwark raised.' It is touching to think of, to those of us who have seen the deserted site, the foundations now being laid bare, the simple objects of the colonists' daily use recovered from the soil, fragments of metal and pottery, if not their bones — for, of course, the whole place is a cemetery, their eloquent memorial. Dale never faltered in his hopes of the colony: he wrote to Robert Cecil, now Lord Salisbury, in 1611, 'I know right well how covetous (if not zealous) your full and absolute meditations are over and concerning this so pious, so heroic enterprise, in these days not employing any state in Christendom with a like work parallel to it.'[3] The old campaigner's phrasing, writing to the great man, was a

---

[1] W. R. Scott, *Joint Stock Companies to 1720*, II. 277.
[2] Hamor, 27, 33.   [3] q. Brown, I. 501.

trifle clumsy, but there is no doubt of his faith in the enterprise. Two years later he writes to Sir Thomas Smythe, 'I have seen the best countries in Europe; I protest unto you, before the living God, put them all together, this country will be equivalent unto them, if it be inhabited with good people.' [1]

At home Sir Thomas Smythe needed every ounce of confidence to keep the Adventurers to the task. In the absence of any return on their money, with repeated calls for further supplies, the discouragements of all these disasters, the persistent run of ill-luck and the rumours circulating against the colony in consequence, Smythe needed courage and statesmanship of the highest order to pull things round. These he possessed. He was a man of immense capacity and experience, of unhurried judgment and weighty decision, a somewhat impersonal man, who had the confidence of both the City and the Court. He was the son of the well-known Customer Smythe, customer of the port of London, and son-in-law of Sir Andrew Judd, one of the founders of the Muscovy Company. In 1604–5 he had been sent as envoy to Russia, to return with a new grant of privileges to the Company. From then on to 1621 he was, with one short break, Governor of the East India Company. He supported further voyages to find a North-West Passage, including Baffin's — an account of which the absurd Purchas omitted to include in his book; Baffin, penetrating farthest yet, gave his patron's name to Smith Sound. From the beginning Smythe had been in charge of the Virginia Company and the affairs of the colony.

Faced with a crisis in those affairs and finding that Bermuda looked now more promising, he called in Bermuda to redress the balance of Virginia. He obtained from the Crown a third Charter for Virginia, extending her bounds three hundred leagues from the Continent to include Bermuda. A Bermuda, or Somers Islands, Company was floated on a joint-stock, began to make profits from an immense piece of ambergris found on the coast and started

[1] q. *ibid.* I. 640.

to colonise. By 1616 there were some 600 in Bermuda to only 350 in Virginia, after the many hundreds that had been sent there. It is interesting to note some of the additional names recruited : Robert and Edward Berkeley, of that family to become famous in Virginia; Sir Samuel Saltonstall, head of a stock to make its name in New England —Massachusetts today is represented in the Senate by a Saltonstall; Sir Carew Ralegh, brother of Sir Walter. What chimes these names set going down the corridors of history!

But the Virginia Company was at its wit's end to know how to raise money. There was the greatest difficulty in getting the subscribers to pay up their promised instalments : actions were set going in the courts to make them. The new Charter permitted a lottery to be started, with prizes, to raise cash. And latterly the Company became chiefly a land-company, 'its one asset the land that had been bought with the sacrifices of the first ten years'.[1] The Company appealed to intending planters with an offer of 50 acres for every person to be sent to the colony; on this basis plantation continued and was extended — whatever the setbacks now, settlement went on.

Within the colony, too, the corner may be said to have been turned with the change from communal arrangements to private ownership. No doubt the first tasks in a new settlement were communal in their nature. But when the soldier-governors allotted every man in the settlement three acres of clear ground, they turned from bowling in the street to cultivating their gardens. Progress was at once to be seen. Captain Smith wrote, 'when our people were fed out of the common store and laboured jointly together, glad was he could slip from his labour, or slumber over his task, he cared not how; nay, the most honest among them would hardly take so much true pains in a week as now for themselves they will do in a day; neither cared they for the increase, presuming that howsoever the harvest prospered, the general store must maintain them, so that we reaped not so much corn from the labours of thirty as now

[1] W. F. Craven, *The Virginia Company of London, 1606–1624,* 32.

78

Sir Edwyn Sandys, Second Son of Archbp Sandys
From an Original Picture.
Published Jan 26 1776.

From Notestein: 'The English People on the Eve of Colonization'.   Harper Bros., New York

SIR EDWIN SANDYS

three or four do provide for themselves'.¹ No doubt. At the same time what was to become Virginia's staple export, tobacco, makes its first appearance. The credit for the first experiments is thought to be John Rolfe's. He made another experiment, too, which has brought him greater fame : he fell in love with Pocahontas, and she with him. After much deliberation with his friends, and some prayer, he married her properly. This favourably impressed the Indians and for some years there was a blissful interval of peace and good relations. Rolfe later brought Pocahontas home to England, where she 'unexpectedly' died — of the climate, perhaps.

Now that the colony had been brought round, the man by whose efforts it had been accomplished, Sir Thomas Smythe, lost control of the Company and received his dismissal, in the usual way of such things. There always had been a division in the Company between the big City merchants and the more numerous small adventurers, between the platform and the floor of the house. (As usual, the platform was generally right, the floor generally wrong.) Again as usual, the discontented majority found leadership among the magnates : in the Earl of Warwick, Shakespeare's Southampton, above all, Sir Edwin Sandys. Robert Rich, Earl of Warwick, was a jovial, rather tolerant type for a Puritan — he later used his influence in New England in favour of religious toleration, as against the Massachusetts Puritans. His illegitimate cousin, Richard Rich, was a planter in Bermuda, whose description of the tempest and wreck on that coast was one of the tracts Shakespeare may have read. This man quarrelled with the governor, who was Smythe's *protégé*, and so the Earl of Warwick joined Sandys in attacking Smythe's administration of the Virginia Company. Captain John Smith, who was no friend to Sir Thomas, tells us that he 'would hold it worse than sacrilege to wrong the Company but a shilling', and there never has been any doubt about the integrity of Sir Thomas's

¹ John Smith, *The General Historie of Virginia, New England and the Summer Isles* (MacLehose edn.), I. 222.

administration.[1] However, that did not save him; when he saw that the coalition had produced a majority against him, he withdrew and in 1619 Sandys became Treasurer.

Sir Edwin Sandys was a remarkable man, too. Educated under Richard Hooker at Oxford, where he became a Fellow of Corpus, and provided with a prebend at York by his father, the nepotistical Archbishop — though the son was never in orders — he was much more of an intellectual than Sir Thomas Smythe. He toured Europe with Archbishop Cranmer's great-nephew and dedicated the book he wrote, *Europae Speculum*, to Archbishop Whitgift. We see that his early associations were archiepiscopal. This did not prevent him from being rather a demagogue in the House of Commons, where he was very forward in opposition, resisting demands for supply, maintaining that the origin of monarchy was by election, that the people gave their consent to the authority of a king on reciprocal conditions and that a king who pretended to rule by any other right might be overthrown. (Is that not, if you will pardon the anachronism, rather an American inflexion?) It is almost enough to make one sympathise, if anything would, with James I and his divine-right nonsense: they both had read too much medieval theology for common sense.

In the Virginia Company Sandys captured the leadership of the lesser shareholders, many of whom, including fifty M.P.s, had not paid up their subscriptions. Sandys thereupon resorted to lotteries; he was very ingenious and resourceful, full of energy and ideas, up to anything and everything to raise money. And we must do him this justice: he did infuse new energy into, gave a fresh impetus to, the colony. After his first year of office James refused to have him renominated: 'Choose the Devil, if you will, but not Sir Edwin Sandys.' So Southampton was elected Treasurer; but Sandys remained the moving spirit. In 1620 the Crown came to the aid of Virginia by granting it the monopoly of the import of tobacco into England. Sandys proposed to help Bermuda — still under the control

[1] q. Scott, II. 267.

of his rival — by allowing her tobacco the English market, where it would pay 6d. a lb. custom, while Virginia's had the foreign market, where it paid little or none. Sir Edwin, I fear, was a sharp customer. When it came to depressing reports from Virginia, he and the Ferrars (later so holy at Little Gidding) doctored the minutes. An adept at manœuvring votes in council, by 1622 he had got into control of both Companies. He now proposed a scheme of salaries for himself and offices for his supporters that was unprecedented : himself as director to receive £500 a year. Smythe, after five years as Governor of the East India Company, had refused to accept more than £400 gratuity. For twelve years' service as Treasurer of the Virginia Company he was rewarded with twenty shares ; Sandys got as much for one year, and John Ferrars as his deputy the same amount for three years. It is not the first time that a reformer has been revealed as self-interested. This aroused bitter opposition and brought Warwick back into line with Smythe. But Sandys managed to ensure control by using the existing majority to 'suspend' the votes of his opponents.

The son of an archbishop had nothing to learn in the distasteful arts of managing committees. He was plausible, artful, restless, scheming, a favourite House of Commons man. Meanwhile, so engrossed were they in these characteristic amenities of committees, idiotic dissensions and personal manœuvres, that the terrible Indian massacre of that year — in which three hundred and fifty were killed and five hundred more died within the twelvemonth — went unnoticed, so far as remedies went. Sandys and the Ferrars suppressed information as to the worst miseries the colony endured, and put about misleading reports. But disquiet about Virginia grew, and Smythe's governor back from Bermuda, revealed the facts of Sandys's feverish overshipping of colonists and the fearful mortality in consequence. He had certainly been energetic. In the four years of Sandys' administration 4000 had been transported ; the net increase to the population was 275. In all, by 1622 some 10,000 souls had gone out to Virginia; of these only 2000 were alive. As to money, under Smythe £80,000 had been expended; in the far shorter period of Sandys, between £80,000 and £90,000. Lest you think me unjust to Sandys, I sum up in the words of an economic historian: 'Sandys should have been able to show very much better results since, when he took office, many of the initial difficulties had been overcome, instead of which, at approximately equal cost, under vastly more favourable conditions, he effected less'.[1]

No: the effective founder of Jamestown colony was Sir Thomas Smythe.

These facts were revealed by a committee appointed by the Crown, which exonerated Smythe's administration, going through all the books and figures, and condemned Sandys. There was furious dissension, for, of course, Sandys retained the support of the Commons. But the government had had enough of it; when Sandys and his allies appealed to the Commons, the Crown recalled the Virginia Charters and resumed the government of the colony into its own hands: henceforth this took the classic shape of royal governors with assistants nominated by the Crown, with a representative assembly. We may take this to end the founding phase in the colony's history. Up to 1624 the whole cost of the plantation of Virginia was about £200,000, with what little return we have seen. We may profitably contrast the money poured out by England to settle her stock in Virginia with Spain's ruthless exploitation of the West Indies, the regular drain of treasure from Mexico and Peru.

Meanwhile, what was the old enemy thinking of the course of events?

From the beginning in 1607 the Spanish ambassador Zuñiga was urgent with his king, Philip III, to dig up the root.[2] 'It will be serving God and your Majesty to drive

[1] Scott, II. 287.
[2] Zuñiga's correspondence is printed in Brown I. 122 foll., from which the above quotations are cited.

these villains out from there, hanging them in time, which is short enough for the purpose.' The Spanish Council of State considered the matter, but held that if, in negotiating the peace, they had demanded the exclusion of the English they would have encountered 'the difficulty that it is more than thirty years since they have had peaceful possession of it'. But the Council agreed that a small fleet should be made ready to windward (in Mexico) to drive them out, since their numbers would make this an easy task. A minute added that there would be delay in getting it ready and that it was not to be relied on. In December Zuñiga writes, 'will your Majesty give orders that measures be taken in time?' He hears that the aim is to put 2000 men in Virginia and then it will not be possible to move them thence.

Among the papers transmitted by Zuñiga was one that stated the official English view with regard to North America. 'The coasts and lands of Virginia were discovered many years ago by the English and we have sent colonies there at different times and without opposition on the part of the natives of the country, nor of any other sovereign, which is sufficient argument for us.' As for Pope Alexander VI, 'we do not acknowledge him as our superior'. It compared the situation at the beginning of the Queen's reign with that at the end, amazed at the contrast and by the fact that, while coming to the aid of her neighbours and maintaining large armies and fleets, nevertheless she had improved the condition of her subjects and increased their wealth immensely, compared with what she had found. 'Our ancestors on account of their lack of foresight and their carelessness lost the first opportunity and the first offering of the greatest treasures of the world, and we tax the omission of it. Yet now the same offering and the same trial is made to their children, Divine Providence having reserved for us this magnificent region and the discovery of this great world, which it now offers to us; and since we have arms to embrace it, there is no reason why we should let it escape us.' Nor did they. After 1607 they never let go, in spite of fearful discouragements, and this was in the end the achievement of London and the London merchants more than anyone. The statement is a fascinating example of the Elizabethan awakening to self-awareness — as fundamental an element in the fruition of Elizabethan literature as in the settlement of North America, the two immortal achievements of the age.

Zuñiga was in touch with Lord Arundell of Wardour, from whom he got information. Lord Arundell was discontented, Zuñiga reported, because as a Catholic they did not confide this business to him. The king warned his ambassador to proceed with caution or Lord Arundell might be *hechadiço* (done in). Lord Arundell offered to take a man from the Canaries to Virginia, to report to Spain the strength and fortifications of Jamestown. Now we know the kind of man Lord Arundell of Wardour was; however, he was not done in. In 1610 Zuñiga reported that a thousand more men were to go over, and this showed how much store the English set by it, 'since with such very great losses as they have suffered . . . they still show so much courage'. When he learned of the losses of the 'starving-time' he returned to the charge: now it would be easy to make an end of it altogether by sending a few ships to finish off what was left of the place. We see that Zuñiga was just like Mendoza had been twenty years before: I suspect that he must have been a stupid Castilian like him, quite unlike the clever, insinuating Galician Gondómar who succeeded.

In 1611 Philip III was still seeking information as to the exact state of the colony before deciding, and asked Zuñiga to place two Catholic spies on board the first ship sailing. That summer the Governor of Havana did send a sloop into the James River to investigate, with an Irish pilot on board, who was captured. On the way home in 1616, Sir Thomas Dale, finding that this man had acted as a pilot to the Armada in 1588, strung him up from the yard-arm. From 1612–13 the colony was at its lowest ebb and Philip III was glad to recline upon the hope that the business might sink of itself. He concluded that the best

thing was to do nothing. It is always easier to do nothing
— as Sir Winston Churchill says of the 1930's. Even the
clever Gondómar got the impression in the autumn of 1613
that the colony would be abandoned. Sir Thomas Smythe
told him that to date they had spent as much as £46,000
on the enterprise, all contributed by the merchants and
with some lotteries, without costing the King a real. And
he regaled Philip with the information we know already
that of the thousand persons sent during the last year and
those who were there, eight hundred had died; there
remained only three hundred in the colony.

We have a state paper drawn up by Hakluyt — his last
service to the great cause of his life — giving in detail the
bounds and limits of Spanish occupation in the New World.[1]
There were 'all those huge coasts and mighty inlands lying
southward of the Tropic of Cancer, which hitherto are
quite free from any Spanish government; all those spacious
countries on the east part of America from 32° to 72° of
northerly latitude have not nor never had any one Spanish
colony planted in them, but are, both by right of first
discovery performed by Sebastian Cabot at the cost of
King Henry VII and also of later actual possession taken
in the behalf and under the sovereign authority of her
Majesty, by the several deputies of Sir Walter Ralegh and
by the two English colonies thither deducted, as likewise by
Sir Humphrey Gilbert, Sir Martin Frobisher, Mr. John
Davis and others, most justly and inseparably belonging to
the crown of England. Which countries being greater than
all Europe and in goodness of soil nothing inferior there-
unto are by no means by us to be given over unto them,
who have already a great deal more than they can well
wield. Lastly on the backside or west of America beyond
Cape California, from 24° of northerly latitude to 43° (all
which coast Sir Francis Drake in his voyage about the
world discovered and took possession thereof for her Majesty
in 38°, calling the country New Albion) they have not one
foot of actual possession, much less more northerly. And

[1] q. *ibid.* II. 669 foll.

therefore in time to come they shall have no pretence of cavillation against a North-West Passage, if it should please God to lay open the same.'

There remained no more to be said. The facts spoke.

Within the colony, after such tribulations, all was at last set fair. Even before the last of them, the Indian Massacre of 1622, a most important development in government took place, from which the ultimate form of American government was shaped : the first representative assembly, based on popular election, met there in the tiny church beside the river at Jamestown. A touching scene in its simplicity and yet in all that it signifies — the heart of the political experience of the English-speaking peoples and the peculiar contributions they have to make to the world. It is the distant consequences that matter, and we see evidence of them even in formal details that speak : 'in selecting a new title in 1609, the adventurers chose the alternate of "governor" which, together with the traditional courtesy designation of "his Excellency", was destined to remain a permanent feature of American colonial and state government'.[1]

At home the interest displayed in very different quarters tells its own story. In matter of policy James I did not depart from the stand Queen Elizabeth had taken on America, though there were people, Sir Edwin Sandys among them, who were afraid that he might give way to the Spaniards. Anyway, in the first years that mattered most, he had Cecil beside him to guide policy on the Elizabethan lines. James's own interest did not amount to much. We have an exchange between Southampton and Salisbury in 1609 which shows what they thought. James had heard of the Virginia squirrels said to fly and asked Southampton whether there were none for him and whether Salisbury had not provided some for him. Southampton would not have told him 'but that you know so well how he is affected to these toys'.[2] One notices the contrast

[1] W. F. Craven, *The Southern Colonies in the Seventeenth Century*, 113.
[2] *Cal. S.P. Col., 1574-1660*, 8.

between the light-headed James in these matters and the profound and tenacious concern of the great Queen. And indeed nothing could have advertised that contrast more signally to the world than James's execution of Ralegh at the behest of Spain.

More worthy of respect is the interest of ordinary Englishmen in all walks of life in the new England rising on the other side of the Atlantic. The bishops raised a fund of some £2000 for an Indian college and for the support of an Indian school, though the Company was too short of funds to use them. One day in November 1620 a stranger stepped into a meeting of the court and presented Ralegh's history of Guiana, with a map and four great books, for the college; twelve months later a stranger again came forward with more books for it.[1] Most moving of all are the collections made on board the East Indiamen for Virginia. In 1621 at the Cape of Good Hope the *Royal James* collected £70 : 6 : 8 towards building a free school, the highest amount ten marks from Captain Pring and so down to 1s. from the mariners.[2] Two other ships collected 100 marks — in all £192 : 1 : 10 that Virginia might have a school. When we think of the hard conditions of those sailors' lives and out of their little pay contributing their shillings, we glimpse something of what America meant for those simple English folk.

On the other hand, there is all that the old country meant for the new. Professor Craven rightly emphasises that the beginnings of American history can only properly be read forward from the Elizabethan England of which it was an extrapolation, not backwards from modern America. He is writing in particular about the South, though what he says also applies with little change to the North: 'the historian who would trace the main threads woven into the pattern of Southern life must, therefore, turn first to England. . . . For it was the Elizabethan Englishman who planned and undertook the settlements to which most of us

[1] C. C. Stopes, *The Life of Henry 3rd Earl of Southampton, 1573–1624*, 427, 429.   [2] Brown, II. 973.

look back on as our beginnings. The Elizabethan tongue
that once rang out across the James and the York may still
be heard in certain out-of-the-way spots of the South. The
Elizabethan devotion to Protestantism, born of a long
defence of Elizabeth's church settlement and fed on the
fiery materials of John Foxe's *Book of Martyrs*, still survives
to shape the fundamental tenets of the great majority of
Southerners. Even the institutional pattern our forefathers
adapted to the peculiar requirements of a new-world
environment was more Elizabethan than anything else.
Though sheriffs, coroners, constables, justices of the peace,
juries and representative assemblies were ancient parts of
the English scene, it was as their place and function had
been defined under Elizabeth that the early colonists understood them. Here, too, has the South, ever prompt to
recognise individual achievement, discovered the first heroic
figures of her history — Elizabeth herself and Ralegh.' [1]

[1] W. F. Craven, *The Southern Colonies in the Seventeenth Century*, 27-8.

THE PORTRAICTVER OF CAPTAYNE IOHN SMITH ADMIRALL OF NEW ENGLAND.

Ætatis 37.
A° 1616.

These are the Lines that shew thy Face; but those
That shew thy Grace and Glory, brighter bee:
Thy Faire-Discoueries and Fowle-Overthrowes
Of Salvages, much Civilliz'd by thee
Best shew thy Spirit; and to it Glory Wyn;
So, thou art Brasse without, but Golde within.

CAPTAIN JOHN SMITH

CHAPTER V

SIR FERDINANDO GORGES AND NEW ENGLAND

WE owe the name of New England to Captain John Smith, so he said, and it seems to be true. This may be surprising, his name is so memorably associated with those first years in Virginia. But in 1614 he made a voyage along the coast of New England, the coasts of Maine and Massachusetts — from the towering cliffs of Penobscot, in and out the islands that form a kind of barrier reef, to the sandy shores of Cape Cod and the Massachusetts coast that reminded him of Devon. The coast of New England in summer conquered him; from that time forward he was its slave and its promoter. Two years later he published his *Description of New England*, and from that time the name stuck. Hitherto it had been known, rather clumsily, as the northern parts of Virginia, or North Virginia.

The name was probably suggested by comparison with Drake's New Albion: 'New England is that part of America in the Ocean Sea opposite to Nova Albion in the South Sea, discovered by the most memorable Sir Francis Drake in his Voyage about the World, in regard whereof this is styled New England, being in the same latitude'.[1] Smith was a sort of journalist-promoter as much as anything else. He published the best map of the New England coast to date, though somewhat marred by his habit of conferring his own names upon places everywhere: for example, Cape Cod, already well known as such, is called Cape James. That name did not stick. He followed this up with *New England's Trials* in 1620, and in 1624 his *General History of Virginia, New England and the Summer Isles*. Nor was this the

[1] John Smith, *The General History* (MacLehose edn.), II. 8.

tale of his publications: as late as 1631 there appeared his *Advertisements for the unexperienced Planters of New England or anywhere*. By this time there were in New England many planters with a longer experience than his own. An Elizabethan, born in 1580 — John Smith was not daunted by that. An eminent American historian, Samuel Eliot Morison, sums up: 'Smith was in Virginia only two years and a half, and left it forever in 1609, at the age of twenty-nine. The remaining twenty-one years of his life were largely devoted to promoting the colonisation of New England.' [1]

Twelve years earlier there was born a West Countryman to whom the actual colonisation of New England owed much more — indeed probably owed more than to any other man, as C. M. Andrews, author of the best history of the colonial period in America, recognises. This man was Sir Ferdinando Gorges. He came of ancient Somerset stock, connected with both the Queen and the Howards and therefore a Court family, which in this generation blossomed into these romantic names. There was a poet in the family named Arthur, whose lifelong friendship with Ralegh began, characteristically, in the Marshalsea, where those young bloods had been laid by the heels for Court offences: Ralegh 'for a fray beside the tennis-court', Arthur Gorges 'for giving the lie to Lord Windsor in the Presence Chamber'.[2] What he gave his sons might also be thought to merit the Marshalsea — the names Timoleon, Egremont, Carew.

Ferdinando was a cousin. Then there was Tristram, another cousin of an older generation, who inherited Budockshide, at the head of a creek of the Tamar below St. Budeaux church, where Drake was married, looking across to Saltash whence his bride came. There Tristram Gorges lies in what is left of a fine Elizabethan tomb, after the Victorians have done with it, hidden behind a nondescript organ and littered with hymn-books. This Gorges was related to Raleghs and Gilberts through his mother.

---

[1] S. E. Morison, *Builders of the Bay Colony*, 9.
[2] Raymond Gorges, *The Story of a Family*, 57.

He was associated with Adrian Gilbert in the patent for the North-West Passage in 1583. His brother Edward was on the famous Grenville expedition to plant at Roanoke in 1585, while a son of his was with Ralegh in Guiana ten years later. It was to him that Drake confided the custody of the distinguished prisoner he captured from the Armada, Don Diego de Valdez, and to him that Cavendish wrote his last letter of touching affection. Tristram Gorges was a near neighbour and good friend to his cousin Ferdinando, during his earlier years as Captain of the Fort at Plymouth. The clan held together and gave each other mutual support. When Ferdinando was in need of a third wife, he took Tristram's daughter Elizabeth Gorges. When he shortly after needed a fourth, he did not go outside the family: he recruited another cousin, also Elizabeth — this time a widow with a useful portion for him to spend on colonisation.

A younger son, Ferdinando Gorges inherited little and went off to the wars in Flanders: we find him at twenty one of the prisoners at Ypres to be exchanged for an equivalent gentleman taken in the Armada.[1] In the 1590's he served under Essex in Normandy, and in after years used often to tell how Henry of Navarre carried him wounded from some breach or other. Certainly Henry had a high opinion of him and wrote recommending him to the Queen for promotion: he 'hath gained very great reputation for his valour and conduct in war'.[2] She responded with the command of the Fort at Plymouth: he was the first there in the citadel looking out over the Barbican and Cattewater where the ships came and went for America. He was a loyal kind of man, and his loyalty to Essex, who made him a knight, brought him into danger: that *homme fatal* brought everybody he was in touch with into trouble. At the time of his outbreak — the 'rebellion *unius diei*' as the Queen contemptuously named it — Essex called Gorges up from Plymouth and he was one of those caught in Essex House. In a meeting with Ralegh in a boat on the Thames, Ralegh tried to get him to go back

[1] S.P. 12/216, 6.   [2] R. A. Preston, *Gorges of Plymouth Fort*, 40.

to Plymouth. When all was lost, it was Gorges who released Essex's eminent hostages, the Privy Councillors, from the house; and at Essex's trial he did not cut a dignified figure. However, he saved himself, or his family and friends at Court saved him; [1] and having burned his fingers badly once, he remained a government man ever afterwards. On James's accession he was restored to his command at Plymouth.

We have already seen that, before the Queen's death, exploratory voyages to the American coast, to both Virginia and North Virginia, were being made. All this time, all through the war, the West Country fishermen were going regularly, and in increasing numbers, to the Newfoundland fishery. But the New England fishery, several hundred miles farther on, was yet to be discovered. In 1602 Captains Gosnold and Bartholomew Gilbert set sail from Falmouth for the New England coast, with the intention of leaving a plantation there. They were much impressed by the climate — in summer — 'as healthful a climate as any can be', and 'had not a man sick two days together in all our voyage'.[2] They named Cape Cod, Martha's Vineyard and Elizabeth's Isle, names that stuck. They nosed up two main rivers that 'may haply become good harbours and conduct us to the hopes men so greedily do thirst after', *i.e.* a North-West Passage. They made effective contact with the Indians, who had already been in touch with Europeans: 'these with a piece of chalk described the coast thereabouts and could name Placentia of the Newfoundland' — that bay to gather such unforgettable memories in our time. They noted the Indians' facility with languages: 'they spake divers Christian words and seemed to understand much more than we, for want of language, could comprehend'. The red men were friendly and even

---

[1] Gorges thought of seeking service abroad again at this time, cf. his letter to Cecil, 18 February 1602: 'how grievous it is to me that — after the expense of so many years in Her service, so much blood lost and my whole estate wasted — I should now be forced to raise a new foundation under a foreign prince'. *Cal. S.P. Dom., 1601–1603*, 153.

[2] Purchas, *Pilgrims*, XVIII. 301 foll.

pressing. On going ashore a chief came to greet them —
Gabriel Archer stepping forth and embracing him, 'his
company then all sat down in manner like greyhounds upon
their heels, with whom my company fell a-bartering. . . .
Our captain gave him a straw hat and a pair of knives;
the hat awhiles he wore, but the knives he beheld with great
marvelling, being very bright and sharp. This our courtesy
made them all in love with us.' The only thing the Indians
did not like was English mustard, 'whereat they made many
a sour face'. A small fort was constructed on shore and
here ten men were left while the ship went off to collect a
cargo of cedar wood. Left to themselves with only three
meals' meat, the ship two days overdue, 'in the mean we
sustained ourselves with alexander and sorrel pottage,
ground-nuts and tobacco, which gave nature a reasonable
content. We heard at last our captain to lure unto us,
which made such music as sweeter never came unto poor
men.' Nevertheless, they did not stay, as they had intended:
there was some dispute whether they had enough victuals
for six weeks, let alone six months, and wrangling between
the planters and the sailors — a foretaste of what became
so frequent, on the *Mayflower* and all. So they agreed to
come home again. A report of the voyage was made to
Ralegh, whose rights in regard to American colonisation
were at this time still in force.

He gave his permission for the voyage inspired by
Hakluyt next year and backed by Bristol merchants, chief
among them Robert Aldworth — whose immense monument one used to see in his 'own aisle' in St. Peter's church
before the destruction of Bristol's churches. The captain
was that excellent navigator, Martin Pring,[1] who made —

---

[1] Pring's memorial in St. Stephen's church is worth recording.
'To the pious memory of Martin Pring merchant, and sometime General
to the East Indies, and one of the fraternity of the Trinity House.

> The living worth of this dead man was such,
> That this fair touch can give you but a touch
> Of his admired gifts. These quartered arts
> Enriched his knowledge and the sphere imparts.
> His heart's true emblem where pure thoughts did move
> By a most sacred influence from above.

so Gorges testified later — 'the most exact discovery of that coast that ever came to my hands since'.[1] He added that it was this, more than anything, that made him and that other Somerset man, Lord Chief Justice Popham, persevere with their efforts in spite of their initial discouragements. It was Pring who first penetrated into and appreciated the amenities of Massachusetts Bay. They took out with them a couple of excellent mastiffs, 'Fool' and 'Gallant', 'of whom the Indians were more afraid than of twenty of our men'.[2] They took back an Indian canoe, which they thought much like a Thames wherry. Contacts with the Indians were as important as geographical discovery or the commodities of the country.

Apparently the savages liked Elizabethan music. 'We had a youth in our company that could play upon a gittern, in whose homely music they took great delight and would give him many things, as tobacco, tobacco-pipes, snakes' skins of six foot long which they use for girdles, fawns' skins and such-like. And danced twenty in a ring, and the gittern in the midst of them, using many savage gestures, singing Jo, Ja, Jo, Ja, Ja, Jo: him that first brake the ring the rest would knock and cry out upon.' The English reported well of the Indian cultivation they saw, the gardens in which were sown 'tobacco, pompions, cucumbers and

Prudence and Fortitude are top this tomb
Which in brave Pring took up the chiefest room.
Hope — Time, supporters, show that he did climb
The highest pitch of hope though not of time.
His painful, skillful travels reached as far
As from the Arctic to the Antarctic star.
He made himself a ship: Religion
His only compass, and the truth alone
His guiding cynosure. Faith was his sails,
His anchor Hope, a hope that never fails;
His freight was Charity, and his return
A fruitful practice. In this fatal wine
His ship's fair bulk is lodged, but the rich lading
Is housed in heaven, a haven ever fading.
Hic terris multum iactatus et undis.
Obit anno salutis }1626
aetatis } 46.'

[1] *Sir Ferdinando Gorges and his Province of Maine*, ed. J. P. Baxter (Prince Soc.), II. 11.   [2] Purchas, XVIII. 322 foll.

such-like; and some of the people had maize or Indian wheat among them'. They noted the timber and fur-bearing capacities of the country; as for trees there was plenty of sassafras, 'a plant of sovereign virtue for the French pox' — and so held in much estimation by Elizabethan sailors. They laded their small bark, the *Discoverer*, with as much as they thought sufficient 'to give some speedy contentment to the adventurers', and sent her home to Bristol ahead of them.

In 1605 Captain Weymouth of Torbay, who had intended a fishing voyage on behalf of some Plymouth merchants, went instead on a prospecting voyage to Maine, set forth by the Earl of Southampton. People were becoming aware of the profits the French were making from the fur-trade, and at the same time Champlain was exploring these coasts. Weymouth collected some furs and skins, but was chiefly interested in prospecting for settlement and in the Indians. The narrator James Rosier wrote, 'the first and chiefest thing required for a plantation is a bold coast and a fair land to fall with. The next, a safe harbour for ships to ride in.'[1] He noted, 'here are made by nature most excellent places as docks to grave and careen ships of all burthens, secured from all winds . . . such that in few places in England, or in any other parts of Christendom, art with great charges can make the like'. The subsequent maritime history of Maine, the part it played for a century and a half in the history of the Royal Navy, showed how true that was.[2] Of the Indians, Weymouth gave an interesting account of their habits and of contacts with them; more important, he brought back five, three of whom he handed over to Gorges on his return. Gorges wrote that 'this accident must be acknowledged the means under God of putting on foot and giving life to all our plantations'.[3]

With the peace of 1604 Sir Ferdinando, like other professional soldiers, some of whom went to Virginia, was

---

[1] *Ibid.* 335 foll.
[2] Cf. W. H. Rowe, *The Maritime History of Maine*, 33.
[3] Baxter, II. 8.

rather at a loose end: he spoke of it as 'this idle time'. He was a modest man, having been at Oxford briefly, and described himself as 'a plain soldier and one that is no scholar'. But he wrote plainly and well, and was interested in the problems of fortification and navigation. An unpublished letter among the Hariot papers in the British Museum shows him to have been a friend both of him and of the mathematician Warner. He sends Hariot a discourse he has written 'Of the manner to observe the variation of the compass, or of the wires of the same, by the sun's rising or setting'.[1] He asks him 'to bestow an hour or two in reading it, for that time will largely suffice, as to my good friend I recommend that pains, and as to a most judicious mind I desire your overlooking of my over-sights'. A more intimate mark of friendship, he entreats Hariot to bring Mr. Carleton and Mr. Warner along with him to be gossips at a baptism. (Hariot, by the way, was usually regarded as an atheist; but *ça n'empêche pas*.)

These three Indians were a godsend to an energetic soldier with time on his hands at Plymouth Fort, and there closely in touch with the fishing voyages to Newfoundland, the ships going to and from America and the West Indies. 'After I had those people sometime in my custody I observed in them an inclination to follow the example of the better sort, and in all their carriages manifest shows of great civility far from the rudeness of our common people.' (Remember, this is ten or fifteen years before the visit of Pocahontas.) 'And the longer I conversed with them the better hope they gave me of those parts where they did inhabit, as proper for our uses, especially when I found what goodly rivers, stately islands and safe harbours those parts abounded with, being the special marks I levelled at as the only want our nation met with in all their navigations along that coast. And having kept them full three years, I made them able to set me down what great rivers ran up into the land, what men of note were seated on them, what power they were of, how allied, what enemies

[1] Add. MSS., 6789.

they had, and the like of which in his proper place.' [1]

Next year, 1606, came together the two companies, the London and the Plymouth Companies, to undertake American plantation in the South and in the North, without a complete separation between each other's areas and with intermingled rights and claims. Support for the Western Company came as much from Bristol as from Plymouth, and here Gorges found common meeting ground with his Somerset neighbour, Lord Chief Justice Popham, who had been Recorder of Bristol. It seems that the idea of a public plantation, instead of a series of individual enterprises, was Popham's and that it was his influence that got the Virginia Charter, combining London and West Country interests. From the beginning the Western ports, with their traditional jealousy and their conflict of interest with London, were displeased: their main interest was fishing, not plantation. And this cast a shadow over the whole future of the Plymouth Company and Gorges's life-long efforts.

However, optimistic and ardent, Popham and Gorges came together to send out a ship, victualled for twelve months, under Henry Challons as captain and with a Plymouth pilot who had been with Weymouth on the coast of Maine the year before. They took with them two of Gorges's Indians from that coast. Their instructions were to make for Cape Breton and then feel their way south and west; instead of which they made for the West Indies, where they were captured and taken off to prison in Spain. This utter 'loss and unfortunate beginning did much abate the rising courage of the first adventurers'.[2] Popham's second ship, under a Dorset connection Captain Hanham and the invaluable Pring, made the coast of Maine and brought back such a promising account that 'the Lord Chief Justice and we all waxed so confident of the business that the year following every man of any worth formerly interested in it was willing to join in the charge for the sending over a competent number of people to lay the ground of a hopeful plantation'.

[1] Baxter, II. 8-9.   [2] *Ibid.* I. 204-5.

Next year 1607 — at the same time as the London Company sent their first colony out to Jamestown — the Plymouth Company sent their first plantation out from Plymouth. This consisted of the usual hundred landsmen, with arms and provisions, in two ships: the *Gift of God* under the stern Chief Justice's kinsman, George Popham, and the *Mary and John* captained by Ralegh Gilbert. Shortly after they left the Lord Chief Justice died.[1] Our old friend Zuñiga reported joyfully to Madrid that, since he was the most active forwarder of the business and in the position to advance it best, he expected it would now drop.[2] And indeed it was a great blow: Gorges writes that his 'sudden death did so astonish the hearts of the most part of the adventurers as some grew cold and some did wholly abandon the business'.[3] In fact, he himself stepped into the breach: from this time forward it was he who most persistently, against all discouragements, kept the idea of New England colonisation to the fore.

The colonists arrived safely in Maine and settled down at Sagadahoc on the Kennebec River for the winter, which proved hard. We derive news of them from Gorges's letters to his kinsman Sir Robert Cecil, who was interested in these first voyages. 'This present day here is arrived one of our ships out of the parts of Virginia with great news of a fertile country, gallant rivers, stately harbours and a people tractable (so discreet courses be taken with them), but no return to satisfy the expectation of the adventurers . . . Plymouth this 1 of December late at night 1607.'[4] News from the colony was not good. 'For first the President himself [George Popham] is an honest man but old and of an unwieldy body and timorously fearful to offend or contest with others that will or do oppose him.' Whereas 'Captain Gilbert is described to me from thence to be desirous of supremacy and rule, a loose life, prompt to sensuality, little zeal in religion, humorous, headstrong and of small judgment

---

[1] He is buried beneath a splendid painted tomb, with all his family gathered round him at the base, in the church of Wellington in Somerset.

[2] A. Brown, *The Genesis of the United States*, I. 111.

[3] Baxter, I. 206.   [4] *Ibid.* III. 154–63.

and experience, otherwise valiant enough'. We see that he was a true son of Sir Humphrey, and now, a generation on, he remembered that his father had had the first grant for North America. 'He holds that the king could not give away that by patent to others, which his father had an act of Parliament for and that he will not be put out of it in haste . . . besides he hath sent into England for divers of his friends to come to him, for the strengthening of his party on all occasions.' Like father, like son : this faction-fighting in the bitter Maine winter, with their store-house burnt down over their heads, much discouraged the planters. One lesson that needed to be learned was that each colony, to be successful, needed one undisputed head : a Governor Bradford or a Governor Winthrop.

Some of the colony had behaved well. The preacher, Richard Seymour, 'is most to be commended, both for his pains in his place and his honest endeavours; as also is Captain Robert Davis and likewise Mr. Turner their physician, who is come over to solicit their supplies'. Of Master Carew nothing is said : probably a supporter of *his* cousin Gilbert.[1] Gorges ends, with an impulse of discouragement, though it expressed his deepest conviction, 'I desire in my soul that it would please God his Majesty would take it into his own hands, unto whom of right the conquest of kingdoms doth appertain'. Three months later the second ship returned with nothing to show from a winter in Maine, except to say that, surprisingly, all the colony were well : not a death among them. However, 'these often returns without any commodity hath much discouraged our adventurers, in especial in these parts'. But Gorges viewed the question of colonisation from a loftier standpoint than immediate profit, and indeed, for himself, he was to spend all his private means and his wives' upon it, many thousands, and impoverish himself in the end.

He pointed out to Cecil that 'in common reason it be

---

[1] I mention him simply to correct his name as given in all the books, Gome Carew. It is evidently Gawen, a name in use in the Carew family at this time.

not to be looked for that, from a savage wilderness, any great matters of moment can presently be gotten, for it is art and industry that produceth those things, even from the farthest places of the world. And therefore I am afraid we shall have much ado to go forwards as we ought, wherefore it were to be wished that some furtherance might be had, if it were possible, from the chief spring of our happiness, I mean his Majesty, who at the last must reap the benefit of all our travail.' But the chief spring of all our happiness, the son of Darnley and Mary Stuart, had other objects on whom to spend his money : not a penny did *he* spend — unlike the great Queen — on what was to give the English their place in the world. As for colonisation, America, the sea — he was vastly more interested in theology.

The soldier in Gorges realised the strategic importance of possession of the coast. Already the French had a settlement farther up the coast in Acadia ; in this year Champlain founded Quebec; the Dutch were sending Hudson to explore the river called by his name and were shortly to occupy Manhattan Island in the finest harbour in the world. Gorges was there in mind before them : he asked if the king 'would be pleased to adventure but one of his middle sort of ships with a small pinnace' — as Elizabeth would certainly have done — 'and I durst myself to undertake to procure them to be victualled by the adventurers of these parts, for the discovery of the whole coast along, from the first to the second colony'. Gorges offered himself for the command, would be proud to accomplish it. If it had been taken notice of, we should have been first on the Hudson. Instead of which : no response.

Gorges and his associates in the West found means to send out two little supply ships from Topsham, and were racking their brains to find the means to send out another of 200 tons the next spring. But there was no return from the colony at all. In mid-December George Popham had written the king a grandiose letter, in Latin, as he thought befitting, from 'the fort of St. George in Sagadahoc of

Virginia', announcing that the Indians 'positively assure me that there is a certain sea in the opposite or western part of this province, distant not more than seven days' journey: a sea large, wide and deep, of the boundaries of which they are ignorant; which cannot be any other than the Southern Ocean, reaching to the regions of China, which unquestionably cannot be far from these parts'.[1] This effort exhausted him. When the *Mary and John* arrived with supplies for another year of it, they found that the President was dead. They brought news that was more disastrous: at home Sir John Gilbert had died, leaving his brother heir to his estate. To claim it Ralegh Gilbert returned home, and the colonists elected to return with him in the *Mary and John*, and the pinnace they had built that winter. She was the *Virginia*, first English ship to be built in North America: she survived to make several voyages to Virginia. Considering that all but two of the colonists had survived, in contrast to Jamestown — the Maine winter had acted as a preservative, perhaps a tonic — it was a most disappointing conclusion.

Thus ended the first plantation in New England — the parallel to Roanoke in 1585–6.

The Western adventurers had lost everything they put into these attempts, and they simply had not the resources of the London Company to go on and on until the plant rooted. (Even so, we know what a near thing it was in Virginia.) However, fishing voyages increased upon the coast and began to creep down to the New England fishery, which had one advantage in that it was much closer inshore than the Grand Banks. From this time forward there were constantly men visiting the coast, some of them remaining there — like Captain Williams from Popham's colony whom John Smith found leading a Robinson Crusoe existence on the mainland opposite the island of Monhegan, the best location for fishing. Gorges continued to send fishing vessels along with others in the hope that 'by our ordinary frequenting that country' it would in time 'yield both

[1] Brown, I. 145-6.

profit and content'. Southampton sent a vessel out in
1611 and another in 1614. The first brought back more
Indians, one of whom, Epenow from Martha's Vineyard,
was sent to join Captain Weymouth's Assacumet from
whom Gorges was learning about the Cape Cod area to
the South.

Some of these Indians had fantastic experiences. Assacumet had been captured on Challons's ship and taken with
him to Spain, whence the Indian managed to escape and
somehow got back to Gorges at Plymouth. Gorges's contacts and conversations with these Indians helped to keep
his interest alive. In 1614 a Captain Hunt seized a score
or more Indians on the coast and took them to Málaga
to sell as slaves. One of these, Tisquantum or Squanto,
managed to get a passage on a Bristol fishing-boat out of
Málaga to Newfoundland on his way home to Cape Cod.
In Newfoundland he met a Captain Dermer, who brought
him back with him to Gorges at Plymouth. His interest
in Indians must have been well known by now, and he was
certainly shocked by Hunt's treacherous conduct, which
naturally made the Indians on the Massachusetts coast
mistrustful and hostile for some time to come.

Epenow, who was a fine-looking fellow, had been shown
in London 'for a wonder', and preferring to get back to
his people, put up a tall story about a gold-mine on Cape
Cod, which persuaded Gorges and his fellow-adventurers
to equip a vessel to take him across the Atlantic — treating
it as his Cunarder, evidently. When he got to the coast,
being a man of great stature and strength, he slipped out
of their clutches over the side and joined his relations. That
ended the hopes of that voyage : dead loss again. Nevertheless in 1618 Gorges tried once more, sending out a Captain
Rocroft with a scratch crew, who, after various adventures
on the New England coast, made him go for Virginia where
his ship was wrecked and himself killed in a quarrel. (It
is the world of *Treasure Island*.) Next year Gorges sent out
Captain Dermer, an able navigator, with friend Squanto
aboard, whom he set ashore among his people, and then

met with Epenow once more. In his exploration of the coast Dermer penetrated into Long Island Sound, got through Hell Gate, proving that it was an island, and followed the coast south all the way to Virginia, where he wintered. Returning in the spring to Epenow's coast, the Indian tried to kill him, and, severely wounded, Dermer struggled back to Virginia to die.

The more amenable Squanto, however, does not seem to have resented his English experiences. When the innocent Pilgrims arrived at New Plymouth in 1620 they were astonished to find a savage who spoke fluent English: they considered him, of course, 'a special instrument sent of God for their good beyond their expectation'.[1] And indeed he made himself invaluable to them as their interpreter, put them in touch with the native chief Massasoit with whom they made peace, 'directed them how to set their corn, where to take fish and to procure other commodities, and was also their pilot to bring them to unknown places for their profit and never left them till he died'. It was Squanto who gave them their contact with the Indians southward in Massachusetts Bay, which enabled them to start up a trade in beaver. On a journey with them to get Indian corn and beans, without which they could hardly have lasted out their second winter, he died, 'desiring the Governor to pray for him that he might go to the Englishmen's God in heaven, and bequeathed sundry of his things to sundry of his English friends, as remembrances of his love; of whom they had a great loss'. It is hard to see how the Pilgrims could have got through their first two years without him: no recognition, of course, of what they owed to the trouble Gorges had previously taken with the Indian.

The Pilgrims were the first to make a permanent plantation, but there were already small settlements on the coast, fishermen wintering there, regular communications with Virginia. Virginia was interested in the New England

[1] William Bradford, *History of Plymouth Plantation, 1620–1647* (Mass. Hist. Soc.), I. 202-3, 283.

fishery, and sent boats up for supplies. The French were already settled on the coast farther north. M. de Monts had moved his original settlement (1604) from the Ste-Croix river to Port Royal in Nova Scotia. Now in 1613 a new settlement was made in the Mount Desert area on the coast of Maine. This was within the latitude of the Virginia Company's charter. They were not going to undertake all those efforts, undergo all those sacrifices, to find themselves forestalled by the French: they ordered Captain Argall up from Virginia to put an end to the settlements. Which he did, effectively, but with complete humanity: no massacres like those the Spaniards committed in Florida, or such as the Dutch were shortly to commit in Amboyna. He took the colony's leaders off into gentlemanly captivity along with Pocahontas at Jamestown. The Jesuit Father Biard pays tribute to Argall's humanity: though 'a very clever and cunning captain' he was 'still a gentleman, with truly noble courage; his men were neither inhuman nor cruel in their treatment of us'.[1]

This is not the full tale of the efforts made by Gorges and others in these years before the sailing of the *Mayflower*. Captain John Smith had come back in 1614 fired by an idea — no doubt others had it at the time, but he made more of it — namely, of combining planting with fishing. The fishing-boats went out and back doubly manned, having to carry men to dry and cure the fish, in addition to the fishermen. What more obvious than that these should remain on shore as planters, supplementing the fishermen at need, instead of being carried to and fro? This became the basis of Gorges's next phase of activity, as also of the Dorchester Company with its brief colony at Cape Ann, out of which the Massachusetts Bay Colony sprang. In 1615 four London ships sailed for New England, only one from Plymouth and that largely provided by Gorges. She 'returned as she went, and did little or nothing but lost her time'. This may have been captained by Sir Richard Hawkins, Sir John's son who had spent several years in

[1] C. M. Andrews, *The Colonial Period of American History*, I. 149.

captivity in Spain. Next year Gorges had better luck with the boat he sent under his servant Richard Vines; for though the ship's company refused to explore but concentrated on fishing, Gorges's men were able to trade along the coast and actually wintered there. Thus it was Gorges who tried out, what Smith had only suggested, the feasibility of winter settlement in New England — the Popham experiment had made people very doubtful. What returns Gorges got from fishing ventures he spent on exploring with a view to settlement, his real passion: 'this course I held some years together, but nothing to my private profit, for what I got one way I spent in another'.[1]

On the basis of all this experience and dearly-bought knowledge Gorges thought he now saw the way to successful plantation: he would secure from the Crown a patent for the northern territory with rights of government and power to grant licences to plant as also to fish on the coasts: the payments for fishing licences would provide funds for plantation. At once he found himself opposed by the Virginia Company under the redoubtable Sir Edwin Sandys.[2] However, the Crown granted the charter for New England, with an extension of boundaries, as had been done for Virginia to include Bermuda — in this case to 48° North to include Acadia. A Council was set up, very different from the Virginia Company: a self-perpetuating body, including seven sleeping Privy Councillors who never attended; it was not under the control of the investors — perhaps that was why it had no investors, or very few, beyond Gorges, his family and a few friends like Argall, Dr. Sutcliffe and Dr. Gooch, successive Deans of Exeter. They were a company of gentlemen. The absence of the merchants was fatal: the New England Council simply never had enough resources, it lived from hand to mouth.

[1] Baxter, II. 19.
[2] The dispute came before the Virginia Company, where Gorges protested against what he considered the infringement of the Plymouth Company's patent. Sandys retorted, plausibly as ever, that the two Companies were one free of the other, and that their patents allowed each to fish within the other, the sea being free. *Records of the Virginia Company of London*, ed. S. M. Kingsbury, I. 277.

The whole idea was the Elizabethan one of a regulated colonial enterprise, already becoming inappropriate in the circumstances of seventeenth-century society.[1]

Checkmated by the Crown Sandys carried the case to the House of Commons. One would hardly expect that body to take long views, and freedom to fish was the popular cause, upheld (of course) by Sir Edward Coke. They considered fishing more profitable to the commonwealth than planting English stock in America. So did the West Country ports, and their M.P.s followed suit. The attack was held up by successive adjournments of Parliament, but the struggle itself increased hostility to Gorges and the New England Council, and support fell away: 'all men were afraid to join with us', he wrote.

Meanwhile, a very different body of men came forward: the Pilgrims. 'In the story of American colonisation', C. M. Andrews says, 'the Pilgrim plantation at Plymouth occupies a place apart from the normal colonising process, in that its origin and purpose were entirely out of touch with the features of settlement characteristic of the time.'[2] They were a religious body, at any rate the nucleus of them was — only thirty-seven of the hundred or so who came over in the *Mayflower*.

The Pilgrims were in origin a Nottinghamshire group who were in the habit of meeting at Scrooby manor, where their Elder Brewster was postmaster. The lease of Scrooby manor was held by Sir Edwin Sandys's brother, Sir Samuel,[3] eldest son of the acquisitive and philoprogenitive Archbishop — he got it from his father, out of the see of York. To enjoy their own brand of religious observance and the ministrations of their pastor, John Robinson, the Pilgrims migrated to Holland. After a decade of that they decided

---

[1] In the *Brief Relation* Gorges points the contrast, evident to 'every well-affected person or any truly loving the public good of our nation', between 'trading by joint stock under government and order and the promiscuous trading without order and in a disjointed manner, as of late they have done to the infinite prejudice of others already'. Baxter, I. 223.

[2] C. M. Andrews, 298.

[3] Sir Samuel's grandson married the widow of Col. Henry Washington, cousin of John Washington, emigrant ancestor of the first President.

on America. They first thought of Guiana, with Ralegh's recent expedition in mind, 'but the jealous Spaniard would never suffer them long, but would overthrow them, as he did the French in Florida'.[1] Spain would have made short shrift of *them*: it would have been the flames of the Inquisition. So they concluded 'to live as a distinct body by themselves under the general government of Virginia'. They sent two emissaries to London, where they 'found the Virginia Company very desirous to have them go thither. And willing to grant them a patent with as ample privileges as they had or could grant to any.' They should have toleration in practice: the King could not openly depart from the law, but he 'would connive at them and not molest them'. King James and even the much-maligned bishops consented to the Pilgrim form of subscription. The Pilgrims were in the habit of regarding themselves as much persecuted in this world, but in fact everybody was very helpful.

At this time, 1619, Sandys gained control of the Virginia Company and gave them every encouragement. They got their patent to settle, the Company approved their plan, declared the thing was of God and, what was more important, loaned them £300 out of its exiguous resources. On this basis they went forward: 'it is not with us as with other men, whom small things can discourage, or small discontentments cause to wish themselves at home again'. And so it proved. They were much aided in making their arrangements by a not very respectable promoter-under-taker, a Mr. Weston, who obtained the patent for them and organised the business end of their affairs in London — which proved largely unremunerative, I may say, to the original investors. However, late in the season, much delayed, the *Mayflower* set sail from Plymouth on 16 September 1620.

They had originally intended to settle, as 'but one particular colony or plantation' within the area of the Virginia Company. As they drew near to the coast they

[1] Bradford, I. 64-8, 76.

thought of the Hudson River, but much-buffeted and exhausted by the voyage they halted at Cape Cod, then
settled across the bay at New Plymouth. They kept the
Mayflower with them that first terrible winter in which —
as at Jamestown — half the colonists died. In one respect
they were lucky: in the two or three years before their
coming most of the Indians on that coast, after bitter inter-
necine war, had died of plague. This was regarded as a
special providence, and it meant that in their weakened
state they were not molested.

We cannot pursue their story here. We must merely
note that they went under a patent similar to all the other
grants made by the Virginia Company, allotting them land
but no powers of government. They never did get any
grant of powers of government — all that was provisional,
dependent upon the measures to be taken by the Crown
for the government of New England when the time came.
The Pilgrims never had the slightest reluctance — unlike
the Massachusetts Puritans — in owning their allegiance and
obedience to the Crown. What they were chiefly interested
in was their separateness and sufficiency to themselves as a
church. Satisfied as to that they entered into a compact
together — that is, the members of the church — to form
a 'civil body politic for our better ordering and preservation'.[1] A lot has been made of that, a whole myth grown
up around the Pilgrim Compact: in fact, it was merely
common sense, operating like any corporate town at home
in England, such as they formed. And it certainly did not
represent the rule of the majority: it merely provided for
popular 'ratification of government by the best men'.[2]
Actually, Governor Bradford, governor for some thirty years,
exercised a benevolent autocracy, as he was well qualified
to do.

Having settled in New England, in 1621, they sued out
a fresh patent from the New England Council, of which
Gorges was the ruling spirit. Gorges made no difficulty
whatever; he had no objection to Puritans, indeed we find

[1] Bradford, I. 191.   [2] Andrews, I. 293.

him working in association with Warwick in the New England Council and he was friendly with other Puritan leaders, Sir John Eliot and Lord Saye and Sele. He was glad to welcome the Pilgrims into his plans for the plantation of New England — always with the proviso of the ultimate governmental rights of the New England Council. When the Pilgrims' agent, John Pierce, got himself a second patent constituting something like a seigniory for himself, and the Pilgrims objected, it was withdrawn. Later they had no difficulty in securing a patent for the Kennebec concession in Maine, where they had their fishery, and in 1630 Bradford secured them a charter with enlarged rights and delimitation of boundaries. So long as the work went forward and there was no challenge to the overlordship of the New England Council, Gorges was content and helpful.

In 1621 Sir Ferdinando, still sanguine, married his second wife, a Cornish widow with a portion, which enabled him to expend some more money on his schemes and undertake the building of a large vessel, the *Great Neptune*, to control the New England fishery. It was time for him to assert the Council's rights. That slippery customer Weston had forfeited his ship for exporting ordnance contrary to the law, and slipped away to Massachusetts Bay with a very mixed crew of people, who were dealing badly with the Indians and causing trouble. This was within the Council's jurisdiction, but it had no funds and therefore effective power to assert it. Gorges fell back on the *pis aller* of land grants to raise cash, and on the device of a grand lottery at Greenwich Palace, with King James amiably drawing lots on behalf of his still sleeping Privy Councillors, by way of attracting publicity. As part of the campaign Gorges published his *Brief Relation of the Discovery and Plantation of New England*, our best authority for the first obscure stages in which he had been a prime mover. The book has the further interest of exposing his idea of colonisation as an extrapolation of the normal English society of the day, with its usual structure and accustomed institutions. Laws were to be enacted by a general assembly :

Gorges was in no way behind the first assembly of Virginia
or the Mayflower Compact.

Among those who had got grants of land on Massachusetts Bay was Robert Gorges, Sir Ferdinando's second
son, and in 1623 he sent him over to assert authority as
Governor-General of New England. There went with him
Captain Francis West — of the De la Warr family so much
interested in Virginia — to assert authority over the fishermen and various others who had taken up land with the
idea of forming a plantation. The whole assumption was
that this was but a forerunner to a larger expedition next
year with the big ship, the *Great Neptune*, which was not yet
ready. Until that happy consummation they had nothing
to assert their authority with, and the realisation of that
gives a certain edge to Governor Bradford's account of their
proceedings, which betrays his satisfaction.

The Pilgrim Governor conducted himself with perfect
propriety and much worldly wisdom. He received the
young Governor-General with politeness, when he came
over from Wessagussett in pursuit of the contumacious
Weston. When Weston perceived that Gorges possessed no
greater power than himself, and was indeed dependent on
the Pilgrims, he grew insolent. Governor Bradford did not
question young Gorges's authority: he contented himself
with pointing out the impossibility of exercising it. It was
a humiliating situation — all the more since Captain West
failed equally to get the fishermen to recognise his authority,
while the clergyman they brought with them did not dare
exercise his ministry in that holy place. Bradford sums up
the episode in his *History*: 'the Governor and some that
depended upon him returned for England, having scarcely
saluted the country in his government, not finding the state
of things here to answer his quality and condition'.[1]

Sir Ferdinando did not blame his son for not having
made a better effort, though he might well have done.
For some of his company remained on there: the incoming
Puritans later found David Thomson living alone on an

[1] Bradford, I. 336.

island in Boston Bay, another comfortable solitary occupying Beacon Hill.[1] Some came back; others floated off to Virginia. Gorges put down his son's failure simply to 'the poor means he had'. Meanwhile, he himself was approaching the West Country towns once more to support his efforts. So far from that, they were only waiting for Parliament to meet to attack what they regarded as a fishing monopoly, upon which Gorges's hopes rested; and when Parliament met the attack broadened into one against the Council's Charter itself. Gorges did his best in Parliament, appearing before the Commons' committees, answering the agitation with his usual reasonableness and patience. But in vain: the government gave way over the fishing rights and that knocked the bottom out of his plan for plantation. There were very few who had given him any support, and these now withdrew. 'These crosses did draw upon us such a disheartened weakness as there only remained a carcass in a manner breathless.'[2]

The next few years, 1624 to 1629, were occupied by desultory wars with Spain and France into which the incompetent handling of affairs by those young men, Buckingham and Charles, muddled the country. Gorges, as governor of Plymouth, had the express confidence of the government, and he was busily employed not only there, struggling to equip and dealing with the *débris* of their ill-managed expeditions, but also in operations at sea. All that is no part of our story; what is, is this. In Canada Quebec was taken, and the whole of French territory fell into British hands. At the peace this was handed back to France, in return for the payment of Henrietta Maria's dowry — to the understandable indignation of Puritan empire-builders, who did not much appreciate her private theatricals or her. Secondly, while Gorges's back was

---

[1] This man, William Blackstone, a Cambridge man told them, 'I came from England because I did not like the Lord Bishops, but I cannot join with you because I would not be under the Lord Brethren.' q. H. C. Porter, *Reformation and Reaction in Tudor Cambridge*, 257.

[2] q. Preston, 233.

turned and he had other things to think about, something happened that turned out to be decisive for the American future : the Massachusetts Bay Company got its charter for territory plumb in the middle of the New England Council's grant, and incidentally overlaying Robert Gorges's perfectly legal grant on the shores of the Bay — prelude to the big Puritan migration that, more than any other factor, made New England what it became. *How* the Massachusetts Bay Company got a patent, which it proceeded to turn into a royal charter, has never been fully clear and will never now come to light. And those legally-minded Puritans, John Winthrop and company, were careful to carry their charter away with them from the English shores so that, when the government asked for it for investigation, it could not be produced.

The story goes back to 1623 and to Dorchester, where John White, a Wykehamist Fellow of New College, was the pastor of Holy Trinity and St. Peter's churches for nearly half a century.[1] (He lies buried there under the porch of St. Peter's — Hardy's St. Peter's.) For most of that time he was an active propagandist of colonisation in America and took a direct hand in equipping and sending out ships and colonists — a Dorset parallel to Gorges, with whom he was roughly contemporary. He was taken with Captain John Smith's idea of combining fishing with plantation, and in 1623 got over a hundred Dorset and Somerset folk to subscribe to a joint-stock for the purpose and form the Dorchester Adventurers, with his parishioner John Humfry as treasurer, subsequently a leading figure in Massachusetts. They got their patent from the New England Council, sent out a colony in that year to Cape Ann and in successive years dispatched further ships with supplies. By 1626 they lost everything they had put into it and more. (It does not seem that anybody ever made any money by these ventures.)

John White found, like Gorges before him, that fishing

---

[1] F. Rose-Troup, *John White, the Patriarch of Dorchester and the Founder of Massachusetts, 1575–1648*, vii.

and planting did not go together. 'No sure fishing place in the land is fit for planting nor any good place for planting found fit for fishing, at least near the shore. And, secondly, rarely any fishermen will work at land, neither are husbandmen fit for fishermen but with long use and experience.' [1]

However, like Gorges, White was undaunted : he wrote, 'as in building houses the first stones of the foundation are buried under ground and are not seen, so in planting colonies the first stocks employed that way are consumed, although they serve for a foundation to the work'.[2] And the Cape Ann venture had important consequences. In its last year Roger Conant moved up there from New Plymouth to take charge. He had come out from Ralegh's parish of East Budleigh, but had been put off by the rigid separatism of the Pilgrims. Now he led the remnant of the Cape Ann settlement back to Massachusetts, where he became the founder of Salem. At home a new idea of signal importance became grafted on to that of plantation : with the gathering conflict between Crown and Parliament, between the Puritans and the Laudian church, that of a Puritan refuge overseas. The idea was very understandable, if one thinks only of the blundering ineptitude of Charles I's conduct of affairs. Even James had not been quite such a fool — though there were West Countrymen who never forgave Ralegh's execution : two of them who had witnessed it outside the Gatehouse at Westminster wrought an almighty revenge upon the Stuarts — John Eliot and, brought up on Tamarside in the home of the Rouses, John Pym.[3]

There now came together three elements : John White and his West Country supporters ; the London merchants who have been shown to be indispensable — chief among them Sir Richard Saltonstall of the Virginia Company, in whose house Captain John Smith died ; and a formidable group of East Anglian Puritans, of whom the leader was

[1] q. Andrews, I. 351.
[2] q. S. E. Morison, *Builders of the Bay Colony*, 29.
[3] For their colonial activities *v.* A. P. Newton, *The Colonising Activities of the English Puritans*.

John Winthrop. His father was Adam Winthrop, cloth-worker of London, who became the squire of Groton in Suffolk. (The manor had been bought, from the estates of Bury St. Edmunds, when the going was good, after the Dissolution.) Adam Winthrop was auditor of Trinity College, Cambridge; his famous son John, born in Armada year, went up to Trinity before the end of the Queen's reign, in 1601.[1] He did not remain long; like all Puritans he was disturbed about his spiritual condition and some other little things, for at seventeen he married. Reading between the lines, I rather think John Winthrop was of an amorous disposition — all within the safe bounds of Christian matrimony, of course : he ran through four wives. Married in April 1605, his first son was born in February 1606 — to become well known as Governor of Connecticut.

Winthrop's Journal reveals him as becoming more intensely religious, as family troubles accumulated, and as the country moved from the balance of the Elizabethan age to that sharpening of conflict, that scission and unbalance that foreboded the lamentable, the destructive, Civil War. All this group were very much under the influence of Puritan theologians, William Perkins of Christ's, William Ames and the rest of them.

A group of such men, friends and relations, gentlemen, men of ability and education — nearly all Cambridge men — came together. There were Isaac Johnson and John Humfrey, who had married the daughters of two Puritan peers ; Thomas Dudley, who, like Gorges, had fought under Henry of Navarre and was latterly a parishioner of the Puritan divine, John Cotton, at Boston. There were Increase Nowell and William Pynchon and Saltonstall. At Cambridge in 1629 they met and signed a compact to go to New England and found a commonwealth. They next decided to take their patent with them, for they meant to be in control themselves. This was the fundamental difference between them and the Pilgrims. These were not simple people content to obey ; these were governing

[1] *The Winthrop Papers*, I. 78, 89, 175.

Puritans who were leaving the country because they could not have their own way. When they got to Massachusetts, from the beginning they made it clear that they meant to have it. People who wanted the Book of Common Prayer were soon given to understand that they had better leave — and indeed the Pilgrims had sent Church of England people away from New Plymouth. They never went over there to set a model of toleration, they never intended it; they went there to have their own way, and to impose it on others. As John Cotton said, 'do ye not know that the Saints shall judge the world?' (Saints = themselves.) 'And Solomon maketh it the joy of a commonwealth, when the righteous are in authority.' [1] In other words, it was a reinforcement of their own egoism — naturally the most vital force in human history. And it certainly succeeded — the central, if not necessarily the final, test in human history.

Governor Endecott, a stern, unattractive Devonshire-man, had gone before in 1628 to prepare the ground. In 1630 no less than fourteen ships left these shores with over a thousand colonists, and — since they had such strong backing and resources — no want of supplies. This was in marked contrast with everything that had gone before, in New England no less than Virginia. It was something exceptional. And there was another thing that was exceptional, too. In the interval they had managed to turn their patent from the New England Council into a royal charter, which confirmed to them not only territorial rights, but rights of government. 'The charter created something that had not existed before, the right of these men as a corporate body to rule and administer the territory under their authority and to exercise complete sway over any colonies or plantations that might be set up on its soil.' [2]

How had they managed it? Nobody knows. One thing is clear: they managed it when nobody was looking. For another: these Puritans were not lawyers, like John Winthrop, for nothing. For a third: there is no doubt at all that the Puritan magnates, the Earl of Warwick and

[1] q. Morison, 85-6.   [2] Andrews, I. 368.

Lord Saye and Sele, were deliberately helping them out with their plans. They got their original patent from Warwick as President of the New England Council, when Gorges was away at the war. There is no evidence of any conflict between Warwick and Gorges over the matter. And surreptitious as the whole thing was, it may have been simply that people thought the New England Council was moribund and were quick to take advantage of it. Once before its rights had been set aside, when James I transferred Nova Scotia to a fellow-Scot, Sir William Alexander. Now again Gorges was forced to acquiesce, saving the rights of his son on Massachusetts Bay. But the New England Council was not moribund, though it was some time before Gorges learned, or appreciated the significance of, what had happened. With the end of the war he married again, so that he could retire from his command at Plymouth and was both free and in a position to take up his colonial projects where he had left them.

Before and during the wars Gorges had been associated with an interesting man, Captain John Mason, who, born in 1586, had served six years as Governor of Newfoundland, 1615–21.[1] In 1622 they took out a joint grant of all the land that subsequently became Maine and New Hampshire. Here Mason settled David Thomson in the first settlement on the Piscataqua, living by the fur-trade and fishing. In 1629 Mason took a grant of the southern half of the territory to himself, becoming thus the founder of New Hampshire. In that year, with Canada conquered and Champlain a prisoner in London, Gorges and Mason set up the Laconia Company, hoping to tap the Canadian fur-trade through the Lake Champlain route to New England. The return of Canada to the French knocked this project on the head and left Gorges and Mason with a dead loss.[2]

Gorges had, however, secured in Mason a valuable and energetic recruit to the New England Council, of which he

---

[1] C. W. Tuttle, *Capt. John Mason, the Founder of New Hampshire* (Prince Soc.), ii.

[2] For a full treatment *v.* R. A. Preston, 'The Laconia Company of 1629', *Canadian Hist. Rev.*, 1950, 125 foll.

became Vice-President in 1632, and which — to the surprise of the Massachusetts Puritans — now burst into renewed activity. A number of individual grants of land were made, Gorges being now careful to make them outside the territory of Massachusetts Bay. We cannot go into them all here, but one of them was made to his grandson Ferdinando, to carry forward the Gorges interests. Others were made to Bristol and Plymouth merchants — we have the correspondence of the latter in the *Trelawny Papers*.[1] Meanwhile people were pouring into the Massachusetts territory 'in heaps' — by no means all of them Puritans; indeed, it is likely that a majority of them were not. But all power was held by the governing Puritan minority — they were a governing class and they knew well how to govern : no nonsense with them about democracy.[2] The Board there arrogated all power to themselves, and they proceeded to show their mettle by driving out of the colony those of whom they disapproved.

It may be said that to this they had a perfect right; but it gave an opening to their opponents in England, who now realised more clearly what they were up to. The extradition of that merry scamp, Thomas Morton of Merrymount, Sir Christopher Gardiner and others, provided a matter to bring before the Privy Council. To everyone's surprise, not least that of the Bay Puritans, Charles I's Privy Council came to their defence and even offered them further support. They did not wish, they said, to discourage a colony that was of potential value to the nation, and anyhow the extruded persons were not very respectable. The Bay Puritans had influences very high up on their side, and thus Gorges's first attempt to assert the general rights of the New England Council over the Bay colony was blocked for the time.

[1] Edited by J. P. Baxter. (Portland, Maine, 1884.)
[2] 'At the first meeting of the General Court, consisting of exactly six Assistants beside the two chief magistrates, it was decided, in direct violation of charter terms, that the Governor and Deputy-Governor be elected out of the Assistants, by the Assistants. In other words, the first Board of Assistants, not one half of the legal number, arrogated to themselves complete legislative, executive and judicial power.' Morison, 85.

It was not until Laud was in the saddle and, realising the implications of the Puritan migration overseas, formed the Commission of Foreign Plantation to control it, that Gorges got his opportunity. He proposed that New England should be divided into a number of provinces under proprietors, with a Governor-General over the whole, appointed by the Crown. Meanwhile the Bay Charter was to be returned home for investigation by due process of law. The Puritans at once prepared to resist; they planned to fortify Boston harbour. The undaunted Endecott defaced the flag of St. George on the ground that it was a Popish symbol, and Massachusetts adopted its own ensign of a red and white rose. Only five years after their first settlement — and how it looks forward to 1776! They accepted all the advantages of the Crown's protection, but they were not going to yield obedience in return.

This opened people's eyes at home, though Laud's respect for the law was such that no steps were taken until the Massachusetts Charter was voided by due process of the courts, and that took two years. Gorges was to go out as Governor-General, with Mason as Vice-Admiral, in a new ship they were building, to control the shipping and trade that were now greatly increasing on the coast. But Mason, nearly twenty years younger than Gorges, died: 'the Lord, in mercy, taking him away', wrote Winthrop, 'all the business fell on sleep, so as ships came and brought what or whom without any question or control'.[1] And, by a further special providence, when the ship was launched it 'fell all in pieces, no man knew how'. Gorges was reduced to sending out a young nephew William to look after the various private family interests that were scattered about there, primarily the northern half of the Gorges-Mason grant, or Maine proper, which he called the province of New Somerset. In these last years Gorges was reduced more and more to his own family for support: after Warwick withdrew, significantly, from the New England Council, Lord Gorges took his place. Young William made no

---

[1] *Winthrop's Journal* (Mass. Hist. Soc.), I. 181.

A VIRGINIA ADVENTURER

success of it in Maine and shortly returned home. Gorges's servant Richard Vines remained on, holding the fort gallantly there as deputy-governor.

At last the courts ruled in favour of the Crown over the Bay Charter, and Gorges was named Governor-General. Massachusetts greeted this news by keeping 'a general fast through all the churches, for seeking the Lord to prevent evil that we feared to be intended against us by a General Governor'. Either this, or perhaps merely terrestrial events in England, in the end turned out efficacious.[1] Gorges sent various conciliatory messages, which Winthrop regarded as mere hypocrisy.[2] (One thing must in fairness be admitted of the best Puritans — they were always ready to believe the worst of other people.) Gorges, on the other hand, always spoke of Winthrop with respect. There is no evidence at all that Gorges was hostile to Puritans as such; several of his friends he found among them, he collaborated in the Laconia Company with the Rev. John Cotton, later a sainted figure in Massachusetts; he was a firm Protestant, a fervent anti-Papist. When his cousin Thomas Gorges went out to govern Maine, he ruled it on rather Puritan lines and actually won the grudging approval of Massachusetts. All that Gorges cared about was the colonisation of America: he was a man of one idea, but that a great one.

He received very little support from Charles's Privy Council — only from Laud. He put forward to them his last and matured ideas on colonisation, continuous with those of the Elizabethans: the special importance to England of an increase of trade and shipping, and consequently of colonies. He adduced the classic argument, borne out by our subsequent history, of the superiority of natural expansion by trading colonies to the imperialism of war and conquest — with Rome and Spain in mind. To

---

[1] *Winthrop's Journal, 1630-1649*, ed. J. K. Hosmer, I. 269.

[2] Cf. Winthrop's summing up : 'Sir Ferdinando Gorges also sided with our adversaries against us, but underhand, pretending by his letters and speeches to seek our welfare; but he never prospered. He attempted great matters, and was at large expenses about his province here, but he lost all.' *Ibid.* II. 10-11.

this the pro-Spanish Treasurer, Lord Cottington, replied: 'Romans, Spanish and Dutch did and do conquer, not plant tobacco and Puritanism only, like fools.' [1] He was evidently a very short-sighted type. When Gorges defended the Puritans by saying that, whatever their humours, their colonising activity brought honour to the whole realm, Lord Cottington annotated, 'What honour, if no profit, but extreme scandal to the whole Christian world?' (He was a crypto-Catholic and became a convert.)

This shows something of what not only Gorges but Laud, too, had to put up with at home. However, in 1639 Gorges got his charter for Maine as a proprietary province, to support his position as Governor-General of New England, if ever he should come to it. It was all too late. He was no longer the man he had been; though capable of taking part in a horse-race in his sixties, he now was 'doubtful of the state of my own body, not able to endure the sea any long time'.[2] He was an old man, his resources spent on his life-long labours to bring about the colonisation of New England. He sent out his young cousin, Thomas, to take his place, writing a last letter to Governor Winthrop to aid him 'in any just and reasonable occasion he shall have cause to use your favour in, I having given him command to be careful to do his best that all fair correspondency be maintained between those two several plantations . . . and when God shall be pleased that I may arrive, I doubt not but you shall perceive my greatest ambition shall tend (next to the service of God) by what ways or means an union or conformity of all parties may be established, or at the least a patient or charitable bearing with each other's errors or self-affections.' That day was not to arrive; at home the country was splitting apart, was on the eve of the Civil War. The Massachusetts Puritans were free to go their own way; certainly the Lord, as they said, seems to have been on their side.

Thomas Gorges did his job well in Maine. While old Sir Ferdinando occupied himself writing his second book,

[1] q. Preston, 314-15.   [2] Baxter, III. 278, 296.

Sir Ferdinando Gorges and New England

A Brief Narration of the Original Undertakings of the Advancement of Plantations into the Parts of America. Especially Showing the Beginning, Progress and Continuance of that of New England, telling the story of the efforts made and expounding once more his ideas, his young kinsman was putting them into practice on the spot. Even Winthrop at last spoke well of him: 'he was sober and well-disposed; he stayed a few days at Boston, and was very careful to take advice of our magistrates how to manage his affairs'.[1] Thomas Gorges brought together the scattered settlements in that wild and beautiful country into a firm and ordered government that lasted, under the faithful Vines, until after the Civil War. For the young man himself came home to fight on the King's side, and even the aged Sir Ferdinando was able to perform some service. In 1647 he died, and after him, two years later, John Winthrop. Perhaps we may judge equitably between these two men: they contributed, in their different ways, more than any others to the building of New England. While John Winthrop made everything he became out of it, Sir Ferdinando Gorges spent everything he possessed on it. For it there was Maine to show — and then, in 1652, the Puritans having won in England, the empire-building commonwealth of Massachusetts annexed Maine outright. After the Restoration they had to make some composition: they acknowledged Sir Ferdinando's rights by buying his grandson and heir out for a miserable £1250.

It has been usual to regard the career of Sir Ferdinando Gorges as a failure. I do not think we need do so, though he has no place in the American tradition commensurate with his contribution. Where Pilgrims and Puritans have always been held high in history, their cherished names entered not only into folk-memory but into myth and poetry, his name is hardly remembered. Except, of course, in Maine, where he is rightly honoured as the Founder. It is only in the careerist sense that he did not succeed, for in fact his efforts did bear fruit, even if others enjoyed the

[1] *Winthrop's Journal*, ed. J. K. Hosmer, II. 8.

121

rewards. Sir Ferdinando Gorges was the man to whom, more than any other, New England owes it that the idea of colonisation there was kept before the mind of the public and attempts made with constancy to carry it out, as the result of which scattered settlements took root before ever Pilgrims or Puritans appeared : the man who held on tenaciously to his fixed idea, in spite of all setbacks, personal losses and discouragements.

He was an Elizabethan, and a more characteristic one than a brilliant and broken man of genius like Ralegh, or an impulsive and rash one like Humphry Gilbert. For he was an average, humdrum person, of fair judgment, dogged and persistent. We know nothing ill of him in all his long life ; the one mistake he made was out of a personal loyalty to an impossible leader, Essex, a man fit to wreck anybody. By his longevity, exceptional for those days, Gorges's life provides not only a bridge between the Elizabethan age and the Civil War, but also between the Elizabethan conception of regulation and control in enterprise and the freer, more variegated individualism of the seventeenth century. The latter, naturally and inevitably, won, and Gorges's inability to control those developments had vast consequences. Though the majority of incomers were not Puritans, the dominating minority were ; and this gave New England its character and temper, of the greatest importance for the future.

The settlement of New England, as we have seen, stands in some contrast to that of Virginia, under the control of the Company, then of the Crown. But there is a deeper contrast. Where Virginia was an extrapolation of normal Elizabethan society, Massachusetts was dominantly an extrapolation of the opposition. We may say that except for the short period of the Interregnum, when Old England fell into step with the New, Massachusetts was always opposition-minded. These two, Virginia and Massachusetts, were the prime seed-beds of the American nation. When Virginia, with its more normal but not less self-governing tradition, joined with New England, against the old country, the new nation was made.

However, it is better to end with poetry than politics, for disagreements, convictions, conflicts of opinion are less interesting than men. In the end we should think of the men themselves, their endeavours and endurances, the harsh rewarding lives they lived, wresting their living from the woods and waters, the soil and the sea. As a modern poet, their descendant, does :

> They died
> When time was open-eyed,
> Wooden and childish; only bones abide
> There, in the nowhere, where their boats were tossed
> Sky-high, where mariners had fabled news
> Of Is, the swashing castle. What it cost
> Them is their secret.

CHAPTER VI

PILGRIMS AND PURITANS: THE
ELIZABETHAN ELEMENT

IT is no part of my purpose to tell again the too often told story of the Pilgrim Fathers and the Massachusetts Puritans. In any case theirs is a story specifically of the seventeenth century, very characteristic of that age split open by religious scission. But not only was their background Elizabethan, the first generation of leaders in New England, the founding fathers, were themselves Elizabethans, their minds formed by that age before its passing. And this whether we take the end of the reign in 1603, or, as is more usual, some such date as 1616, in which both Shakespeare and Hakluyt died, as a dividing line.

John Winthrop, the great governor of Massachusetts, was born in Armada Year, 1588; even his son, the governor of Connecticut, of the second generation, was born in England as early as 1606. Of the first leaders Thomas Hooker, Richard Saltonstall and Francis Higginson were born in 1586, John Cotton and Miles Standish in 1584, Peter Bulkeley 1583, Nathaniel Ward 1578, Thomas Dudley 1576, and Elder Brewster as early as 1567.[1] All these we may regard without question as Elizabethans. And it would not be straining the point to regard those born in the earlier 1590's as Elizabethans too: Governor Bradford, Increase Nowell, William Pynchon born in 1590, William Vassall, Charles Chauncey and Samuel Gorton in 1592, George Phillips 1593, Governor Haynes 1594, Edward Winslow 1595. It is when we come to those leaders born in the early 1600's, with Roger Williams born in 1603 and Thomas

[1] Others who died early, like Isaac Johnson, d. 1630, or William Wood, d. 1635, may belong to this group or the next.

Shepard 1605, that we mark a real difference. In the famous controversy between John Cotton, 'the unmitred Pope of a pope-hating commonwealth',[1] and Roger Williams, the apostle of toleration and freedom of thought, the essential difference was in the cast of their minds, for they were mutually exclusive — and one physically excluded the other. All the same, it is not usually noticed that one was nearly twenty years older. John Cotton was an entire Elizabethan, who believed in an ordered society possessing full authority over its members, himself looking to the past. Roger Williams regarded the individual's conscience as supreme, with no authority higher than that (save God — a reflection of it) : himself entirely a man of the seventeenth century, he looked very much to the future. May we not suppose that the difference of generation between them counted for something? It is certainly apt to do so; it is only natural.

The New England Puritans had already behind them almost a century's experience of Protestant effort and thought; it was not in this realm that they had anything new to contribute. A leading authority on the subject tells us, 'the major part of Puritan thought was taken bodily from sixteenth-century Protestantism. From the great reformers came the whole system of theology, definitions of terms, orientation of interests, interpretations of Scripture, and evaluations of previous scholarship. Puritan thinking was fundamentally so much a repetition of Luther and Calvin, and Puritans were so far from contributing any new ideas, that there is reason to doubt whether a distinctly Puritan thought exists.'[2] What was new, and of extreme importance, was the opportunity to carry these ideas into practice, erect upon the unencumbered soil of the New World a Bible commonwealth free of the corruptions and adhesions of the Old. In this we see a fundamental and continuing element in the American experience, and in America's conception of her rôle in history.

There can be no doubt at all, after a generation of

---

[1] M. C. Tyler, *A History of American Literature*, I. 212.
[2] Perry Miller, *The New England Mind: the Seventeenth Century*, 92.

historical controversy, that the realisation of this ideal was the dynamic motive that drove the Puritans across the Atlantic. We might go so far as to say that Charles I and Archbishop Laud made New England; for it was during the decade of personal rule 1630–40, and as a consequence of it, that the great migration of many thousands took place. After the meeting of Parliament in 1640 this ceased, with the prospect of the Puritans getting their own way in the old country; and for the next two centuries there was little migration to change the essential character of New England.[1] Left to themselves and their own breeding, they produced that stock with its so recognisable idiosyncrasy, which became the strongest factor in the making of the nation and has formed the most efficacious agent in the formation of its mind.[2]

The Puritans, even in New England, were a minority; when one considers effective church membership, which was apt to coincide with full citizenship, a small minority. All the decisive movements in history are made by minorities. And the Puritans carried with them these irresistible elements of strength, that they knew quite clearly what they wanted, the character their polity should take was already formulated in their minds and in their writings, the structure of belief and discipline worked out. There were only minor adjustments to be made in accordance with conditions on the other side of the Atlantic, for in the New World, in the wilderness, they were essentially free to have their own way — that was what they had gone there for. (If they could have had their way at home they would not have gone.)[3] A perfectly clear-minded and determined minority, provided it is agreed and united, can usually impose its will on the rest. Hence, by the way, the emphasis on unity, the determination of Massachusetts to inflict uniformity on all within its borders.

[1] *Winthrop's Journal, 1630–1649*, ed. J. K. Hosmer, I. 3.
[2] Massachusetts supplied probably more than a quarter of the fighting men in the Revolutionary war. *Ibid.* I. 4.
[3] In the controversy as to the motive-force behind the migration, this consideration seems to me to clinch the matter.

The conception of a Bible commonwealth was already clear to them: they had entered into a covenant with God to erect a polity according to the pattern they conceived laid down in the New Testament, without the subsequent excrescences of history, without a hierarchy in church and state-government. They did not at all question the hierarchy of social classes. In his famous sermon on board the *Arbella* on the way over John Winthrop laid down that God had ordained that 'in all times some must be rich, some poor, some high and eminent in power and dignity; others mean and in subjection'.[1] This was the usual Elizabethan conception of society — except that these people had no use for episcopacy, or for a nobility above them, or even, for that matter, of a monarchy when Christ was their king. I think we may say that there was an incipient republicanism in Massachusetts from the beginning. As for the hierarchical organisation of society, they were not keen to recognise any order above themselves, though quite clear that there were people below them. It is a very middle-class point of view, and the Puritans were essentially middle class: John Winthrop was unlikely to see over there anyone more 'high and eminent in power and dignity than himself'. Q.E.D. (Modern America is likewise a society essentially governed by the middle-class, in which middle-class standards and values are dominant.)

To achieve the ends of this Bible commonwealth they had entered into a covenant with each other: 'we have professed to enterprise these actions upon these and these ends. . . . We must be knit together in this work as one man, we must entertain each other in brotherly affection.' [2] They were embarked upon a mission: 'for we must consider that we shall be as a city upon a hill, the eyes of all people are upon us'. If they failed in their endeavour, God will 'make us a story and a by-word through the world, we shall open the mouths of enemies to speak evil of the ways of God and all professors for God's sake'. (God means themselves, of course.) On the other hand, if they succeeded,

[1] q. Perry Miller, *Errand into the Wilderness*, 5.   [2] q. *Ibid.* 5, 11.

men would say of later settlements, 'the Lord make it like
that of New England'. We recognise thus early that
exemplary element, so different from other colonies, the
sense of mission that is so strong in the American make-up
today.

That came from the Bay Puritans, not from the Plymouth
Pilgrims.

The corner-stone of all their churches, as Perry Miller
tells us, was a covenant; and 'the covenant doctrine
preached on the *Arbella* had been formulated in England'.
We find it clearly stated by one of their mentors, the Elizabethan Henry Jacob, a generation before: 'a free mutual
consent of believers joining and covenanting to live as
members of a holy society together in all religious and
virtuous duties as Christ and his apostles did institute and
practise in the Gospel'.[1] Upon this they were all agreed,
with their religious experience in the Old World, whether
in England or Holland, behind them. As John Cotton
afterwards said, the churches that they established on
coming to New England were naturally 'one like to another
. . . I do not know that they agreed upon it by any common
consultation'.[2]

Actually, while John Cotton was minister of the parish
church of Boston in Lincolnshire he entered into a covenant
with some members of his congregation. It seems a little
invidious and it did give rise to some question; but we
are told that 'almost the entire twenty years that he spent
at Boston he was treated with great leniency and consideration by his bishop'.[3] It is not surprising that during his
pastorate, though apparently not by his responsibility, the
Puritans defaced the sculpture and monuments and broke
all the stained glass in that splendid church — so that two
or three centuries later the Victorians had to be at the pains
of replacing it all with much worse glass. Those of us who
attach more value to what men create in things of beauty,

---

[1] q. C. Burrage, *The Early English Dissenters*, II. 157.
[2] q. *Ibid.* I. 361.
[3] *Dictionary of National Biography*, under Cotton.

rather than the varieties of nonsense they are apt to think,[1] find cause for regret in this.

It was this corner-stone of a congregational covenant that made them Congregationalists. The Pilgrims at Plymouth were rather a different case, though it seems to be questioned today whether they were absolutely and determinedly separatists, willing to be regarded as utterly separated from the Church of England. Their mentor, John Robinson, at Leyden rather changed his position about this, under the influence of Henry Jacob, who was never a separatist: Robinson came back to the idea of being still members of the Church, agreeing in Christian beliefs, though not in Church government. And though the enemies of the Pilgrims called them Brownists — Robert Browne had been very vituperative about the Elizabethan bishops — in fact the Plymouth Pilgrims did not descend from Browne: they had an independent ancestry of their own in the Scrooby congregation, and its pastors and mentors, John Smyth, Richard Clifton, John Robinson, Elder Brewster. As for the vastly more important Massachusetts Puritans, nobody could mistake them for Brownists: 'they never begat us, either to God, or to the Church, or to their Schism . . . so we have ever borne witness against it, since our first knowledge of it'.[2] They held themselves to be Puritan congregations of the Church of England and regarded separation as a sin. They were out to set a better model, away from the corruptions of the Old World, and by their example to convert the Church at home, upon which they had their eyes fixed.

As the *Arbella* drew away from Land's End in 1630 — a more important ship than the *Mayflower*, for she carried Winthrop and the Massachusetts leadership on board — Francis Higginson gathered the passengers in the stern to take their last sight of England. He spoke these words, 'We will not say as the Separatists were wont to say at their leaving of England, Farewell Babylon! Farewell

---

[1] Cf. William James, *The Varieties of Religious Experience.*
[2] q. Burrage, I. 362.

Rome! But we will say, Farewell dear England! Farewell the Church of God in England, and all the Christian friends there! We do not go to New England as Separatists from the Church of England, though we cannot but separate from the corruptions in it; but we go to practise the positive part of Church reformation, and propagate the gospel in America.'[1]

We have already seen that there was this difference between the Plymouth people and the Bay Colony, that the Pilgrims were self-effacing exiles who only wanted to escape attention to worship and live in their own way; the Massachusetts Puritans were a governing body going forth to convert others to their way and impose it on others, so far as they could. After a generation of historical discussion we now understand much better the relation between the one and the other. The nineteenth century immensely exaggerated the importance of the Pilgrim Fathers. Their story was told in countless books and then put into verse by Longfellow. To judge from its literature anyone would think that America started with them, and I wonder whether that is not the popular belief still. This book has shown to what diverse sources it goes back, way beyond Jamestown in the generation before the Plymouth colony, to two generations earlier — the 1580's, high-water mark of the Elizabethan age, when everything begins together, including the colonisation of America, to prove in the fullness of time the most spacious achievement of the age.

The Pilgrim Fathers are much more important in American folklore and myth than they are historically[2] — and no country is so addicted to myth where its history is concerned. Even for New England the seed-bed is not Plymouth, but imperious and imperial Massachusetts.[3] Samuel Eliot Morison tells us, 'by any quantitative standard, the Plymouth Colony was one of the smallest, weakest, and

---

[1] q. C. M. Andrews, *The Colonial Period of American History*, I. 377 n.

[2] S. E. Morison, 'The Pilgrim Fathers: their Significance in History', in *By Land and By Sea*, 233-4, 238.

[3] I should explain that the words 'imperial' and 'imperialism' are not used in any pejorative sense.

least important of the English colonies, even of those in New England'. On the other hand, 'in spiritual quality it was second to none in the New World'. Of course, it was no more democratic than Massachusetts: only one-third of its menfolk were freemen with a vote, and even so 'from 1627 to 1639 there was one minor group that had greater power than the whole body of freemen, the "Old Comers", who had the exclusive power to allot land'. Governor Bradford would have agreed with Governor Winthrop that 'the best part of a community is always the least, and of that best part the wiser is always the lesser'.[1] It is difficult to see how anyone can disagree with that. The Pilgrims' own mentor, John Robinson, left behind at Leyden, instructed them, 'it behoves the elders to govern the people, even in their voting, in just liberty, given by Christ whatsoever. Let the elders publicly propound, and order all things in the Church . . . let the people of faith give their assent to their elders' holy and lawful administration.' [2]

It seems to bother American historians that New England did not come up to modern democratic standards. In their disappointment they have failed to observe what an advance all the colonies made in this respect on the Elizabethan England they came out of.

The Pilgrims had the advantage of priority, and thereby exerted an influence by the example they set of civil marriage and in the registering of deeds. Theirs also was the first Congregational church, a working model already in being when the Massachusetts Puritans began to arrive. But in every other respect the influence was all the other way. The size, power and importance of the Bay Colony began to tell, until ultimately it absorbed Plymouth. It does not appear that it absorbed the Pilgrim spirit: 'towards other-minded persons, the Pilgrims, considering that the Plymouth Colony was their colony and that there was plenty of room for the otherwise-minded elsewhere in New England, behaved with singular kindness, forbearance and justice'.[3]

---

[1] *Winthrop's Journal*, ed. cit., I. 125.
[2] q. Perry Miller, 22.   [3] Morison, 240.

The religion, and thereby the mentality, of New England was essentially the product of Elizabethan Cambridge. When one considers the formative influence of that upon America, I suppose one must regard it, along with nuclear physics, as the cardinal contribution of Cambridge to the making of the modern world. New England Puritanism was entirely English in its sources, in spite of the Pilgrims' sojourn in Holland. It has been noticed that in their libraries English theological works were much more numerous even than those of Luther and Calvin; and of them Cambridge theologians like William Perkins and William Ames, especially the former, came first. Elder Brewster, in his remarkable library at Plymouth, had more books by Perkins than any other author.

It is already significant that it should be Perkins who had such a marked influence on New England, and not Cartwright. Cartwright, who dominated the earlier Cambridge Puritanism, was a Presbyterian. Perkins, the foremost Cambridge theologian of the end of Elizabeth's reign, though a Puritan, always kept within the bounds of the Church of England. Though a rigid Calvinist, he had a certain catholicity of spirit; his ability and candour were recognised on all sides. Preaching was the key to success with Puritans, and Perkins was a prodigious preacher. In addition he was a voluminous writer. The secret of his power was probably that, in spite of high intellectual ability, he had a way of expressing himself simply; he did not allow himself to get bogged down with merely intellectual problems, he directed his intellect to the main issues of Christian teaching and the problems of the conscience.[1] Not unnaturally, this became also the inflexion of his pupil William Ames, also of Christ's, whose chief work *De Conscientia* adumbrated Christian morality applied to specific cases — thereby absolving Puritan lambs from the necessity of resorting to the wisdom of the Egyptians.

[1] Thomas Fuller tells us how Perkins 'would pronounce the word *damn* with such an emphasis as left a doleful echo in his auditors' ears a good while after'. This would, of course, give him pleasure.

These men exerted more influence, through their disciples, than any others, on Pilgrims and Puritans alike. Let us indicate something of it. The influences upon the Pilgrims, partly because they went underground in Holland, used to be a somewhat confused matter; but I think the affiliation can be made clear.

The original congregation at Scrooby followed the lines suggested by John Smyth, another fellow of Christ's, who had already established a congregation at Gainsborough. Leaving the country for Amsterdam in 1608, his arrival there set off further dissensions in the English community, for he frequently changed his position, disputing hotly as he went. He became a Baptist; but no sooner had he baptised himself and his congregation than he perceived it was all an error. The disappointed congregation thereupon excommunicated him, and when he died joined the Mennonites. I believe he is respected by the Baptists as a forerunner.

The Scrooby flock looked up and were fed by Richard Clifton, a beneficed minister who apparently neglected his living for the purpose: to whom the celebrated John Robinson attached himself as assistant. Clifton removed to Holland in 1608, where he joined Francis Johnson's church as teacher. Johnson, another fellow of Christ's, was singular in that he was a follower of Cartwright and had therefore a Presbyterian colouring, if colouring is the word. After making trouble at Cambridge and being frustrated of his intention of settling with other sectaries on an island off Newfoundland, he had removed to Holland. John Smyth now brought over a Lincolnshire congregation and they all quarrelled like mad over their absurdities. Smyth insisted on a rigid separation from the Church of England, for which the others attacked him in a corporate work, *The Profane Schism of the Brownists, with the impiety, dissensions, lewd and abominable vices of that impure Sect discovered.*

Amid these enthusiasts John Robinson was distinguished, comparatively, by sense and moderation. He, too, was a

Cambridge man, also influenced by Perkins.[1] Bishop Hall, a truthful person, makes no doubt that Robinson was disgruntled, or not particularly gruntled, at not getting a preferment to the hospital at Norwich, and that this was the cause of his separation. Having joined the Scrooby flock, he followed Clifton with a number of them to Holland. They showed sense, or a preference for quiet, in not joining the church at Amsterdam, where the pot was now boiling over, dissensions, preachings against each other, pamphlet-warfare, law-suits — a very unholy resort to Baal.

The Scrooby flock settled at Leyden, where John Robinson was publicly ordained as their pastor; Brewster became their ruling elder. Here Robinson corresponded agreeably with Ames, and took a full share in the controversies against Smyth and the Baptists on one side, Johnson and the Presbyterians on the other. While rejecting the rude names of Brownist or Barrowist, Robinson advocated a moderate Congregational position, what became the 'Congregational way'; like Elizabeth I, comparing herself with Mary, Queen of Scots, he was exactly 'the right height'.

In the discussions prior to emigration it was agreed that if a majority of the congregation volunteered, Robinson should go as their pastor. To his disappointment only a minority volunteered. Only thirty-seven of the hundred or more passengers on board the *Mayflower* were Pilgrims from Leyden;[2] we do not know who the rest were, but some of them we learn from Bradford were profane fellows. Robinson remained behind to minister to the majority; after his death further groups from his congregation did go to New England. Meanwhile he refused to sanction the administration of the sacraments by Elder Brewster at Plymouth: not being ordained, Brewster might preach and pray, but not baptise or give communion to the flock. Robinson kept hoping that he might be able to join them; he sent them spiritual advice and consolation, but he was

---

[1] Robinson was a Nottinghamshire man, born 1576, matriculated from Corpus Christi 1592. J. A. Venn, *Alumni Cantabrigienses*, Pt. 1, Vol. III. 470.
[2] Morison, 239.

removed shortly to a better world. The state of the Pilgrims at Plymouth may be described as one of 'Waiting for Robinson'.

However, they seem to have got on very well without him. Elder Brewster, a mature man of fifty-three when they landed at Plymouth, had already had a wide and varied experience. He had been for a short time at Peterhouse, where he acquired nonconforming ideas.[1] For several years, 1583–9, he was in the household of Secretary Davison, whom he accompanied on missions abroad, hence his acquaintance with Holland. In 1590 he succeeded his father as postmaster at Scrooby where he remained as pillar of the congregation till 1608. 'After some investigation of their proceedings by the High Commission at York, which clearly did not amount to persecution, they decided to leave so ungodly a land.'[2] They found Amsterdam uncongenial, so they went on to Leyden; when they found Leyden not altogether congenial, only the wilderness would do. To the wilderness they went.

Social life in Plymouth has been described as 'undoubtedly quiet in the extreme'; but Brewster, according to Bradford, was 'of a very cheerful spirit, very sociable and pleasant amongst his friends'. He had an excellent library of some four hundred books, more than half of which he took over with him.[3] Mostly theology, since he had to preach thrice a week; the rest practical — herbals, books of surveying and medicine, works on the culture of silkworms and varieties of timber. But, in addition, were these worldly authors, Machiavelli's *Prince*, Bodin's *Republic*, Bacon's *Advancement of Learning*, and Ralegh's *Prerogative of Parliaments*.

For company there were Miles Standish and a much younger man, Edward Winslow; above all Governor Bradford, to whom Elder Brewster stood second in the little colony. Miles Standish was born about 1584, of a younger

[1] He matriculated from Peterhouse in 1580, but did not take a degree. Venn, Pt. 1, Vol. I. 213.
[2] *Dictionary of American Biography*, under Brewster.
[3] S. E. Morison, *The Intellectual Life of Colonial New England*, 133.

branch of the old Lancashire family, probably the Duxbury branch, after which he called his place in New England. Before 1603 he was already a lieutenant under Vere in the Netherlands. A professional soldier, he joined the Pilgrims as such, for in religion he was never one of them. He was given command of parties exploring the country and to defend the colony against suspect Indians — on one occasion being responsible for a deed of blood against some Indian chiefs. It fell to him to take the merry-andrew Thomas Morton of Merrymount. In 1621 he was made Captain of the colony, and was frequently an assistant to the governor. Next to Standish in dealing with the Indians was Winslow, also a man of good family, who when travelling on the Continent fell into the Leyden community, it may be said, since he married into it. Above all there was Governor Bradford: impossible to overestimate what the Plymouth plantation owed to him, for he was, like Winthrop, ideally suited to govern. They would not have been the great men they became, if they had remained at home in England: no scope, no opportunity. Bradford brought with him the same Elizabethan ideas of authority that Winthrop enjoyed: the generality share in government 'only in some weighty matters, when we think good'.[1] Queen Elizabeth I might have subscribed to that. Bradford and Winthrop were good and just men, of a marked moderation and lenity in government; Bradford had further to recommend him that he was accustomed to answer mildly 'the harsh insolence which the Pilgrim colony sometimes received from the Bay authorities'.

These two were of an age: Winthrop born in 1588, William Bradford in 1590, of substantial Yorkshire yeoman stock. As a youth affected by the preaching of Richard Clifton, he joined the Scrooby flock and went with Robinson to Leyden. Bradford was of a spirit to dislike sectarian labels and wished to retain fellowship with all reformed churches. This was too much for some, but Bradford thought it 'a great arrogancy for any man or church to

[1] *Dict. Amer. Biog.*, under Bradford.

think that he or they have sounded the word of God to the bottom'. Re-elected governor thirty times, almost continuously in fact — in spite of the fear of the New England colonies of a governor for life — it is obvious that the Pilgrims could not get on without him: his long rule was really one of a benevolent autocracy.

Though not a university man, he was well read, and indeed as an historian to better purpose; for his *History of Plymouth Plantation* is, by all counts, a masterpiece. In his well-stocked library he, too, had Bodin, Guicciardini's *History of Florence*, and Peter Martyr's *Decades of the New World*. It is nice to think that this Puritan governor, so wise, so sober, so restrained, an 'achieved spirit', as his age would say, also owned a red waistcoat with silver buttons, a coloured hat and a violet cloak. But it is by his *History* that he lives, for it offers us the perfect mirror of the life of the Pilgrim colony to all time.

His book has been much admired by a great American historian, Samuel Eliot Morison, and by an eminent English one, Richard Pares, foremost of our scholars on the colonial history of America: their judgment I am bound to respect. It has indeed the qualities that give enduring life to a book: absolute fidelity, lifelikeness and trustworthiness; its moral purity shines through, the selflessness, submission and control. Its tones are, however, those of a New England winter, russet and grey and white; where I prefer colour and poetry. Perhaps there is a sober, subdued poetry in Bradford, as it might be Cowper — the parallel is really Anne Bradstreet; and the book certainly has charm: like all living work it carries the personality of its author. C. M. Andrews warns us that we must be careful about accepting his opinions about those whom he criticises: that is merely human, and anyway he has more justice of mind than most. Morison pays tribute to the distinction of the style, a perfect instrument and manner for expressing all that the governor wishes to convey; he points out the superiority of the style of this first generation in New England, who were born and bred in Elizabethan England, to that of the next generation who had Jacobean complexity and quaintness for their background.

Let us cite two passages from Bradford significant for their content. The first, on the colony's experience of communal arrangements, we may compare with Captain Smith's account of Virginia's experience. 'At length, after much debate of things, the Governor (with the advice of the chiefest amongst them) gave way that they should set corn every man for his own particular, and in that regard trust to themselves; in all other things to go on in the general way as before. And so assigned to every family a parcel of land, according to the proportion of their number for that end, only for present use (but made no division for inheritance), and ranged all boys and youth under some family. This had very good success; for it made all hands very industrious, so as much more corn was planted than otherwise would have been by any mean the Governor or any other could use, and saved him a great deal of trouble, and gave far better content. The women now went willingly into the field and took their little ones with them to set corn, which before would allege weakness and inability; whom to have compelled would have been thought great tyranny and oppression. The experience that was had in this common course and condition, tried sundry years, and that amongst godly and sober men, may well evince the vanity of that conceit of Plato's and other ancients, applauded by some of later times: that the taking away of property and bringing in community into a commonwealth, would make them happy and flourishing; as if they were wiser than God.' [1]

Bradford is in still livelier vein in dealing with the misdoings of Thomas Morton of Merrymount. 'After this they fell to great licentiousness and led a dissolute life, pouring out themselves into all profaneness. And Morton became Lord of Misrule, and maintained (as it were) a school of atheism. . . . They also set up a maypole, drink-

[1] William Bradford, *History of Plymouth Plantation, 1620–1647*, (Mass. Hist. Soc.), I. 300-2.

ing and dancing about it many days together, inviting the Indian women for their consorts, dancing and frisking together (like so many fairies, or furies rather), and worse practices. As if they had anew revived and celebrated the feasts of the Roman goddess Flora, or the beastly practices of the mad Bacchanalians. Morton likewise (to show his poetry) composed sundry rhymes and verses, some tending to lasciviousness and other to the detraction and scandal of some persons, which he affixed to this idle or idol Maypole.' (Though the Puritans had not read Freud, they knew what a maypole meant.) 'They changed also the name of their place, and instead of calling it Mount Wollaston, they called it Merrymount, as if this jollity would have lasted ever.'[1] The Massachusetts Puritans, under the uncongenial Endecott, saw to it that it did not: they soon brought those junketings to an end.

For the Elizabethan background of Massachusetts we could not do better than look at the life lived at Groton in the years before John Winthrop left for America. All the Winthrops were given to writing, letters, diaries, journals, so it is well documented. We derive an agreeable impression of their family life in the pleasant undulating pastures in that nook of East Anglia.

The Winthrops were originally clothiers, connected with the celebrated Springs of Lavenham.[2] One of them was a favourer of the Reformers under Mary, to whom the martyr Philpot confided his papers and these were used by John Foxe. So advanced Protestant sympathies were endemic in the family. Adam Winthrop, the governor's grandfather, who died in 1562, described himself in his will as clothworker of London, gentleman of Groton — where he lies again under his brass, taken away to America in the last century, restored in this. His son Adam, bred to the law, became auditor of Trinity College. His diary shows him

[1] *Ibid.* II. 48-9.
[2] For details in these paragraphs, *v. Winthrop Papers*, I, 1498–1628 (Mass. Hist. Soc.) *passim.*

paying his obligations in Groton church porch, for the poor
or to the collectors of a subsidy or for setting forth a soldier
to the wars. We note his payments indoors and outdoors,
for a new plough or half a dozen skins of parchment, for
settles for the hall, for shoes and books for young John.
He notes the coming and going of men and maids in service;
on April Fool's day 1596, 'Thomas Bond ran his way for
that he had gotten a maid with child'. The diary reveals
Adam Winthrop's bookish interests; he constantly lends
books to friends, the Rheims Testament to the vicar of
Acton, or he lends Lambard's *Perambulation of Kent*, Petrarch's
Works, Jewel's *Defence of the Apology*, Eusebius and Socrates
in English. The Biblical commentaries of Nicholas de Lyra
are much in use; but so is Googe's Husbandry. An interesting geographical item is Munster's *Cosmography*, for which
he paid five shillings; while his *Theatrum Terrae Sanctae* his
son subsequently gave to Harvard.

It is unexpected to come across the curious, the asinine
William Alabaster, who went to and fro like a weathercock
in his religious opinions; but he was a nephew of Adam
Winthrop, who, I must say, treated him with marked forbearance for all the trouble he gave. The first mention of
him is characteristic: 'William Alabaster departed from
my house towards Cambridge, 9 July, malcontent'. And
malcontent he remained all through; we do not need to
take his religious opinions seriously, he was just a psychological case. In 1597 'my cousin William Alabaster fate-
batur se esse papistam', and they rode together to London.[1]
Unable to keep his mouth shut and publishing a contro-
versial tract, Alabaster found himself in the Tower, whence
he was removed in 1600 to Framlingham Castle — more
convenient, or perhaps less, for his unfortunate relatives. In
August next year, sister Alabaster and sister Veysey came
to the house, 'where five of us that are brethren and sisters

[1] Elizabethans sometimes used the word 'cousin' for other relationships.
Alabaster had been a chaplain on Essex's expedition to Cadiz in 1596. After
the capture of the city there was a discussion between the English ministers
and some Spanish priests, as a result of which Alabaster found himself converted. *v.* my *Expansion of Elizabethan England*, 309.

met and made merry, which we had not done in sixteen years before'.

Then brother Alabaster turned up and 'told me that he made certain English verses in his sleep which he recited unto me', on the strength of which he borrowed forty shillings. We see where the silliness in William Alabaster came from: not from the Winthrop side — nor the poetry either. In 1603 Alabaster submitted, received his pardon and came to show it off to his uncle. In summer next year — the complaint seems to have been seasonal — he was committed to prison again for popery. On his release he went abroad, where he published a treatise on cabalistic divinity; the Jesuits persuaded him to go on to Rome, where the Inquisition at once threw him into prison. When he got away, Winthrop heard from Sir William Waldegrave that his nephew 'was revolted from the Pope's religion, quod vix credo, licet verum esse libenter vellem. But since he came into England and revolted from the Pope 1610, 20 November.' In the end it remained for the despised Church of England to provide for him, with a prebend in St. Paul's cathedral and a nice living in Hertfordshire.

Adam Winthrop was better justified in his sensible son. John was admitted to Trinity College in 1601; but he left early, to be married at the age of seventeen. From his 'Experiencia' it seems that he was already beginning to burn, or rather, felt the impulses of nature rising. So he was safely married by the religious Ezekiel Culverwell, and on his return from his honeymoon his father made the young couple a marriage-feast, 'with Sir Thomas Mildmay and his lady my sister present'.

In the last decade of Elizabeth's reign we observe in the Winthrop family an illustration of a general theme — the increasing wealth and standards of comfort in these smaller landed gentry. Adam Winthrop buys himself a great bedstead of walnut for his great chamber, costing him £5, a livery cupboard of walnut for the same; a framed table of wainscot and a pair of green curtains; a long table of wainscot for his great parlour, a dozen buffet stools and 'a joined cupboard standing in my hall', with a couple of settles for the chimney corner there. There follow purchases of a salt of silver and gilt, a dozen silver spoons, three silver bowls, pewter porringers, a bason and ewer. Evidently there is no want of money, or of comforts, when we read of unpuritanical cushions, and lute strings, taffeta and lace for a sweet-bag, a box of tobacco and half a dozen pipes in a case. Then, in 1610, Adam Winthrop resigns his auditorship for which he receives £20 — multiply by thirty for a contemporary valuation.

Now it is John Winthrop's turn. In the son we observe a more intense and introspective religious consciousness: John was much under the influence of the gloomy Ezekiel Culverwell.[1] And this state of mind was not improved by the deaths of two wives in eleven years, for John Winthrop was distinctly uxorious. Of the second he writes, 'for her carriage towards myself, it was so amiable and observant as I am not able to express; it had this only inconvenience, that it made me delight too much in her to enjoy her long'.

It was at this time, in this year 1616, that he began to keep a record of his spiritual state, from which we gain an authentic picture of a Puritan's inner mind.[2] John Winthrop felt that his heart halted between God and the world, that he was not yet 'resolved upon the denial of this world and myself'. His 'Experiencia' shows us how hard he tried. After the affliction of his second wife's death he thought he 'had brought under my rebellious flesh and prettily tamed it by moderate and spare diet and holding it somewhat close to its task, by prayer, reading, meditation and the works of my calling'. He was a busy Justice of the Peace, but at sessions he refrained his 'mouth, eyes, and ears from vanity as well as I could while I was there'. And 'whereas I was wont to lose all my time in my journeys my eyes running upon every object and my thoughts varying with every occasion, it pleased God that I now made use of my time, both in praying, singing and meditat-

---

[1] For this man cf. *Two Elizabethan Puritan Diaries*, ed. M. M. Knappen.
[2] *Winthrop Papers*, I. 190 foll.

ing with good intention and much comfort'.

Nevertheless, when he tried to settle down to his ordinary tasks again, he found that 'the flesh had gotten head and heart again and began to linger after the world; the society of the saints seemed a contemptible thing, meditations were few, prayer was tedious, and fain would the flesh have been at an end before I began'. He put himself on a spare diet again and set himself to read the devout Mr. Rogers and, of course, Perkins. After some time at this, he was surprised to find that he 'grew very melancholic and uncomfortable', especially since he had refrained from any 'outward conversation in the world'. In this condition he began to enjoy experiences more like that of a Counter-Reformation mystic, St. John of the Cross or St. Theresa. He had such 'a heavenly meditation of the love between Christ and me as ravished my heart with unspeakable joy; methought my soul had as familiar and sensible society with him as my wife could have with the kindest husband. I desired no other happiness but to be embraced of him.' And, very shortly, he was: 'O my Lord, my love, how wholly delectable art thou! Let him kiss me with the kisses of his mouth, for his love is sweeter than wine; how lovely is thy countenance! how pleasant are thy embracings!'

This state of exaltation seems to have ended with his third marriage — and perhaps it was about time — in 1618, when this spiritual diary comes to an end. Winthrop got away from this disagreeable intensity of morbid introspection; his impulses found normal channels of expression; he was able to turn himself to the extrovert tasks of a legal career. He became an attorney in the Court of Wards and a member of the Inner Temple. It would seem that it was external considerations that decided him to go to America, the state of the country, the loss of his post; the king's decision to dispense with Parliaments, his embarking upon personal rule, meant that there was no future for Puritans while that lasted.[1] The outlook was indeed gloomy;

---

[1] Cf. *Dict. Nat. Biog.*, under Winthrop. His admission to the Inner Temple 'seems to indicate that his emigration was not the result of long

Winthrop's response to it may be read in a letter to his third wife, 'I am verily persuaded God will bring some heavy affliction upon this land, and that speedily. . . . If the Lord seeth it will be good for us, he will provide a shelter and a hiding-place for us and ours, as a Zoar for Lot.' [1]

Of those who met together at Cambridge in August 1629 and entered into an agreement to go, Thomas Dudley was eight years, Richard Saltonstall two years, Winthrop's senior; William Pynchon and Increase Nowell his junior by two years, William Vassall by four years. Such men were Elizabethans, formed in that age. They were followed by others, more important.

Dudley, born at Northampton in 1576, was the son of a captain 'slain in the wars'. Left an orphan, but with a sufficient maintenance, he went to a grammar school and became a page in the household of the Earl of Northampton. In turn he went to the wars to serve as captain under Henry IV, but saw no fighting for peace was made: that, then, would be 1598. In 1603 he married, according to Cotton Mather, 'a gentlewoman of good estate and good extraction'. Becoming steward to the Puritan Earl of Lincoln, in nine years he succeeded in paying off £20,000 debts and arranged a marriage of the young Earl with a daughter of the still more Puritan Lord Saye and Sele. Now well off, Dudley retired to Boston to enjoy the ministrations of the Rev. John Cotton. In close touch with all the discussions preparatory to the move, he sailed on the *Arbella* with Winthrop. Though Winthrop's deputy-governor, Dudley had a violent quarrel with him over the decision to move from their first site to Boston. They exchanged some very ungodly, though not necessarily unpuritanical, words: the fact was that the two men were hardly congenial to each other.

Dudley was dogmatic and overbearing; he had none of Winthrop's moderation, judgment, charm — for there is a

previous deliberation. John Winthrop had not joined any of the colonial companies as an adventurer, and the earliest intimation of his leaving the old world for the new is conveyed in the letter above.

[1] *Winthrop Papers*, II. 91-2.

certain charm in the personality of Winthrop. Once and again they came into conflict — there were people who disapproved of Winthrop's wise lenity; but the terms of mutual submission with which they terminated their dispute are a tribute to the efficacy of Puritan discipline in self-restraint and self-control. A man of fifty-four when he landed in New England, Dudley was tough physically: he produced progeny at the age of seventy. He was four times elected governor, thirteen times deputy-governor; he was one of the first governors of Harvard, one of the two Massachusetts commissioners that formed the New England Confederation. He was something of a scholar and, like most Elizabethans, wrote verse. A last poem, found in his pocket after his death, spoke his mind on toleration:

> Let men of God in courts and churches watch,
> O'er such as do a *toleration* hatch.

These lines were not without application to such as Saltonstall. Nephew to Sir Richard Saltonstall, who had been Lord Mayor of London, owner of the manor of Ledsham and a J.P., he was one of the Puritan governing-class who went over on the *Arbella*. But he did not see eye to eye with the rigid exclusiveness of the theocracy, and was twice fined for backslidings in regard to church matters. Perhaps this helped to persuade him to return home next year: *he* had not burnt his boats. He never went back to Massachusetts, though he obtained a grant of land in Connecticut; a son continued the line in New England. From wicked Old England he remonstrated later with the Rev. John Cotton and the Rev. John Wilson for their harsh attitude to the Quakers.

Of those only just junior to Winthrop, Pynchon, Nowell, Vassall, all three had trouble with the ruling authorities. Pynchon became a member of the first court of assistants and helped to found Roxbury. In 1636 he withdrew from Massachusetts along with the Rev. Thomas Hooker, who found the infallibility of the Rev. John Cotton too much for him. They were then charged by Cotton with breaking their covenant by departing. Later, Pynchon, who had founded Springfield, withdrew it from the rule of Connecticut. Thereupon Hooker accused him of breaking the covenant, in the same terms Cotton had used. (Q.E.D. There is no objectivity in these people's arguments: they are merely rationalisations of what suits their interests.)

In England, Pynchon, like Winthrop, had been the squire in his parish; and, as Morison puts it, 'the squire of Springfield in Essex had become the squire of Springfield in Massachusetts'.[1] Treasurer of the colony 1632–4, Pynchon was granted the fur-trading privilege of Roxbury for one year for his service. When Pynchon decided to leave, he opted on the Connecticut river as the best location for the fur-trade and planted opposite Agawam. But he could not get along with Hooker, who unfairly accused him of cornering the corn trade and of breaking his oath. Hooker pursued Pynchon unjustly, pressing for his excommunication. Pynchon took his opportunity on the commission of confederation to secede from Connecticut. Hooker protested furiously to Cotton, with aspersions on Pynchon's character. There seem to have been no substance in the specific complaints with which he was charged. I suspect that the objection to Pynchon was at bottom anti-squirearchical, and that Hooker was the mouthpiece of the community, jealous of any eminence above them. For Hooker certainly had the people with him, condemning Pynchon unheard; the air they breathed in the New World was thus early egalitarian.

Pynchon had no better luck with Massachusetts. When later he wrote a book controverting the Calvinist view of the Atonement, the General Court ordered the book to be burnt and the author to appear before them. This he refused to do; 'instead, he decided to return to England, where he might enjoy that liberty of opinion which was denied him in the colony he had helped to found'.

[1] For this account, *v.* S. E. Morison, 'William Pynchon, the Founder of Springfield', in *Mass. Hist. Soc.*, vol. 64, from which the quotations above are taken.

Increase Nowell arrived with Winthrop, to whom he became an assistant. A ruling elder of the church at Boston, he developed the libertarian view that it was improper to be both a magistrate and an elder, as he was. He was thereupon dismissed from the pastorate, and went off to found the church at Charlestown. William Vassall, whose father was a member of the Virginia Company, accompanied Winthrop, but, unable to agree with the elect, left after a few months. In 1635 he returned to join the Plymouth colony, where he prospered financially. However, still not at ease in Zion, he returned to England and finished his earthly course, a rich man, in Barbados. Isaac Johnson, the wealthiest to go over, avoided these difficulties by dying almost immediately. His wife, the Lady Arbella, daughter of the Earl of Lincoln, had died even sooner : one glimpse enough for her. The ship that took these magnates over, the *Arbella*, had been renamed in her honour ; the *mystique* did not work as with the *Mayflower*.

In 1633 there went over the two authoritative religious leaders of the first generation, Cotton and Thomas Hooker. The same boat contained them, though the same pulpit on arrival did not. They had been invited over together, but it was wisely decided that 'a couple of such great men might be more serviceable asunder than together'.[1] Samuel Stone accompanied them, so that it was possible to say, in the punning manner of the time, that in Massachusetts they now had 'Cotton for their clothing, Hooker for their fishing, and Stone for their building'. With them went Edmund Quincy and John Haynes. John Haynes, born in 1594, was a gentleman of good estate in Essex — one sees how easterly New England was — who signalised himself by attacking Winthrop's government as too mild. He himself removed with Hooker to Hartford, where he became the first governor of Connecticut.

The important Cotton was probably the leading non-conforming clergyman in, if it is not paradoxical to say so, the Church of England. Born at Derby, where his father

[1] *Dict. Amer. Biog.*, under Hooker.

was a lawyer, he went up to Trinity and took his degree in 1603. As a normal undergraduate Cotton heard the bell tolling for Perkins with relief that 'he should now be rid of him who had (as he said) laid siege to and beleaguered his heart'.[1]   However, his heart was forced by another clergyman and so he qualified to become a fellow of Emmanuel — that paradise of Elizabethan Puritans. We have seen that he became vicar of Boston, where he at once began to simplify the services in the interest of more preaching — he was a great preacher; we did not note that the bishop had to be squared to approve of his somewhat irregular appointment. He soon developed a faithful following, dependent on his ministrations; he, like Winthrop, was a leader — and this was given full scope in Massachusetts where Roger Williams said there were people 'who could hardly believe that God would suffer Mr. Cotton to err'.[2] Everybody else erred at some time; Mr. Cotton never. Cotton had journeyed down to Southampton to preach the farewell sermon at Winthrop's embarkation. It is not surprising that in Massachusetts those two formed a solid front in church and state, which nothing could break or by-pass.

They were both Elizabethans in their point of view; they were both men whose minds were geared to government. Cotton's chief works were in defence of the civil power's right to interfere in support of the truth. (This was just what the government believed in in England.) What Cotton pronounced was apt to become the law of the land — except when, given the job of drawing up a code of laws, he came out with the complete Mosaic system, of a draconian severity, appropriate to unpleasant tribes of two thousand years earlier. This had to be rejected by the laity, who showed more sense. But Cotton had no more illusions than Winthrop as to the people's fitness to govern: 'Democracy', he wrote, 'I do not conceive that ever God did ordain as a fit government either for church or state.' This

---

[1] q. H. C. Porter, 'Alexander Whitaker', *William and Mary Quarterly*, 1957, 328-9.   [2] q. Tyler, I. 212.

was what the rejected Church of England held, without breaking stained-glass windows — or for that matter Rome, without breaking anything, except men's heads. Nevertheless, there was in Protestantism an inner dynamic that led on to democracy — in particular in Congregationalism with the emphasis on the consent of the congregation, if highly select; and this became shortly evident in New England.

John Wilson, three years younger than Winthrop, had accompanied him over in 1630. Born at Windsor, where his father was a canon — his mother was a niece of Archbishop Grindal — he was at Eton and King's, where he was converted by William Ames, became troublesome and refused to conform. He was made teacher at the first church of Boston and, when Cotton arrived, was sometimes at odds with him; yet the pulpit managed to hold them both, if at different times.

This was hardly the case with Hooker — too near a rival for the great Cotton. We now know that there was no real divergence of opinion between these two, as used to be thought; it was simply that both could not be first. A couple of years junior to Cotton and senior to Winthrop, Thomas Hooker was the son of a Leicestershire yeoman, was a student at Queens' and became, like Cotton, a fellow of Emmanuel. At Esher, to which living he was presented by Francis Drake, his patron's wife lay under the impression that she had committed the unpardonable sin — whatever that was (something sexual and absurd, no doubt: one can imagine). Hooker succeeded in comforting her, where Ussher and John Dod had failed. Hooker had a way with him — to the soul — and married the lady's waiting woman: the proper social status for a clergyman's bride, as we learn from Elizabethan Injunctions.[1] Then, falling under the influence of John Rogers of Dedham, he ceased to conform and left his living. He took to schoolmastering in the country in Essex, with John Eliot, later Apostle to the

---

[1] These amusing facts, from the *Dict. Nat. Biog.* under Hooker, are unaccountably omitted from the *Dict. Amer. Biog.*

Indians, as assistant.[1] Then Hooker went to Holland, where, undergoing the influence of William Ames, he wrote a preface for Ames's book against ceremonies. (The effect of all this we can still observe in the simplicity that is a keynote of New England worship.)

Hooker and Stone were called as pastor and teacher of Newtown. But they and their congregation became restive under the self-sufficient autocracy of Massachusetts. It used to be thought — one of the many myths of American history — that they were democrats. As to that, Samuel Stone, whose later life was embittered by a long controversy with the ruling elder of his church, spoke succinctly: he held the essence of Congregationalism to be 'a *speaking* aristocracy in the face of a *silent* democracy'. Hooker's resolution to move away into Connecticut was preached against by Cotton as a breach of the covenant and opposed by the General Court in consequence. Hooker refused to discuss the matter and settled at Hartford, where there was greater freedom than in Massachusetts — though, as we saw, *he* took the same line as Cotton when William Pynchon wished to withdraw in turn from Connecticut.

Hooker's sermon at the making of the Connecticut constitution used to be thought a democratic declaration, when he stated that the 'foundation of all authority is the free consent of the people'.[2] But we recognise in that the traditional social contract doctrine as the base of society, which appears in the far greater Hooker of the *Laws of Ecclesiastical Polity*. 'They who have the power to appoint officers and magistrates', wrote Thomas Hooker, 'it is in their power also to set the bounds and limitations of the power and place unto which they call them.' We recognise in that a continuing element in American society, the heart of Ameri-

---

[1] One of the treasures of the library at Jesus College, Cambridge, is an original edition of John Eliot's translation of the New Testament into the language of the Massachusetts Indians, with the inscription:

Pro Collegio Jesu. Accipias mater quod alumnus humillimus offert Filius, oro preces semper habere tuas.   *Johannes Eliot.*

[2] For a re-statement of the traditional view that Connecticut was more democratic, *v.* D. H. Fowler, 'Connecticut's Freemen: the First Forty Years', *William and Mary Quarterly*, 1958, 312 foll.

can political conviction. And it did fall to Hooker to formulate the classic statement of the 'Congregational way' in his *Survey of the Sum of Church Discipline*.

The bent of Hooker's mind was, however, evangelical, in what is called saving souls: his books bear such titles as *The Soul's Preparation for Christ*, *The Soul's Vocation*, *The Soul's Implantation into Christ*, etc. From Connecticut Hooker was called to take part in the controversies that raged in Massachusetts over the tiresome Roger Williams and the exceptionally self-satisfied Mrs. Hutchinson, the antinomian.[1] That far from quiet Quietist, spilling her spiritual favours all round her, played a part in New England comparable with that of Madame Guyon at the court of Louis XIV. The New England theocracy had no more hesitation in shutting up the one than the French bishops had the other: the New England version of an episcopate was no less responsible for keeping order in the nursery. The matter was ended happily with their condemnation of eighty-two specifically erroneous opinions.

Roger Williams did not agree, but then he never agreed with anybody, including himself, for long. As for order in the nursery, in a sense he never emerged from it. Since he was a man entirely of the seventeenth century, we do not have to go into his career — only in so far as his conflict with the Elizabethan views of Cotton brings out the character of the latter. No sooner had Williams landed in Massachusetts than he discovered that he was 'once more in a land where the non-conforming were unfree'. He responded by declaring that civil governments had no right to enforce religious injunctions, and when the civil authorities showed that they had the power he took refuge in

[1] We can hardly blame Winthrop for his credulity about the monstrous births produced by Mrs. Hutchinson and her friend Mrs. Dyer, for the gruesome details of which *v. Winthrop's Journal*, I. 266-7, 277; or as to the witchcraft of Mrs. Hutchinson's bosom-friend Mrs. Hawkins, who 'had much familiarity with the Devil in England, when she dwelt at St. Ives, where divers ministers and others resorted to her and found it true', *ibid.* II. 8; or for the execution of Mrs. Dyer, which took place in 1660, long after Winthrop was dead. These things were true to the mind of the age, and anyway regrettably Elizabethan.

Plymouth. He inconveniently attacked the 'imperialism' of the Puritan colonists, for of course their pushing out the Indians was 'imperialism' of an uncompromising sort. This troubled the sensitive conscience of Roger Williams, who adored Red Indians. Banished from Massachusetts, he escaped in mid-winter to their friendly shelter and founded a settlement at Providence, the beginning of Rhode Island. Imperial Massachusetts sought to extinguish Rhode Island and invaded it; only an appeal to Old England secured a patent and freedom for it to exist.

It was while enjoying the freedom of the old country that Roger Williams engaged in his famous controversy with Cotton. Cotton had issued his encyclical, *A Letter concerning the Power of the Magistrate in Matters of Religion*. To this Williams replied with *The Bloody Tenet of Persecution for the Cause of Conscience*, putting forward the shocking doctrine that 'God requireth not an uniformity of religion' and urging that all individuals and religious bodies were entitled to liberty as a natural right.[1] The affronted Cotton rejoined with *The Bloody Tenet Washed and Made White in the Blood of the Lamb*. Williams, inexplicably unabashed, wound up with *The Bloody Tenet yet more Bloody by Mr. Cotton's Endeavour to wash it white in the Blood of the Lamb*. (One begins to perceive that the Blood of the Lamb also = what one happens to think.) This was the kind of thing that New England delighted in bothering its head about. Yet these were real issues, and Roger Williams's ideas lived on to win the battle at a later date. In the dichotomy between John Cotton and Roger Williams much of America's subsequent history consists — not least in the twentieth century.

Perry Miller tells us that 'such a learned and acute work as Hooker's *Survey of the Sum of Church Discipline*, which is specifically about the régime set up in America, is written entirely within the logical patterns and out of the religious experience of Europe'.[2] But, of course. Logical patterns are much the same in all times and places — would one expect Hooker to write outside them? As for the religious

[1] *Dict. Amer. Biog.*, under Williams.   [2] Miller, 10.

experience of Europe, this was all they had to proceed on.

The Puritans went out to set a model of a godly commonwealth for the world to see and follow. They suffered the fate of all who make an egoistic, a conceited assumption as to the course history will take: the course it takes is never what they suppose it will be. They are always disappointed — but they ask for disillusionment, to assume so boldly, so confidently, that things are going to go the way they think. The godly in England, like Milton, suffered the bitter surprise that the country did not want them, but the King again, the ungodly Restoration. Similarly with New England — the second generation there wondered what had gone wrong.[1]

Nevertheless, all experience does not go for nothing; not everything — the heroic effort, the sacrifice — had been in vain. The continuing legacy of the Elizabethan Puritans to New England — though different from what they expected — was a matter of the highest importance in the constitution of the greatest of modern nations. It did not turn out the New Jerusalem, but it did provide the strongest of bonds to bind together a continental society of a new sort and kind. Something very strong, even astringent, was needed to hold together so vast a country — the New England mentality, something very wiry and taut and idiosyncratic; something which, when it lost the narrowness of its early beliefs, retained a distinguishing element — strongly ethical, seeing life in terms of obligation and duty rather than pleasure, social responsibility and doing good, neighbourliness and goodness. Though the theology and belief had gone, the metaphysics broken down, the Puritan character remained — the strongest factor in survival; for, in history, to survive is what matters.

The overwhelmingly, the excruciatingly theological

---

[1] Cf. Miller, 6 foll.; and Morison, *Builders of the Bay Colony*, 341: 'there is much evidence that the proportion of church members to population fell off rapidly after 1652, and that Palfrey's estimate of 20 to 25 per cent may be substantially correct for 1670. This falling off was not, however, caused by immigration, but by the decline of religious interest in the new native-born generation.'

complexion of the intellectual culture of New England did but reflect, not so much Elizabethan England as Elizabethan Puritanism. Massachusetts was the realisation of the dreams of its later, rather than earlier, generation. We must not underrate their intellectual energy, if we disrelish the forms it took. The Puritans were intolerant in their day, and in consequence they have met with an intolerance in ours reluctant to do them justice for what they achieved.[1] Samuel Eliot Morison tells us that 'the dominant Puritan clergy, far from being indifferent to culture, did everything possible under the circumstances under which they lived, to stimulate, promote and even produce intellectual activity. Moreover, it was largely the clergy who persuaded a poor and struggling people to set up schools and a college, which continued to serve the community in later centuries.' [2]

Their handicaps in keeping civilised standards going were tremendous — theirs was a pioneer country strenuously engaged in the struggle for existence, a whole Atlantic away from the centres of learning. 'New England was a poor country, even by the standards of the day, struggling with a niggardly nature for livelihood.' It is all the more astonishing what they achieved, whether one likes it or not. Within ten years of its founding Massachusetts had a vigorous intellectual life of its own, 'expressed institutionally in a college, a school system, and a printing press; applied in a native sermon literature, poetry and history'. No other English settlement until the nineteenth century attempted to provide for learning so soon after it was founded — not even the States of the Union two centuries later, as the frontier advanced. But New England had Elizabethan England behind it, with its enthusiasm for education, fortified by the Puritan belief in the intellect.

---

[1] The classic instance of this may be seen in James Truslow Adams's *The Founding of New England*, of which Morison says handsomely that though 'fundamentally unsympathetic to the Puritans . . . it is still the best general history of seventeenth-century Massachusetts that we have, and a salutary one for New Englanders to read'. *Builders of the Bay Colony*, 347.

[2] For the content of the above pars. I am indebted to S. E. Morison's brilliant lectures on *The Intellectual Life of Colonial New England*, from which the quotations are taken.

New Englanders proved their belief not only in their precepts but in their works: they were ready to tax themselves for things which in Old England were provided by endowment.

These were things of the mind, and their mind was formed by the English universities, especially by Cambridge, from which nearly all the leaders came, notably from those Puritan seminaries, Emmanuel and Christ's. The Puritan migration contained a very high proportion of university men: up to 1646 there were a hundred Cambridge men to some thirty from Oxford.[1] It was the university of Cambridge to which the leaders looked back, the Elizabethan Cambridge of Perkins and Ames, Preston and Chaderton.[2] There was an average of one university man to every forty or fifty families — much higher, we may say, than in Old England. The standards they set themselves to reproduce were naturally those they had imbibed at home. At Harvard the programme of education laid down was 'very similar to that which many founders of New England had studied at Old Cambridge'. Similarly the Elizabethan grammar school curriculum was repeated in New England: it was what the founders 'understood to be the proper secondary education of a boy'.

Puritanism throve 'under conditions of vigour, hardship and isolation'; the tensions within the New England mind resulted in a higher average of intellectual activity, which in fact was 'conspicuously absent in other colonies'. Morison tells us that Puritanism 'preserved far more of the humanist tradition than did non-Puritanism in the other colonies'. It devoted more attention to classical scholarship, and had an interest therefore in making verses, such as all English students were taught to write. 'This tradition and, to a surprising extent, the amorous poetical fashion of Elizabeth's

[1] S. E. Morison, *The Founding of Harvard College*, 40. 'If we would know upon what model Harvard College was established, what were the ideals of her founders and the purpose of her first governors, we need seek no further than the University of Cambridge. It was there that the greater part of them had their education.'

[2] For a brief treatment of the Cambridge contingent in New England, *v.* H. C. Porter, *Reformation and Reaction in Tudor Cambridge*, 255 foll.

reign, crossed to New England together with other things of which the stricter Puritans did not approve.' So, too, with literary form and style : Morison points out that 'the older generation of New England grew up in the age of Shakespeare and the King James Bible', and in consequence these men 'wrote prose superior by any standard to that of the later native-born writers'.

However, we must not allow ourselves to be over-persuaded by the charm of a great historian. Shakespeare was precisely what the New England Puritans excluded ; and the Cambridge they looked back to was the Cambridge of Perkins, not of Spenser and Marlowe, Greene and Thomas Nash, or even of Bacon and the scientist William Gilbert. The Puritans cared for none of these things. As the historian of their literature, Moses Coit Tyler, allows, the Puritan was 'at war with nearly every form of the beautiful. . . . In the logic and fury of his tremendous faith, he turned away utterly from music, from sculpture and painting, from architecture, from the adornments of costume, from the pleasures and embellishments of society.' [1] They would have suppressed the Elizabethan drama if they could. They had no appreciation of the majesty of the Catholic Church, the Rome of Sixtus V, the music of Palestrina — they are not called on to admire their opposite numbers, St. Ignatius Loyola and the Jesuits. They had nothing but dislike for the grave and ordered beauty of the Anglican Church, the cadence of the Book of Common Prayer, the music of Byrd and Orlando Gibbons, their contemporaries ; there is no evidence that they had any liking for the music of that golden age, the wonder of their time, Tallis and Dowland and Wilbye. (The Catholics had : they contributed largely to it.) Nor did they respond to painting, the contemporary world of Tintoretto and Veronese, El Greco and Velasquez, or even the very English charm of Nicholas Hilliard and Isaac Oliver ; let alone the delights of sculpture, a Michelangelo or a Bernini, or even the chaste marbles of Nicholas Stone.

[1] *Op. cit.* 264.

No civilised person who cares for the arts can have much liking for them. Nor can one forgive them for their attitude to the dear Church of England — though no doubt some of the bishops were proud, pompous, and prelatical.

If we do not like them, we must give a reason why — a rational one. The Puritans' attitude involved a profound contraction of response to life, in some ways a denial of life. They were enemies to the glorification of the natural man, with all his instincts and appetites, that characterised the Renaissance and the great Elizabethans, the discovery of a new world of riches in himself to match that in the outer world across the oceans. Shakespeare expresses its inspiration: 'what a piece of work is man! how noble in reason! how infinite in faculties! in form and moving how express and admirable! in action how like an angel! in apprehension how like a god!' The Puritan stood at the opposite pole: 'the doctrine of the total depravity of man', Tyler tells us, 'lay in his mind under a light of absolute certainty'. He expressed it in the usual appalling language. Here is the Rev. Thomas Shepard, who with Cotton and Hooker, stood, according to Tyler, 'apart, above rivalry, above envy' — though not among each other. Here is Shepard on man's mind: 'thy mind is a nest of all foul opinions, heresies, that ever were vented by any man; thy heart is a foul sink of all atheism, sodomy, blasphemy, murder, whoredom, adultery, witchcraft, buggery . . .' [1] We observe the Puritan obsession with sex, the natural concomitant of repression; they had not very nice minds. Their dominating art was of the pulpit, and pulpit oratory is a vulgar art.

We cannot rank very high their voluminous expressions in this kind, or even such a tract as Nathaniel Ward's *Simple Cobbler of Agawam*, which stands out rather by the flatness of the surrounding country. The literature of social objurgation is not rated so highly today as it was in the day of Carlyle and Ruskin. Their early literature shows best

[1] I should have hesitated to quote this passage, if it had not already been cited by the respectable Moses Coit Tyler in his *History of American Literature* which, Morison tells us, 'has never been surpassed'. For the quotations above, *v.* Tyler, I. 193, 201, 208.

in the writings of their historians — the sincerity and truth-fulness, prime qualities for an historian, of Bradford and Winthrop. But what a story they had on hand to write! Then, shortly, after the winter, they would be putting forth shoots of poetry, naïve, musical, delightful as a bird's song with Anne Bradstreet.

On the other hand, some contraction of response, some repression, some inhibition produces greater strength and energy with which to face the ills of life, particularly in the harsh sad conditions of pioneer life in the wilderness. One sees, with more imaginative sympathy, what it all meant for them as one stands in the Museum devoted to them at Plymouth, surrounded by the rude objects of their daily use, or by the graveyards, touching in their simplicity, by the roadside in country places or in the village streets of New England. And for the life of their community, in probity and public spirit, in moral responsibility and uprightness, in humaneness as to punishment and in mutual help in need, in simple godliness — whether we believe or no, regarding it as a human fact — they did exemplify higher standards than any other English society. And theirs' more than any others' was the making of the nation.

CHAPTER VII

NEWFOUNDLAND, NOVA SCOTIA AND THE NORTH-WEST PASSAGE

THERE remain for consideration the further efforts to find a short cut to Asia by the North-West, the goal of all these endeavours, in the course of which they had stumbled upon America; the plantations in Newfoundland and Nova Scotia, the first British holdings in what was to become Canada. And first for Newfoundland — until recently, with its absorption into Canada, for long the oldest dominion of the Crown.

It is here that Bristol came first to the fore with the Cabot voyages and moved back effectively into the picture, with the Newfoundland efforts, at the end of our period.

Attempts from Bristol to find rumoured islands in the Atlantic go back to the decade before Cabot, with the voyage set forth by John Jay as early as 1480.[1] He was a merchant engaged in trading with both Portugal and Iceland, and these trades, with their rumours of Atlantic islands and Greenland, made Bristol the natural focus for the first attempts stretching out towards the continent lost in the mists of the Atlantic. Every year from 1491 to 1498 some voyage of this kind went out from the port, and again in 1501 and 1502. Cabot's voyages — it is now held that there were three, including a preliminary unsuccessful reconnaissance in 1496 [2] — fit naturally into this series. What lured him to Bristol was not commerce so much as the prospects of discovery.

These voyages found that, with a favourable wind, the

---

[1] Cf. J. A. Williamson, *The Voyages of the Cabots*, 132 foll.
[2] Cf. L. A. Vigneras, 'The Cape Breton Landfall: 1494 or 1497', *Canadian Hist. Rev.*, 1957, 225.

nearest land on the other side of the Atlantic could be made in some twenty days. It is usually held that Cabot made his first landfall at Cape Breton, though there is an interesting note attached to Cape Bonavista, in the first map of Newfoundland, made by Captain Mason, saying 'a Caboto primum reperta'.[1] This is a century later, but it must represent some element of tradition.

What these voyages also discovered was that the waters off Newfoundland were alive with fish; though these English and Anglo-Portuguese expeditions[2] were voyages of discovery, and others — Normans and Bretons, Basques and Biscayans — were earlier engaged in fishing, certainly in greater numbers. But by 1522 we find a casual mention of the Newfoundland fishing fleet, so that by then it had become a regular thing, though until the middle of Elizabeth's reign it lagged far behind the foreigners in those waters. From first to last the English interest in the matter was, naturally, a West Country concern. The West Country fishing interests came to dominate not only those waters but the development of Newfoundland, and even to exert something of a stranglehold upon it. After all, the historian of the island tells us, 'the Newfoundland trade was by far the greatest English enterprise in America up to 1630'.[3] This was reflected in England by the prominence of that element in Bristol's trade over centuries,[4] while, Edmund Gosse tells us, Poole in the early 1800's was almost an off-shoot of Newfoundland. It is well recognised that one reason for the English taking possession of the coast was their adherence to dry-fishing — curing the fish on land; and in the West Country of my childhood, dryfish, pronounced familiarly like that, was an accustomed diet of the people in winter (though not much in favour with me).

---

[1] Prefixed to Sir William Vaughan's *The Golden Fleece*, see below, p. 173.

[2] For the Portuguese background see S. E. Morison, *The Portuguese Voyages to America in the Fifteenth Century*.

[3] D. W. Prowse, *A History of Newfoundland*, xiv.

[4] By 1667 the Mediterranean products brought in to Bristol in exchange for Newfoundland fish accounted for £40,000 customs duty at the port. J. Latimer, *The Annals of Bristol in the Seventeenth Century*, 345.

We have to see the efforts to come to grips with Newfoundland, in shape like a crab, against the background of those harbours on the Avalon peninsula at the southeastern end increasingly swarming with fishermen in the summer season. The reign of Henry VIII saw two voyages that made an unwilling acquaintance with the island. John Rut set out from Plymouth in 1527 to seek the passage to Asia, but found himself in St. John's harbour and got no farther. Master Hore in 1536, with a cargo of no less than thirty gentlemen weighing him down, got farther and fared worse. Somewhere on the coast of Newfoundland or Labrador they were stranded on an inclement shore with no food, and were just being reduced to cannibalism, when they managed to lighten a French ship of her cargo by a stratagem and struggled home in sad straits. Hakluyt rode two hundred miles to get an account of this affair from its last survivor, then an old man. How well Hakluyt deserved the tribute to his 'burning zeal' and 'good nature which is so ready pressed to benefit your country and all such poor men as have any spark in them of good desires', which the Bristol merchant Anthony Parkhurst paid him in his 'Report of the True State and Commodities of Newfoundland', written in 1578.[1]

Parkhurst tells us that at this time there were 'above a hundred sail of Spaniards that come to take cod, who make all wet and do dry it when they come home, besides twenty or thirty more that come from Biscay to kill whale for train [*i.e.* oil]. These be better appointed for shipping and furniture of munition than any nation saving the Englishmen, who commonly are lords of the harbours where they fish, and do use all strangers' help in fishing if need require, according to an old custom of the country, which thing they do willingly.' Apparently this was due to the English ships, though fewer, being better armed and fought, and the foreigners' submission to them was in return for 'protection of them against rovers or other violent intruders, who do often put them from good harbour, etc.'. Life in

---

[1] R. Hakluyt, *Principal Navigations, ed. cit.* V. 343 foll.

those waters was a scuffle and a scrimmage, out of which the West Country fishermen emerged on top, before ever Queen Elizabeth I effectively clinched matters and made their supremacy permanent. This move was only five years ahead. Now, in 1578, there were about fifty Portuguese sail, and a hundred and fifty French and Breton, 'the most of their shipping is very small, not past forty tons, among which some are great and reasonably well appointed' — better than the Portuguese, but not so strong as the Spaniards. Parkhurst was in favour of strengthening our position there; by fortifying the strait at Belle Isle, 'we shall be lords of the whole fishing in time, if it do so please the Queen's Majesty'. It shortly did please the Queen's Majesty, and by a more direct measure.

This same year Sir Humphrey Gilbert advocated the scuppering of the Spaniards and their extrusion from the fishery there. His visit to the island in 1583 and taking formal possession of it in the Queen's name in St. John's harbour had no real influence upon its history, though it has left its charming memorial in Edward Hay's narration of the voyage. The fisher-folk were the men, and until Gilbert produced his commission from the Queen were prepared to resist his entrance. There were in harbour at that moment some thirty-six sail, over whom were 'the English merchants, that were and always be admirals by turns interchangeably . . . for our English merchants command all there'.[1] Hay illustrates for us what a mart the harbour had already become, with the opportunities of exchanging fish against Mediterranean delicacies. 'Insomuch as we were presented, above our allowance' — so magical was the Queen's commission — 'with wines, marmalades, most fine rusk or biscuit, sweet oils and sundry delicacies. Also we wanted not of fresh salmons, trouts, lobsters and other fresh fish brought daily unto us.' Embedded in his account is a brief relation of Newfoundland and its commodities, the climate, the soil and its products. 'The soil along the coast is not deep of earth, bringing forth

[1] Hakluyt, VI. 16 foll.

abundantly peason small, yet good feeding for cattle. Roses passing sweet, like unto our musk roses in form, raspberries, a berry which we call whorts, good and wholesome to eat. The grass and herb doth fat sheep in very short space, proved by English merchants which have carried sheep thither for fresh victual and had them raised exceeding fat in less than three weeks.' And so on.

Sir George Peckham, the chief adventurer in Gilbert's voyage, added to the growing literature about America with his *True Report of the late Discoveries*, written after the return of one of the captains from it and upon his information, before Gilbert's fate was known. It is concerned chiefly with the general question of America, setting forth the Queen's title to North America and discussing the rights of traffic with the natives, which 'the savages may not justly impugn and forbid in respect of the mutual society and fellowship between man and man prescribed by the law of nations. . . . For who doubteth but that it is lawful for Christians to use trade and traffic with infidels or savages, carrying thither such commodities as they want, and bringing from thence some part of their plenty?' [1] His informant gave him an account of their coasting the south of Newfoundland, where off Cape Race they were becalmed and took large quantities of cod. 'And from thence, trending the coast west toward the bay of Placentia, the general sent certain men ashore to view the country, which to them as they sailed along seemed pleasant. Whereof his men at their return gave great commendation, liking so well of the place as they would willingly have stayed and wintered there.' [2] It was on their course to the mainland that, in a fog, the flagship the *Delight*, was lost with all Gilbert's supplies, his books and charts, and Hakluyt's room-mate at Oxford, Stephen Parmenius, the geographer. On the way home Gilbert himself was drowned in the little frigate, the *Squirrel*. The Queen was only too much justified in her fear that he was a man 'not of good hap by sea'. Peckham lost everything he had put into the venture, and later

[1] *Ibid.* 49.   [2] *Ibid.* 44-5.

forfeited his family estate for his debt to the Crown.

As a first strategic move, with the opening of the war in 1585, Bernard Drake was sent to round up the Spanish fishing fleet in Newfoundland. This was a very profitable enterprise and six hundred fishermen were brought back to be taken care of. Henceforth no Spanish fishing fleet went to Newfoundland, and 'out of the whole number of fishing vessels England had more than double the fleet of her rivals and all quietly submitted to her control'.[1] Already the Queen had furthered a more settled state of affairs with a wise ruling in 1582, that the master of a vessel might retain his space on the foreshore so long as he kept buildings on it. The fishing fleet was achieving regular organisation, with charter-parties, licences to export and even insurance policies by 1603. And the first settlements made on the coast were those of the fishermen, winter crews harbouring there to prepare flakes, stages, cellars for the spring fishery. They remained hostile to any idea of plantation : they felt that they had conquered this water-world and it was theirs. Bristol and Hakluyt had been to the fore in promoting Gilbert's tragic voyage. Walsingham had written to a leading merchant, Thomas Aldworth, asking for support, and upon Hakluyt's information an assembly of merchants put up a thousand marks to furnish a bark.[2] A decade later Hakluyt gives us an account of the voyage of a Bristol and a Topsham ship into the Gulf of St. Lawrence 'to flay the morses or sea-oxen'. The Topsham bark returned with an interesting report of Indian life and habits upon Cape Breton. 'One thing very strange happened in this voyage : to wit, that a mighty great whale followed this ship by the space of many days as we passed by Cape Race, which by no means we could chase from our ship, until one of our men fell overboard and was drowned, after which she immediately forsook us and never afterward appeared unto us.' Thus early, in the Elizabethan age, appears the theme of *Moby Dick*.

Hakluyt gives us accounts of three voyages into the Gulf in these years, with the characteristic note, 'because

[1] Prowse, 79.   [2] Hakluyt, VI. 79, 93 foll.

they are the first, for aught that hitherto is come to my knowledge, of our own nation that have conducted English ships so far within this gulf of St. Lawrence and have brought us true relation of the manifold gain which the French, Bretons, Basques and Biscayans do yearly return from the said parts; while we this long time have stood still and have been idle lookers on, making curtsy who should give the first adventure or, once being given, who should continue or prosecute the same'. In 1594 the *Grace* of Bristol, under Sylvester Wyatt, went up to the north-west of Newfoundland and into the mouth of the St. Lawrence as far as Natiscotec (Anticosti) island. In Placentia bay they met with over threescore sail of fishermen from St.-Jean-de-Luz and Biscay, 'whereof eight ships only were Spaniards, of whom we were very well used and they wished heartily for peace between them and us'. In 1597 two London barks, the *Hopewell* and the *Chancewell*, had a very exciting time of it in the Gulf, being chased and giving chase, pillaging a Basque ship and being threatened with mutiny by one of their crews, catching lobsters to the number of a hundred and forty in one place 'with a little draw net', and ending up with a Spanish prize of two hundred tons. 'The Newfoundland we found very subject to fogs and mists.'

In the wake of this tradition of interest and enterprise, it was not surprising that, when peace came, Bristol should look to Newfoundland as its special province. When we say Bristol we mean the circle of its leading merchants, Aldworths, Slanys, Guys, Colstons. When Popham and Gorges approached the City Council to subscribe to the Plymouth Company, they got little response except from the mayor, the sheriff John Guy, who promised twenty marks and Robert Aldworth £12 : 10.[1] But in 1609 Bristol began to favour a plan of its own. John Guy put forth a tract 'to animate the English to plant in Newfoundland', and a number of merchants joined with associates in London to petition the Privy Council for a patent. Bright was that dawn: with peace all the colonising ventures were taking

[1] Latimer, 27, 38.

shape together — Jamestown, Bermuda, New England, Newfoundland. In 1610 a patent was granted to 'The Company of Adventurers and Planters of London and Bristol for the colony or plantation of Newfoundland in the southern and eastern parts'.[1] A number of grandees were added to grace the document: the Earl of Northampton, Sir Francis Bacon, Sir Lawrence Tanfield, Sir John Doddridge; the work fell upon the Guys, Slanys, Aldworth and Colston.

There was already a sprinkling of settlers in the neighbourhood of St. John's and spread about Conception bay. John and Philip Guy, with their brother-in-law William Colston, went out in 1610: three small ships carrying thirty-nine persons, including a few women and children. Their first instruction was to assemble the fishermen and assure them that there was no intent to deprive them of their rights in fishing. On that understanding the fishermen amicably supplied their wants. But Guy was careful to settle out of their way, in a secluded and defensible spot, Cupid's or Cupert's cove, at the head of an inlet, where he proceeded to build a little fort, with stockade and battery, and to erect cottages, farm-buildings, grist- and saw-mills. Here they spent an exceptionally mild winter, 'small brooks were not the whole winter frozen over so thick as that the ice could bear a dog to go over it, which I found by good proof', Guy wrote home; 'for every morning I went to the brook which runneth by our house to wash'. All that winter the colony remained in health.

With the spring Guy as governor proclaimed his orders for the fishermen to keep, and this at once aroused their hostility: they were accustomed to regard the isle as their own and rule as they pleased. They petitioned the king against the planters, and meanwhile attempted to destroy their mills. The planters' reply to the petition, later on, stated the view mildly that 'it is conceivable to be lawful for them the inhabitants to make choice of their fishing place and not to leave the benefit thereof to the uncertain comers thither'.[2] Here was the fundamental conflict of

[1] Purchas, *ed. cit.* XIX. 406 foll.   [2] Prowse, 100.

interest thus early, that proved so discouraging to colonising efforts in Newfoundland. In the autumn of 1611 Guy returned to England, leaving Colston as his deputy. In the spring of 1612 Guy took over peasants and artisans, horses, cattle and poultry, and also an aggressively Protestant preacher, the Rev. Erasmus Stourton, who later was banished by Lord Baltimore for his troublesomeness.

That summer they were visited by Captain Easton, a celebrated pirate, who robbed fishermen and planters alike. 'In October John Guy with thirteen others in the *Endeavour* and five in the shallop went upon discovery.'[1] In the north of Trinity bay they made contact with the elusive Indians of the island. When the bark and shallop rowed towards them, the Indians made off; 'whereupon the bark wheazed unto them and flourished the flag of truce and came to anchor, which pleased them, and then they stayed. Presently after the shallop landed Master Whittington with the flag of truce, who went towards them. Then they rowed into the shore with one canoe, the other standing aloof off and landed two men, one of them having the white skin in his hand; and coming towards Master Whittington, the savage made a loud speech and shaked the skin, which was answered by Master Whittington in like manner. And as the savage drew near he threw down the white skin on the ground, the like was done by Master Whittington. Whereupon both the savages passed over a little water-stream towards Master Whittington, dancing, leaping, and singing; and coming together, the foremost of them presented unto him a chain of leather full of small periwinkle shells, a spitting knife, and a feather that stack in his ear.' These were the preliminaries to friendly contact with the braves, who commonly 'have no beards; behind they have a great lock of hair platted with feathers like a hawk's lure, with a feather in it standing upright by the crown of the head'. We recognise the familiar picture, so clearly described in excellent Elizabethan English, to prevail over the course of so much history to come.

[1] Purchas, XIX. 419 foll.

In 1613 Guy returned to his busy life in Bristol, becoming mayor in 1618, member of Parliament in 1621 and 1624. Stow describes him as 'a man very industrious and of great experience'. By 1626 he was dead, not old, leaving four sons under age.

In Newfoundland Colston remained as deputy-governor during the winter of 1613–14, and when he went the colony was left without law or order. Nor was there any means for such a small band, with no authority, to enforce order upon thousands of fishermen. By 1615 there were some two hundred and fifty English sail engaged in the fishery, a tonnage of fifteen thousand, taking fish and making train-oil to the annual value of £135,000.[1] One sees the enormous increase since Queen Elizabeth I's pounce upon the Spanish fishing fleet thirty years before — an unrecognised achievement of the age in the New World.

On the other hand, tiny as the colony was, it became the parent of further plantations in the temperate south-eastern peninsula. In 1616 the Bristol Company sold a band of territory running across the Avalon peninsula to Placentia bay to Sir William Vaughan of Golden Grove, and that brought an interesting Welsh fantastic, with his public spirit and poetry and nonsense, upon the scene. In the previous year two men of mark arrived: Captain Whitbourne, later Sir Richard, arrived in the *Trinity* in Trinity bay on Trinity Sunday, to hold an Admiralty court and enforce some order upon the swarming fishermen; and Captain John Mason, who remained as governor of the parent colony for the six years, 1615 to 1621. He was succeeded as governor by Robert Hayman, who wrote his *Quodlibets* while there — the first book of original English verse, for Sandys in Virginia was engaged in translation, to come out of America. All these four wrote books dealing with Newfoundland: it is curious how literary its early history appears — or perhaps it reflects the unabashed expressiveness of Elizabethan colonisers.

In 1618 some Bristol merchants — Robert Aldworth

[1] Purchas, XIX. 437.

continuing his interest — purchased a grant for plantation not far from Guy's location, at Harbour Grace. It was known as Bristol's Hope, but it proved none. Vaughan planted his settlement at Trepassy. Besides the original settlers in and around St. John's, Falkland planted his colony on Trinity bay, and there was Calvert's, Lord Baltimore's: altogether some six settlements came into existence in James's reign.

We have already come across the excellent Captain John Mason as an associate of Gorges in the New England Council and as founder of New Hampshire. Born at King's Lynn in 1586, he was taken early to Portsmouth where he spent most of his life, latterly in the house where Buckingham was assassinated. Hence he seems to have looked upon himself as a Hampshire man. In 1610 he equipped two ships and spent fourteen months in subduing the rebellious Redshanks in the Hebrides on behalf of James I, who left him to foot the bill.[1] (By 1629 the bill, with interest, amounted to nearly £12,500 and was never paid, of course.) Perhaps as some kind of recompense, he was appointed governor of Newfoundland; he at once set about exploring all round it and constructing a map. When completed, a careful and charming work, it was prefixed to Vaughan's book *The Golden Fleece*, published in 1626. Mason was no poet, but he wrote some commendatory verses for the book:

> O how my heart doth leap with joy to hear
> Our Newfound Isle by Britons prizèd dear!
> That hopeful land which winters six I tried
> And for our profit meet at full descried . . .

To Vaughan's volume celebrating Charles I's marriage called *Cambrensium Caroleia* with its word-play upon the crab-like shape of the island (*caris* means sea-crab), Mason contributed a Latin poem, 'In Cambriolae Plantationem',

> Quae deserta Novae quondam fuit insula terrae
>   Curis et musis nunc viget alma tuis . . .

---

[1] *Captain John Mason*, ed. J. W. Dean, with Memoir by C. W. Tuttle (Prince Soc.), 10 foll.

Mason had not been at Magdalen College for nothing — or else Vaughan wrote the verses for him.

In 1620 he published his *Brief Discourse of the Newfoundland* with the idea of 'inciting our nation to go forward in that hopeful plantation begun'.[1] It is a pleasant little tract, giving his experience of the climate and an account of the products, the herbs and roots he managed to raise in his garden. As with most of the Newfoundland promotion-literature he was at pains to answer the prevalent idea that the winter-climate was too cold for settlement. However, he admits the pest of mosquitoes in summer — 'small flies bred of the rottenness of ruined wood and moisture, like as in Russia'. The advantages of Newfoundland for settlement that he enumerates are four: though the soil and climate are inferior to Virginia, it is only half the distance there; it costs only ten shillings to transport a planter, and twenty shillings for victual, to Newfoundland, five pounds to Virginia; the fishery employs three thousand seamen a year, freighting three hundred ships, and providing for twenty thousand people in England; the security of the island was complete and plantation on it, there being but few Indians in the north and none in the south.

The admirable sailor Richard Whitbourne followed with his *A Discourse and Discovery of Newfoundland* in 1622. The historian of the island calls him the Captain Smith of Newfoundland, and certainly his is a pleasant little book, written, as the *Dictionary of National Biography* observes, 'with a literary skill hardly to be looked for in one who had been a mariner from fifteen years of age'.[2] But, then, we may observe — he was an Elizabethan mariner. He was born, just over the hill from Ralegh's Budleigh, at Exmouth. He made several Newfoundland voyages and knew it well, having made his first in 1579 in a ship set forth from Southampton, bound for whaling in the Gulf. 'But this our intended voyage was overthrown by the indiscretion of our captain and faint-heartedness of some gentlemen of our company; whereupon we set sail from thence

[1] *Captain John Mason*, 139 foll.   [2] *D.N.B.*, under Whitbourne.

and bare with Trinity harbour in Newfoundland.' [1] Four
years later he was there in command of another Southampton
ship at the time of Gilbert's taking possession of the country,
'whereof I was an eye-witness'. Two years later he was
present when Bernard Drake rounded up the Spanish and
Portuguese fishing fleets. In 1588 he served in a ship of
his own against the Armada, and made several more Newfoundland voyages in the Queen's reign.

Whitbourne was there again in 1611 when the celebrated pirate Captain Easton replenished his fleet of ten
ships and kept Whitbourne in his custody for eleven weeks,
making the virtuous sailor many offers and golden promises.
The West Countryman resisted these blandishments, re-
questing Easton only 'to release a ship that he had taken
on the coast of Guinea, belonging to one Captain Rashleigh
of Fowey in Cornwall, a man whom I knew but only by
report; which he accordingly released. Whereupon I
provided men, victuals and a freight for the said ship, and
so sent her home to Dartmouth in Devon, though I never
had so much as thanks for my kindness therein.'

In 1614 Whitbourne was back in Newfoundland, when
another well-known pirate or privateer, Mainwaring, was
upon the coast and compelled his company for a time.
Next year Whitbourne went back with a commission from
the Court of Admiralty to hold a court and rectify disorders
among the fishermen. In 1616 he had a ship of his own
returning thence rifled by a French pirate, the voyage
overthrown to the loss of more than £860, for which he
never got any recompense. From all this we perceive that
Whitbourne was fairly regularly engaged in the Newfoundland trade and what a thing it had become in the country's
trade in general, the West Country's in particular. In 1618
he went out in a ship of his own, partly victualled by Sir
William Vaughan, to take charge of the latter's unsatisfactory
settlement on the Avalon peninsula, for which he had got
a grant from the London and Bristol Company. And this
brings an interesting Welsh character upon the scene.

[1] Purchas, XIX. 425 foll.

Dr. Vaughan was born in 1577 and matriculated, like a good Welshman, at Jesus College, Oxford, in 1592. A gentleman of some estate, he then travelled abroad to France and Italy, and became a doctor of laws at the university of Vienna. He married and settled on his estate at Torcoed in Carmarthen, where lightning struck the house and killed his wife. This increased his eccentricity somewhat and implanted a streak of religious, or perhaps persecution, mania that led him to write a mystical work to answer the 'disgraceful libels dispersed far and nigh' about his wife's death. (Did the Welsh think that this man of learning was a wizard who could make lightning?) However, the Doctor was a public spirited man, who was much depressed by the poverty and unemployment in Wales, the redundant population many of whom died of want, though one cannot credit his figures. 'I am sorry to find so many hopeless in my country of Wales, whereas close by us in Devonshire a hundred and fifty ships go to Newfoundland transporting from thence those commodities without which Spain and Italy can hardly live.'[1] In 1616 he purchased his grant and at his own expense sent out a colony to settle at Trepassy, at the southernmost tip of the peninsula.

For all his pains the colonists were not less hopeless than they had been at home. Whitbourne wrote of them as he found them: 'for certainly I have already seen and known by experience that the desired plantation can never be made beneficial by such idle fellows as I found there in 1618, which people had remained there a whole year before I came there or knew any of them and never applied themselves to any commendable thing, no, not so much as to make themselves a house to lodge in, but lay in such cold and simple rooms all the winter as the fishermen had formerly built there for their necessary occasions the year before those men arrived there.'[2] Nothing could be expected of such people, but they attracted in addition the ill-luck of those who will not help themselves. Whitbourne

[1] q. Prowse, 136.   [2] q. *Ibid.* 112.

went out as Vaughan's deputy to govern the colony, taking a further recruitment of people. He was interested in the venture and anxious 'to advance that work'. He and Vaughan set forth an additional ship for a fishing voyage and carrying victuals to the colony, but this ship was captured by an 'erring captain' from Ralegh's last Guiana enterprise: 'whereby our intended fishing voyages of both our ships were overthrown and the plantation hindered'.

This seems to have been the end of Whitbourne's interest in Newfoundland, and we are not concerned here with the rest of his career of service. It is nice to think that for it he was eventually knighted.

Vaughan himself went out in 1622 and remained a couple of years, patriotically calling the settlement Cambriol and conferring the names of the South Welsh counties upon the places. But it was all to no purpose, and the very names disappeared. Vaughan found the burden 'too heavy for my weak shoulders' and assigned the northerly portion of his grant to Falkland, the rest to Lord Baltimore. That was the end of Cambriol — except that one of his Welshmen, 'Captain Wynne, a Cambro-Briton', took on the job of settling Baltimore's plantation at Ferriland. We are not called upon to go into that; for all these failures the inhabitation of Newfoundland was now begun, though it proceeded slowly and always with the hostility of the fishing interests. It was not until the arrival of the imperialist Puritans to power and the rule of Cromwell that Newfoundland got able and upright administration from their governor, John Treworgie — to be betrayed, of course, at the Restoration.

Vaughan came back with a couple of books to add to the literature of Newfoundland. In 1626 he published *The Golden Fleece*, by Orpheus Junior.[1] The device of a modern pursuit of the golden fleece, as reported before a court of the ancient gods, enabled him to traverse a number of contemporary questions upon which he expressed strong

[1] He is best known by his book, *The Golden Grove*.

opinions: tithes, celibacy of the clergy, Rome and so on. One may judge the style of the thing from the preface: 'my masters, you that slight the first lesson of the Psalms, you that plot at home like crafty crowders, to reap the fruits of all painful trades without wetting your cat's feet, though the fish be never so dearly prized, you who repose your chiefest felicity in playing on the viol of fraud, and in idolizing a painted strumpet, come not at Colchos, nor presume ye once, more than Tantalus, to touch the golden apples of the Hesperides'. One observes the instinctive Welsh alliteration and the exaltation of temperament that goes with it.

The golden apples of the Hesperides were to be found in Newfoundland; but it is not until the third book that we are allowed to arrive there. Its recommendations turn out pedestrian enough, for they are naturally the same as those already advanced on behalf of plantation there. But Vaughan's literary device enables him to call upon all those concerned to give their evidence in the court of Apollo: John Guy as to the climate, since he was 'the first Christian that planted and wintered in that island', John and Humphrey Slany as to its commodities, Mason as to its advantages; while Gorges, accused by the western fishermen of hindering their stages for drying fish, replies to the anti-planters that it is for the good of the commonwealth that there should be an outlet for surplus population. Guy and Mason were called in to write commendatory verses, while the latter contributed his delightful map. Guy wrote:

> We need not now complain for want of trade
> Sith from the West we golden wares may lade;
> Which Orpheus shows in this his golden fleece,
> A trade more rich than Jason brought to Greece
> From Colchos land; if by our slothful ease
> And wanton peace we lose not the increase.
> What I first chalked two years at Cuperts cove
> New Cambriol's planter sprung from Golden Grove
> Old Cambria's soil up to the skies doth raise.
> For which let Fame crown him with sacred bays.

Perhaps the learned Doctor wrote these verses himself under the Bristol merchant's name? We cannot help feeling that that may have been the case with the Latin poems of Guy and Mason prefixed to Vaughan's volume of Latin verses, *Cambrensium Caroleia, reportata a Colchide Cambriola ex australissima Novae Terrae Plaga*. Here again, as in Vaughan's prose-work, he traverses numerous contemporary themes exposing to the full, in true Celtic fashion, his views and prejudices, without restraint: that the old country will gain by transporting felons to the Newfoundland colonies; on the advantages of plantation there; the North-West Passage; *De Tobacconistarum prodigalitate comprimenda*.

Nor was this the end of Vaughan's interest. Some years after his return he wrote a little work, *The Newlander's Cure*, on the complaints prevalent there, with his suggested remedies. Pleasant and idiosyncratic a writer as Vaughan was, we could dispense with a measure of his opinions for a little more about his days in Newfoundland. He must have spent a good many of them writing Latin verses, and then, himself unwell and his colony not prospering, came home again. Anyhow, Vaughan's interest was not that of a practical man but of a projector, a combination of public spirit and fantasy.

Perhaps it was the climate, and the loneliness, that turned men's thoughts to literature. For Vaughan's contemporary, Robert Hayman, while in charge of Bristol's Hope at Harbour Grace wrote his volume of *Quodlibets* and translated four books of John Owen's Latin epigrams into English verse. Hayman was a Devonshire lad who matriculated at the age of eleven from Exeter College in 1590:[1] so he too was an Elizabethan, a couple of years junior to Vaughan. He was a student at Lincoln's Inn at the time of the capture of Cadiz; years afterwards in far Newfoundland he would think of the festival days and grand nights in the hall, the young men taking the guests by the hand and trooping round the fire singing a song, 'which I could never sing'. A still earlier memory from childhood came back to

[1] J. Foster, *Alumni Oxon.*, II. 681 (early series).

his mind, of Drake, home from a voyage, enquiring for his
father at his house in Totnes:

> As he was walking up Totnes' long street:
> He asked me whose I was? I answered him.
> He asked me if his good friend were within?
> A fair red orange in his hand he had;
> He gave it me, whereof I was right glad,
> Takes and kissed me, and prays God bless my boy.

These simple and artless verses bring to mind many
names from the West Country circles interested in Newfoundland, Hayman's early friends at Oxford, among the
citizens and churchmen of Exeter and Bristol, the literary
men of London. The first poem in commendation of
Hayman's volume is by Vaughan, 'to my dear friend and
fellow-planter', ending

> Thus he who borrowed twice sweet Orpheus' name,
> Poor Cambriol's lord, adds to your rising fame.

In turn Hayman salutes 'the admirably witty and excellently
learned Sir Nicholas Smith, knight, of Larkbeare near
Exeter, my ancient friend'; and the Cornishman, 'the
right worshipful William Noy esquire, one of the benchers
of Lincoln's Inn, long since of my acquaintance both in
Oxford and London' — to become Charles I's Attorney-
General. Among other lawyers are Nicholas Duck, Recorder of Exeter, Arthur Duck, Chancellor of London and
of Bath and Wells — Hayman's cousins — and also William
Hakewell. Among clergymen, there was Archdeacon George
Hakewell, Dean Winnise of Gloucester, 'anciently of my
acquaintance in Exeter College, Oxford', and the Cornish
incumbent, chaplain to the Rouses, 'the reverend, learned,
acute and witty Master Charles FitzGeoffrey, B.D., my
especial kind friend, most excellent poet' — of whom we
learn:

> Featured you are like Homer in one eye.

Among the bright young men who had been at Exeter
College together was one Taylor, a turncoat, for he had
turned Jesuit, 'sometime my familiar friend in Oxford'.

Hayman proceeds to write some skeltonics in praise of Newfoundland, and it is a pleasant enough picture of life there that he gives:

> Although in clothes, company, buildings fair
> With England Newfoundland cannot compare,
> Did some know what contentment I found there —
> Always enough, most times somewhat to spare,
> With little pains, less toil and lesser care,
> Exempt from taxings, illness, lawing, fear,
> If clean and warm no matter what you wear,
> Healthy and wealthy if men careful are,
> With much much more than I will now declare —
> I say, if some wise men knew what this were,
> I do believe they'd live no other where.

A poem to Captain John Mason celebrates the wholesome air, 'the fire as sweet as any made with wood', the waters teeming with fish — in fact, the four elements.

Among those similarly involved in plantation Hayman remembers the Slanys at Bristol, the mayor and one or two merchants in the city; Lord Baltimore, Sir Richard Whitbourne, Sir William Vaughan — a poem from which we learn of his illness. There is the Rev. Erasmus Stourton, parson of Ferriland, and a poem for Thomas Rowley, 'who from the first plantation hath lived in Newfoundland, little to his profit'. But for this poem, we should not know of his existence: it shows that there were planters, however, who did not give up. Two poems were addressed to Sir William Alexander, interested in Nova Scotia.

Last, there were Hayman's literary friends, Bishop Hall at Exeter, Donne now Dean of St. Paul's, Ben Jonson and George Wither. And there is 'my right worthy friend Master Michael Drayton, whose unwearied old Muse still produceth new dainties': with him we are back again in the heart of the Elizabethan age.

After the Welsh and Cambriola, the Scots and Nova Scotia.

Welsh feeling had largely impelled Vaughan in his

schemes; a similar element of Scottish feeling moved Sir William Alexander to look for an outlet for Scottish over-population in America. Just as Vaughan's heart had been touched by the spectacle of poor Welsh folk dying of want, so Alexander tells us that Scotland was overswarming with people (in relation to available livelihood), and if new habitations were not provided for them they would miscarry for want or turn drones.[1] Nevertheless, 'my countrymen would never adventure in such an enterprise, unless it were as there was a New France, a New Spain, and a New England, that they might have a New Scotland . . . which they might hold of their own Crown and where they might be governed by their own laws'.[2]

They were both poets: Vaughan in the fantastic Welsh manner, Alexander in the prolix Scots manner — his poem *Doomsday* is in twelve books and has eleven thousand lines. Alexander was in fact a whole decade senior to Vaughan, being a contemporary of Elder Brewster, and had been, like him, at Leyden, but at the university. Most of Alexander's poems were written in the decade after 1603, though they were not published till later : of a grave and didactic beauty, in a Scots manner. A laird of old family, towards the end of his life he was made Secretary of State for Scotland, where, for his breadth of view and tolerance, he was naturally unpopular. He was made Earl of Stirling and Viscount of Canada, but this did not prevent him from dying poor — like so many of these colonial pioneers.

In 1611 James I had created his new order of baronets to raise money for the plantation of Scots in Ulster. Alexander suggested the application of the scheme to America, and in some ten years over a hundred Nova Scotia baronets were created to raise cash. James disregarded the prior rights of Gorges's New England Council to make Alexander an immense grant of the land south and east of the St. Lawrence, and from Cape Breton to Maine. This land had been opened up and fairly well explored by the English

[1] E. F. Slafter, *Sir William Alexander and American Colonisation* (Prince Soc.), 56.　　　　[2] *Ibid.* 196.

voyagers in the first decade of the century, as we see from a 'Description of the Country of Mawooshen' which Purchas found among Hakluyt's papers.[1] So far from objecting, Gorges did all he could to encourage Alexander, who pays him this tribute, 'Sir Ferdinando Gorges hath been a chief man for the furtherance of all things that might lend to the advancement of New England, having been at great charges these many years past for the discovery thereof'.

Sir William Alexander got his patent for Nova Scotia in 1621, and immediately granted a charter to Sir Robert Gordon for Cape Breton island as New Galloway. Nothing of this took effect, and when Alexander sent out a ship with his colonists next year they were driven back by storm and forced to put in at St. John's to winter. Next spring Alexander sent a supply ship, which found the colonists already dispersed, some gone a-fishing, to return home with their catch. The supply ship decided to explore the coast of Nova Scotia, whence they returned with the usual glowing reports, upon which Alexander based his tract, *An Encouragement to Colonise*, published in 1624. This went right back to the beginning of colonisation with the exodus of the Jews, Phoenicians, Greeks, Romans. It recited the history of colonial efforts in America, from the good fortune of the Spaniards, who were 'of all others in regard of their scarcity of people most unfit for planting thereof'. On the other hand, 'Scotland by reason of her populousness being constrained to disburden herself did every year send forth swarms, whereof great numbers did haunt Pole [Poland] . . . till now they were compelled . . . to betake themselves to the wars against Russians'[2], etc. And now that the great current of Scottish emigration to Ireland had run dry, there remained America.

America appealed to Alexander's poetic imagination : to think 'how it hath pleased the Lord to lock it up so long amidst the depths, concealing it from the curiosity of the ancients, that it might be discovered in a fit time for their posterity'.[3] He thought that there must be some narrow

---

[1] Purchas, XIX. 400 foll.   [2] Slafter, 205-6.   [3] *Ibid.* 208-9.

sea towards the north, a passage whence the original inhabitants came from Asia — or perhaps they came floating
on the mountains of ice that float every spring along the
Newfoundland coast. 'But this is a matter that can hardly
be determined by demonstration or reason . . . (all men
forming that which they know not according to the square
of their own conceits) we must leave this to the unlimited
liberty of the imagination of man.'

With the set-backs he had endured, like Gorges and so
many others, Alexander's schemes languished. But with the
outbreak of war with France and the remarkable exploits
of the Kirke brothers, to be crowned by the capture of
Quebec, Sir William revived his interest. He made an
agreement with the formidable trio for an Anglo-Scottish
descent on Nova Scotia — which to the French was Acadia.[1]
In 1628 Alexander's son headed a party of Scots colonists
to occupy Port Royal, of whom thirty died that winter.[2]
In 1629 Lord Ochiltree landed a party on Cape Breton,
but these were held off by the French.[3] In spite of the
Kirkes' brilliant success in capturing Quebec and Champlain
in it, by the Treaty of St.-Germain Charles I handed over
his subjects' conquests and their claims for the payment of
his wife's dowry. It was not until this that the effective
French colonisation of the St. Lawrence began.[4] As for
Nova Scotia–Acadia, this turn of events led to the complex
and disputed history of the territory later. The shape of
the long conflict for Canada was thus early prefigured.

We have had constant indications of the extreme importance to the Elizabethan English of finding a route to
the East by North-East or North-West : if they could discover it, it would be *their* route. Moreover, the southern
routes were already occupied. Some idea of the importance

---

[1] Donald Creighton, *Dominion of the North*, 35.
[2] T. C. Haliburton, *An Historical and Statistical Account of Nova Scotia*, I. 45.
[3] W. O. Raymond, 'The Acadian Settlements and Early History, 1604–
1713', in *Canada and its Provinces*, ed. A. Shortt and A. G. Doughty, XIII. 15
foll.
[4] Claude de Bonnault, *Histoire du Canada français*, 1534–1763, 22.

of the question may be gained when we reflect that the opening of trade and communications with Russia and their first acquaintance with America were by-products of the quest. Nothing is more impressive, in that age in which so much impresses us with their energy, than the pertinacity with which they pressed on with the pursuit, returned again and again to it, in spite of all set-backs and losses of life and fortune. The sequence of efforts began with the Queen's reign, and when it ended hope had not yet faded out in the far North-West.

The effective broaching of the matter, putting it on the map politically, as it were, we owe to the fruitful, the originating mind of Humphrey Gilbert. He held a disputation, in formal academic style, with Anthony Jenkinson, the exponent of the idea of a North-East Passage, before the Queen herself and some of her privy councillors in the winter of 1565–6. It was at this time that Gilbert wrote his celebrated *Discourse of a Discovery for a new passage to Cathay*, though it was not published till 1576, to coincide with Frobisher's first voyage to the North-West. It has not been realised that Gilbert himself hoped to lead a voyage to those waters as early as this.

Professor Quinn says that the fact that 'it was largely out of date by the time it was published should not obscure its significance at the time it was written. It was the first considerable English treatise on a project about which, for forty years, many had thought'.[1] That is only just. In addition to the argumentation from classical authorities, *de rigueur* in this time of the Renaissance, Gilbert had equipped himself with a wide reading in contemporary geographers — for he was very much of an intellectual, besides being a soldier — and had researched into the original materials, documents and maps, left by the Cabots. Impossible as it is to traverse the whole *Discourse* here, we may note some shrewd observations tending to the conclusion, thus early, that America must be an island : 'if that America were

[1] *The Voyages and Colonising Enterprises of Sir Humphrey Gilbert*, ed. D. B. Quinn (Hakluyt Soc.), I. 8.

not an island, but a part of the continent adjoining to Asia, the people which inhabit Mangia, Anian and Quinsay [*i.e.* present-day British Columbia and Alaska], being borderers upon it, would before this time have made some road into it.' [1] Conversely, Gilbert has a whole section 'to prove that the Indians . . . came only by the North West, which induceth a certainty of our passage by experience'.

The idea of a colony arose consequentially, as a trading base and a half-way house between England and Asia 'about Sierra Nevada', *i.e.* California. Shortly after, Gilbert entered upon his period of service in Ireland; it was his experience there that emphasised the colonising aspect of his schemes. And it is indeed to be noticed that it was the group of West Countrymen concerned with colonising in southern Ireland, Gilbert, Ralegh, Grenville, who were first to stretch their minds and arms across the Atlantic to Virginia.

We have seen that Frobisher's voyages were disappointing from a geographical point of view, though even more so from that of their hunt for gold. The first effective search for a North-West passage comes also out of the Gilbert circle, with John Davis's three attempts in 1585, 1586, 1587. Gilbert's *Discourse* was approved of by John Dee, who was acquainted with Adrian Gilbert and John Davis, though they quarrelled like everybody who came within the aura of the occult philosopher. They made it up, however, for we find in Dee's Diary, 23 January 1583: 'Mr. Secretary Walsingham came to my house, where by good luck he found Mr. Adrian Gilbert, and so talk was begun of North West straits discovery. 24 January: I, Mr. Adrian Gilbert and John Davis went by appointment of Mr. Secretary to Mr. Beale's house, where only we four were secret, and we made Mr. Secretary privy of the N.W. passage, and all charts and rutters were agreed upon in general. 6 March: I and Mr. Adrian Gilbert and John Davis did meet with Mr. Alderman Barnes, Mr. Towerson and Mr. Young and

---

[1] *The Voyages and Colonising Enterprises of Sir Humphrey Gilbert*, I. 141, 153.

THE SEARCH
FOR A
NORTH-WEST PASSAGE.
1602-1632.
Scale 1:50 000 000
├────────────────────┤ 100 Leagues

1. Hakluyt Island.   2. Cary Islands.
3. Cape Dudley Digges.   4. Cape Comfort.
5. Mansell Island.   6. Nottingham Island.
7. Salisbury Island.   8. Savage Islands.
Tracks of Explorers.
H. Hudson, 1610.   **Bu.** Button, 1612-13.
B. Baffin, 1615.   **Ba.** Baffin, 1616.

Mr. Hudson, about the N.W. voyage.' [1] These discussions led to Adrian Gilbert's obtaining a patent next year for North-Western discovery,[2] though when John Davis set out it was with the backing principally of the merchant William Sanderson, Ralegh's faithful friend and supporter.

John Davis was one of the best and most scientific navigators of the age; we derive the impression that he was also a charming man. He was born about 1550 at Sandridge in the parish of Stoke Gabriel by the waters of the Dart: the yews in the churchyard go back to him, his pew in the church still awaits him. His close neighbours, the gentry of the neighbourhood, were the Gilberts then living at Greenway with its view of the river opening out to sea.

Davis left Dartmouth, 7 June 1585, with two little barks, the *Sunshine* and the *Moonshine*, of fifty and thirty-five tons only, though they carried four musicians on board. These came in handy when they got across the Atlantic, into what is now Davis Strait and made contact with the Eskimos upon the islands. 'The people of the country, having espied us, made a lamentable noise, as we thought, with great outcries and screeching: we hearing them thought it had been the howling of wolves.' [3] A party landing from the ships, 'we brought our musicians . . . purposing by force to rescue us, if need should so require, or with courtesy to allure the people. When they came unto us, we caused our musicians to play, ourselves dancing and making many signs of friendship.' Thus they made contact: 'we were in so great credit with them upon this single acquaintance that we could have anything they had. We bought five canoes of them; we bought their clothes from their backs, which were all made of sealskins and birds' skins; their buskins, their hose, their gloves, all being commonly sewed and well dressed.' On this first reconnaissance they got up as far as 66° 4', finding the sea 'altogether void from the pester of ice'. Here they named the features around them,

[1] *The Private Diary of Dr. John Dee*, ed. J. O. Halliwell (Camden Soc.), 18, 19.   [2] Hakluyt, V. 276 foll.   [3] *Ibid.* 285-6.

Mount Ralegh, Capes Walsingham and Dyer, Exeter Sound and Totnes Road, and were back at Dartmouth by the end of September.

For the second voyage, also supported chiefly by Sanderson, the *Mermaid* of 120 tons was added, and a little pinnace called the *North Star*. In Davis Strait the Eskimos gave the English an engaging welcome, and after exchanging presents they took to leaping together and wrestling, in which 'we found them strong and nimble, for they cast some of our people that were good wrestlers'.[1] For their religion 'they are idolaters and have images great store, which they wear about them and in their boats, which we suppose they worship. They are witches and have many kinds of enchantments, which they often used, but to small purpose, thanks be to God.' When it came to property it seems these primitive people made no nice distinctions, stealing anything they could lay hand on, cables, calivers, oars, spears, swords. 'They brought us seal-skins and salmon peal, but seeing iron they could in no wise forbear stealing; which, when I perceived, it did but minister unto me an occasion of laughter to see their simplicity, and I willed that in no case they should be any more hardly used.' They remained among these islands collecting their cargo of seal-skins and much pestered with ice-banks so that they did not get higher than 66° 33' in latitude before returning.

However, on his third voyage, in 1587 Davis penetrated as far as 72° 12' along the Greenland coast, 'the sea open all to the westwards and northwards', before the wind changing to the north forced them to run across to the opposite coast, where they found themselves greatly impeded by an immense ice-bank.[2] On his return Davis was able to report, 'I have been in 73 degrees, finding the sea all open, and forty leagues between land and land. The passage is most probable, the execution easy.' But this was Davis's last chance of trying it. Frustrated along this route he joined Cavendish's second expedition to the Straits of Magellan, with the hope of tackling the problem from the

[1] Hakluyt, V. 294-5.   [2] *Ibid.* 313, 316-17.

Pacific end. This, too, was the motive of his going east with the first East Indiamen. It is sad to record that in his absence the Gilberts tried to wrest his livelihood from him in his old homestead — one would not put it past them.[1] Then, as we read in his will, he was 'bound to the sea for the coast of China in the *Tiger* of London and uncertain of my return'.[2] Davis's wife being dead, he left one-fourth of his estate to Judith Harvard, 'unto whom I have given my faith in matrimony, to be solemnized at my return'. He did not come back: in 1605 he was killed in a treacherous attack by Japanese pirates in the Straits of Malacca.

Davis left behind him a tradition.[3] It seems that James Hall of Hull, who piloted three Greenland voyages in 1605–7, on behalf of the King of Denmark, had served with Davis. In 1607 a licence was granted to Richard Penkivell of Roserrow in Cornwall to make a journey to discover the North-West passage.[4] Nothing came of this. But Penkivell's family in the previous generation was closely connected with the Gilberts.[5] Back in 1576 William Carnsew, brother-in-law of the Penkivells and their neighbour at Bokelly, close acquaintance of Adrian Gilbert, was reading the *Discourse*.[6] One sees how tenacious was the attraction, the lure of what lay beyond the horizons of the far North-West opening out from Padstow haven or Dartmouth.

Davis's true successor, a man of his own stature and devotion, who shared his fixation on the Arctic, was Henry Hudson. He would have been about ten years junior, born before 1570, and a close relative of the Muscovy Company merchant whom we met discussing the North-West passage in 1583. In 1607 Hudson commanded the *Hopeful*, set forth by the Muscovy Company, to sail across the Pole, if

[1] *Salisbury MSS.* (H.M.C.), XIII. 599. In the patent of 1583 Adrian Gilbert is described as 'of Sandridge'; it is probable then that Davis's family had been tenants, and that the later dispute related to the property.
[2] *The Voyages and Works of John Davis*, ed. A. H. Markham (Hakluyt Soc.), lxxii.
[3] This is best set out in C. R. Markham's excellent *Life of John Davis, the Navigator*.   [4] *Cal. S.P. Dom., 1603–10.* 344.
[5] Quinn, I. 2.   [6] Cf. my *Tudor Cornwall*, 427-9.

possible, as Robert Thorne had advocated long ago to Henry VIII. Hudson skirted the coast of eastern Greenland, struck the ice-barrier and then followed it round in fearful storms and fogs to the east of Spitzbergen, honourably naming a headland for Hakluyt on the way. Next year he attempted the North-East, finding it impossible to get past Vaigatz; and in 1609 when he tried again, in Dutch service, his crew refused to attempt it. So, stretching across the North Atlantic, he searched the Delaware and Hudson entrances for an opening. In 1610 the *Discovery* was fitted out by Sir Thomas Smythe and other merchants, and Hudson sailed for the strait now named after him. He entered it at the end of June; the last words in his journal read, 'then I observed and found the ship at noon in 61 degrees 20 minutes, and a sea to the westwards'.[1]

Hudson must have thought that he had discovered the passage, and he determined to winter in the bay in order to explore to the west for an outlet in the spring. After a desperate winter of fearful hardships his crew thought otherwise, and next June, having reached open water in James Bay, they mutinied and cut him adrift in the shallop to die. His life's work is, however, sufficiently commemorated and constantly before our attention with those famous names, Hudson's Bay and Strait, the Hudson River. News of the discovery of that sea reached England and in 1612 Thomas Button went out, with over a hundred adventurers on board, confident that they had only to sail due west to reach Asia. They sailed due west, found themselves up against the impenetrable west coast of the bay, sailed south to winter and home again in the spring.

We may regard William Baffin as in the true succession to John Davis, in his life, his character and navigational skill, as in his end. Baffin had made several Arctic voyages to Spitzbergen and Greenland, in the series set forth by that imaginative magnate Sir Thomas Smythe. In 1615 he accompanied Bylot on a reconnaissance of North-Western waters; Parry, in the nineteenth century, bore witness to

[1] q. J. B. Brebner, *The Explorers of North America, 1492–1806*, 209.

the accuracy of his observations. In 1616 Baffin sailed on his fifth and most important Arctic voyage, which was backed again by Smythe and his East Indies and Virginia associates, Sir Dudley Digges and Wostenholme. Indeed, we must appreciate how in their minds these objectives hung together — Virginia and the East Indies, with the hope of a North-West passage to connect them. This time Baffin followed Davis along the route to his farthest north, Sanderson's Hope, and beyond into Baffin Bay to 78° N., farther than anyone had yet penetrated. Here in this northern sea Baffin conferred names deservedly honoured : Smythe Sound, Hakluyt Island, Lancaster Sound. Baffin's conscientiousness as a navigator made him conclude that these sounds were but bays, and that there was no passage through. Actually two of them, Lancaster Sound and Jones Sound, afford channels through to the so much desired Pacific. Concluding that an attempt was more feasible from the east, Baffin, like Davis before him, signed on for the Orient, where he too was killed.

Actually there is a channel, also, at the northernmost extremity of Hudson's Bay, but neither Luke Foxe, who had been 'itching after it ever since 1606', nor Captain James of Bristol discovered it in the voyages that brought this cycle of effort to an end.[1] James's voyage indeed has more literary than geographical interest, for his desolating narrative inspired the seascapes of *The Ancient Mariner*.

[1] Brebner, 216-17.

CHAPTER VIII

AMERICA IN ELIZABETHAN LITERATURE, SCIENCE AND THE ARTS

LITERATURE, in earlier times, naturally has a closer association with the events of history and often adheres recognisably to their rhythm. This is noticeably so with regard to America. More's *Utopia* is the first, and a most distinguished, reflection of the New World in the literature of the Old; and if More reflects Columbus as much as he does Cabot, there is no doubt that his brother-in-law Rastell gives voice to Cabot in the *Interlude of the Four Elements*, with its Tudor nationalism and its early expression of resentment at the great chance that had been left to the Spaniards. And just as the Cabot voyages tailed off into the half-hearted attempts of Henry VIII's reign and then, for a time, nothing — so we are faced with a blank in the literature until the revival of interest in America in Elizabeth's reign. That is, after an interval, given expression in the literature; as the interest in and knowledge of America gather momentum, so the reverberation in literature and the arts becomes louder, more frequent and more varied.

If we wish to make distinctions, we may make a useful one between the direct expression of America in writing and the indirect. On the one hand, there were the writings and reports of those who had been there, as collected by Hakluyt and Purchas, the books written by people like Captain Smith and Morton and Strachey, the histories and journals of Bradford and Winthrop, the numerous tracts and sermons devoted to the subject. On the other, there is the reflection of America in the mirror of the imagination, in the poetry and prose of Spenser and Sidney, Ralegh and Chapman, Shakespeare and Drayton, Bacon and Donne.

Sometimes these things run into one another : in the case of Ralegh, for example, who always straddles all fences. But it is fascinating to observe how not only the content but the very phrases of the voyagers will appear in the lines of the poets : how the words of Ralegh's sea-captain Barlow take wing in the verse of his master, or reappear in Drayton's Ode, or how Strachey's account of the hurricane off Bermuda is echoed in *The Tempest*.

We may observe another practical distinction. The reawakening interest in America, from the middle of the century, had at first to feed upon translations, from Spanish, French, Latin. When the English began to go to Virginia themselves in the 1580's, they were able in turn to contribute new information to other peoples, whom we find beginning now to translate from them. Hariot's *Brief Report* was republished in Latin by De Bry, and had no less than seventeen printings in the next quarter of a century : [1] an indication not only of Europe's interest in North America, but of people's turning to England now for information : Hariot remained the leading, the most scientific, authority for the best part of a century. The transition from the one to the other came about in the late seventies and early eighties — those years of heightening geographical interest — and may be seen incarnate in the career of Hakluyt. He began as a translator, with the *Divers Voyages* translated out of other people's accounts of the New World, but ended by collecting the narrations of the English voyagers, by which he is chiefly known to posterity.

Again, the transition from the factual world of translation to the effect upon the realm of the imagination may be seen first, as in so many things, in the circle of Philip Sidney, to whom Hakluyt dedicated the *Divers Voyages*. In his preface to the *Principal Navigations* Hakluyt acknowledged his indebtedness to Sir Edward Dyer for putting him in touch with various people who forwarded the work. It was Dyer who encouraged Frampton, a Bristol merchant who had spent many years in Spain, to translate Monardes'

[1] W. F. Craven, *The Southern Colonies in the Seventeenth Century*, 52.

Joyful News out of the Newfound World with its account of the plants found there and their medicinal qualities. A courtier who is a Somerset man, a Bristol merchant, a prebendary of the cathedral there — such are the natural groupings observable all through our story.

When we read the *Arcadia*, whose author was so much interested in America and several times thought of going there, we recognise the atmosphere of the voyages. It begins with a shipwreck, with the wrack floating in a sea of very rich things and 'many chests which might promise no less'. The capture of prizes dominates the first chapters, with the arrival of Musidorus in a strange country, having lost his friend Pyrocles, who subsequently turns up. It is like the beginning of *The Tempest*, or episodes of *A Winter's Tale* and *Pericles*. The influence of the voyages speaks in them all, inciting the imagination to strange scenes and countries across the seas.

The atmosphere of *Arcadia* has something in common with that of *The Faerie Queene* — the dream-like timelessness of a fairy world of romance. But Spenser, who had been a friend of Sidney, made the acquaintance of Ralegh in Ireland, and the introductory stanzas to Book II acknowledge the impulse of the expansion, in answer to the complaint

> That all this famous antique history
> Of some th' abundance of an idle brain
> Will judged be, and painted forgery
> Rather than matter of just memory. . . .

But here is 'matter of just memory' :

> But let that man with better sense advise
> That of the world least part to us is red ;
> And daily how through hardy enterprise
> Many great regions are discovered,
> Which to late age were never mentioned.
> Who ever heard of th' Indian Peru ?
> Or who in venturous vessel measured
> The Amazon huge river now found true ?
> Or fruitfullest Virginia who did ever view ?

> Yet all these were when no man did them know,
> Yet have from wisest ages hidden been ;
> And later times things more unknown shall show.

Canto XI, Book IV, reflects the geographical excitement of the time in the recital of the names of the great rivers of East and West. Stanza xxii turns to the country of Ralegh's later fixation, Guiana, with a rebuke to those who

> quail in conquest of that land of gold.
> But this to you, O Britons, most pertains
> To whom the right hereof itself hath sold,
> The which, for sparing little cost or pains
> Lose so immortal glory and so endless gains.

Here we have the complaint of Hakluyt and a hundred others, which they never tired of enforcing. It was American gold and silver, which gave Spain her ascendancy in Europe, that made other people so envious. And this theme constantly crops up in the literature.

With people in general America is always regarded as overflowing with gold : it is what it chiefly meant to people in the Old World — as it still does to some. Marlowe has several references to this in *Tamburlaine* :

> Desire of gold, great sir ?
> That's to be gotten in the Western Ind :

i.e. America. (We might rephrase that now with some exchange of alliteration : to 'desire of dollars', etc.). The thought is expressed by Greene, Peele, Lyly, Massinger, Chapman. It appears in Shakespeare, where sooner or later everything gets expression. We must remember that America, in this connotation, often appears as India, with or without the adjective 'Western'. This is made sufficiently clear by the dominant association with 'mines'. 'As bountiful as mines of India', he writes ; Henry VIII's meeting with Francis I at the Field of the Cloth of Gold

> Made Britain India ; every man that stood
> Showed like a mine.

In *Twelfth Night* when Maria appears to lay down the letter that entraps Malvolio, Sir Toby belches, 'How now, my metal of India', *i.e.* piece of gold. When Malvolio falls into the trap and is utterly bemused, Maria reports, 'he does smile his face into more lines than is in the new map with the augmentation of the Indies'. That was the map that went with the first volume of the enlarged edition of Hakluyt appearing in 1598 and gives us a useful date for the play. Shakespeare derived inspiration and profit from reading Hakluyt. The theme of digging for gold is an important element in *Timon* — at a time, too, when the Jamestown colony was temporarily given over to a frantic search for it. Todkill declared in 1608 that there was then 'no talk, no hope, no work but to dig gold, wash gold, refine gold, load gold'.[1] And this was about the date when *Timon* was written. The combination of the gold-theme with digging for roots for subsistence comes straight from the voyages.

The theme is extended in the scenes that Chapman, Ralegh's poet, contributed to Jonson and Marston's *Eastward Ho!* The absurd Sir Petronel Flash's money is bestowed on a ship bound for Virginia. Security comments: 'We have too few such knight adventurers: who would not sell away competent certainties to purchase, with any danger, excellent uncertainties?' This was precisely what many did for Virginia and New England too. Seagull helps with a lot of mariner's tales about Virginia to gull the public. 'Come, boys,' he says, 'Virginia longs till we share the rest of her maidenhead.' That was a regular phrase with the voyagers — Ralegh's phrase for Guiana. On this Spendall asks: 'Why, is she inhabited already with any English?' Seagull: 'A whole country of English is there, man, bred of those that were left there in '79.' (Actually the date was '87; but we do not go to dramatists for dates any more than to historians for dramatics.) 'They have married with the Indians and make 'em bring forth as beautiful faces as any we have in England, and therefore

[1] E. G. R. Taylor, *Late Tudor and Early Stuart Geography, 1583–1650*, 159.

the Indians are so in love with 'em that all the treasure they have they lay at their feet.' Scapethrift: 'But is there such treasure there, captain, as I have heard?' Seagull: 'I tell thee, gold is more plentiful there than copper is with us; and for as much red copper as I can bring, I'll have thrice the weight in gold. Why, man, all their dripping pans and their chamber pots are pure gold; and all the chains with which they chain up their streets are massy gold; all the prisoners they take are fettered in gold; and for rubies and diamonds they go forth on holidays and gather 'em by the sea-shore . . .'[1] Scapethrift asks: 'And is it a pleasant country withal?' Captain Seagull replies: 'As ever the sun shined on: temperate and full of all sorts of excellent viands.' And then, in the spirit in which Cobbett enumerated the advantages of America, ending up with 'No Wilberforces! Think of that: no Wilberforces!', Seagull admits that there are a few industrious Scots there: for his part he would 'a hundred thousand of them were there'. For this abuse of the new King's fellow-countrymen the authors served a turn in prison.

Perhaps it was the closeness of Chapman to the dangerous Ralegh that added to the objectionableness. Chapman had written his *De Guiana: Carmen Epicum* to celebrate Ralegh's voyage and urge the Queen to take over the country:

> What work of honour and eternal name
> For all the world to envy and us to achieve . . .

Chapman was a friend and admirer of Hariot, to whom he addressed his translation from the *Iliad, Achilles' Shield*:

> Virtue must wait on wealth; we must make friends
> Of the unrighteous Mammon, and our sleights
> Must bear the forms of fools or parasites.
> Rich mine of knowledge, O that my strange muse
> Without this body's nourishment could use
> Her zealous faculties, only to inspire
> Instructive light from your whole sphere of fire.

Perhaps a more accurate description of Chapman's muse, which he himself describes as 'strange' and 'stifled',

---

[1] This passage is adapted from More's *Utopia*.

'struggling for birth' would be 'costive' or 'constipated'.

These leads, Spenser, Marlowe, Chapman, all point to Ralegh, as they were all his friends: he stands at the cross-roads in literature as he did in these actions. The captains he sent to reconnoitre Virginia in 1584 reported as follows — and we may note in passing how their report, and indeed all the prose recorded in Hakluyt, contradicts Virginia Woolf's view of the lumbering complexity of Elizabethan prose. 'The second of July we found shoal water, where we smelt so sweet and so strong a smell as if we had been in the midst of some delicate garden abounding with all kind of odoriferous flowers, by which we were assured that the land could not be far distant. . . . We viewed the land about us, being, whereas we first landed, very sandy and low towards the water's side, but so full of grapes as the very beating and surge of the sea overflowed them; of which we found such plenty, as well on every little shrub as also climbing towards the tops of high cedars that I think in all the world the like abundance is not to be found. . . . Under the bank or hill whereon we stood, we beheld the valleys replenished with goodly cedar-trees, and having discharged our arquebus shot, such a flock of cranes arose under us, with such a cry redoubled by many echoes, as if an army of men had shouted all together.' [1]

In the poem Ralegh was writing some years later to recover the Queen's favour (but never finished), *Book of the Ocean to Cynthia*, we read:

> On highest mountains where those cedars grew
> Against whose banks the troubled ocean bet
> And were the marks to find thy hoped port
> Into a soil far off themselves remove.

And when we come to Drayton's [2] *Ode to the Virginian Voyage*, we find:

[1] R. Hakluyt, *Principal Navigations*, VI. 122-3.

[2] Drayton was an intimate of the Rainsford family, whose head, Sir Henry, was a considerable shareholder in the Virginia Company and a constant supporter of Sir Edwin Sandys. C. C. Stopes, *Life of Henry Third Earl of Southampton*, 422.

When as the luscious smell
Of that delicious land
    Above the sea that flows
    The clear wind throws
Your hearts to swell
Approaching the dear strand.

And the ambitious vine
Crowns with his purple mass
    The cedar reaching high
    To kiss the sky,
The cypress, pine,
And useful sassafras.

Of the motives that could lead men to leave home
Ralegh speaks, in his own case:

My hopes clean out of sight with forced wind
To kingdoms strange, to lands far off addressed . . .

And he sums them all up in one famous line,

To seek new worlds for gold, for praise, for glory.

Naturally we turn to the drama for a more realistic, not to say cynical, ascription of motive.[1] A prodigal spendthrift in Middleton's *Spanish Gipsy* implores, 'Then send me to the West Indies; buy me some office there'. In Massinger's *City Madam* the unscrupulous Luke suggests shipping his sister-in-law and her daughters off to America.

Lady Frugal: How! Virginia!
    High Heaven forbid! Remember, sir, I beseech you,
    What creatures are shipped thither.
Anne: Condemned wretches, forfeited to the law.
Mary: Strumpets and bawds, for the abomination of their
    life spewed out of their own country.

This suggests one reason for the greater success of the godly at New Plymouth and Massachusetts Bay. It was certainly one of the reasons for the troubles of early Virginia. We recall Bacon's censure: 'it is a shameful and unblessed thing to take the scum of people and wicked condemned

[1] Cf. for some of these and further illustrations, R. R. Cawley, *The Voyagers and Elizabethan Drama*.

men to be the people with whom you plant'. Hakluyt, however, gave expression to an humanitarian consideration on the other side.

In a play of Jonson's, someone in the toils of a usurer, bursts out, 'I'll to Virginia, like some cheating bankrupt, and leave my creditor in the suds'. Others beside Sir Petronel Flash thought of carrying off the lady of their choice to Virginia. A character in Middleton's *Roaring Girl* warns, 'take deliberation, sir, never choose a wife as if you were going to Virginia'. Aurelia in Mayne's *City Match* imparts the information,

> I do mean to marry,
> Like ladies in New England, where they couple
> With no more ceremony than birds choose their mate
> Upon St. Valentine's day.

But I cannot think this refers to those virtuous Puritan matrons, Mistress Bradford or Mistress Winthrop, the spouses of Miles Standish or Saltonstall — perfect Longfellow heroines : it must refer to naughty Indian ladies.

There was a whole succession of literary men who went as officials to Virginia : William Strachey, John Pory, Christopher Davison, George Sandys. Donne, who was hard up before he condescended to take orders, sought to be made Secretary. Strachey, an Emmanuel man, moved in a literary and dramatic circle in London.[1] He wrote a sonnet for Jonson's *Sejanus*, in which Shakespeare acted. He was a shareholder in the Children of the Queen's Revels and so came to Blackfriars two or three times a week, where he would meet Shakespeare. In 1609 he went out with Gates and Somers in the *Sea Venture*, which was famously wrecked on Bermuda, though all were saved and spent an agreeable winter there. The extraordinary happening made a strong impression on people's minds at home, and several accounts of it appeared, the most detailed being Strachey's letter to a Noble Lady, which circulated in manuscript.

[1] W. Strachey, *The Historie of Travell into Virginia Britania*, ed. L. B. Wright and Virginia Freund, xviii foll.

It is not surprising that the most impressionable mind in that circle was struck by it : for this was the germ of *The Tempest.*[1]

It is somehow right that just as More's *Utopia* provides the first expression of genius of the New World in our period, so *The Tempest* provides the last, that these two transcendent minds should have risen to the full height of the theme. For there is far more of the New World in Shakespeare's play than the original suggestion coming from Strachey's letter — the storm with its veracious details, St. Elmo's fire flaming amazement along the main-mast, the wreck and not a hair of the people hurt, the enchanted island full of noises, for Bermuda was believed to be haunted by evil spirits. The whole play sings of the sea ; the loveliest songs are of the sea :

> Come unto these yellow sands,
>   And then take hands :
> Curtsied when you have and kissed,
>   The wild waves whist . . .

and the most haunting song, surely, ever written :

> Full fathom five thy father lies,
>   Of his bones are coral made ;
> Those are pearls that were his eyes :
>   Nothing of him that doth fade
> But doth suffer a sea-change
> Into something rich and strange.

It is not only that, but with the creation of Caliban, the primitive savage, possessor of the island, and his relation to Prospero, the very civilised and lordly person who dispossesses him, the whole question of what happens when civilisation makes its impact upon primitive society is placed before us in a way we can never forget. Our sympathies are not with Prospero — and perhaps in the subconscious corridors of the mind we think of what happened to the

[1] Shakespeare, like Drayton, had a number of close friends in the Virginia Company. Cf. Leslie Hotson, *I, William Shakespeare*, c. ix, and *The Arden Shakespeare, The Tempest*, ed. Frank Kermode, xxvi foll.

redskins.   There is something affecting about Caliban :

> When thou camest first,
> Thou strok'dst me and mad'st much of me, would'st
>   give me
> Water with berries in't, and teach me how
> To name the bigger light, and how the less,
> That burn by day and night.

This is what happened time and again, generation after
generation, with tribe after tribe, all along the coasts of
America when the Indians came in contact with the white
men and their superior knowledge.   We read in Hakluyt
and Captain Smith with what avidity they learned about
the stars and the firmament, watched the white men's
instruments, were impressed by loadstone and magnet,
optic glass and clock.

> And then I loved thee
> And showed thee all the qualities o' the isle,
> The fresh springs, brine-pits, barren place and fertile.

That, too, had often happened — we remember how Squanto
showed the Pilgrims where best to take their fish, how to
set Indian corn and enabled them to subsist through the
hard first years.   In one sense, the Indians were quick to
learn ;   in another, they never learned — the gulf between
their primitive cast of mind and that of the white man was
too deep to bridge.   And so the red man lost in the struggle
for existence.   Nor did he profit from his knowledge, in
spite of his experiences at the hand of the white man.   After
Prospero comes the drunken Trinculo :

> *Caliban* : I prithee, let me bring thee where crabs grow ;
>   And I with my long nails will dig thee pig-nuts ;
>   Show thee a jay's nest and instruct thee how
>   To snare the nimble marmoset ; I'll bring thee
>   To clustering filberts and sometimes I'll get thee
>   Young scamels from the rocks.

In spite of what he has suffered at the hand of Prospero,
Caliban now wants Trinculo to be his god :

> I'll show thee every fertile inch o' th' island :
> And I will kiss thy foot : I prithee, be my god.

We are reminded of the native Californians who embarrassed Drake and his men by taking them for gods.

We come to the brink of an ambivalent and difficult theme, that of the golden age some people saw in the primitive state of nature these Indians lived in. Captain Barlow reported of the Roanoke Indians, much like the impression Drake derived of those of California : 'we found the people most gentle, loving and faithful, void of all guile and treason, and such as live after the manner of the golden age'.[1] First impressions of other voyagers were similar — until further experience corrected their illusions. Opinion then swung to the other extreme, as with Captain John Smith who, in spite of Pocahontas, held a harsh view of them, and even the sainted Pilgrims were driven to a deed of blood against them. Captain John Smith tells with some gusto what happened to the religious-minded George Thorp, who 'did so truly affect their conversion that whosoever under him did them the least displeasure were punished severely. He thought nothing too dear for them, he never denied them anything, in so much that when they complained that our mastiffs did fear them, he to content them in all things caused some of them to be killed in their presence, to the great displeasure of the owners.'[2] We recognise an early type of the Liberal illusionist : he was one of the first to be murdered in the Indian massacre of 1622. Caliban had another side to him.

Shakespeare, with indefeasible justice of mind, presents both sides. Caliban is a savage, yet Gonzalo reports of the people of the island that

> Their manners are more gentle-kind than of
> Our human generation you shall find
> Many, nay, almost any.

And it is Gonzalo who speaks the passage about his ideal state of nature, that comes from Montaigne's essay on the Cannibals, as translated by Florio.

[1] Hakluyt, VI. 128.
[2] Smith, I. 281.

I' the commonwealth I would by contraries
Execute all things : for no kind of traffic
Would I admit ; no name of magistrate :
Letters should not be known ; riches, poverty,
And use of service, none : contract, succession,
Bourn, bound of land, tilth, vineyard, none ;
No use of metal, corn, or wine or oil ;
No occupation : all men idle, all ;
And women too, but innocent and pure —

Gonzalo forgets himself, is carried away into caricature, so
that we see Shakespeare did not share these fantasies, any
more than the practical Captain Smith or Governor
Bradford did.

> *Gonzalo* : All things in common nature should produce
> Without sweat or endeavour : treason, felony,
> Sword, pike, knife, gun, or need of any engine,
> Would I not have ; but nature should bring forth,
> Of its own kind, all foison, all abundance,
> To feed my innocent people.

We see what nonsense Shakespeare thought it : the kind of
nonsense idealists cherish — though why passes compre-
hension.

The idea of an original state of nature was to have a
long and important development in political speculation
and theorising about society, and it was given an immense
forward impetus by what men discovered in the New
World. We cannot go into it here. It was brought home
vividly to me years ago when I saw John Locke's library
as it had come down in the possession of his representa-
tives : we take it for granted that he was a generalising
and abstract thinker, as he was, but his library was full
of the American voyages. There, made visible, was an
example of the way early anthropology went into political
theory.

Tudor folk were fascinated by the trappings of Indian
life and the spectacle of Indians, from the time Cabot
brought back some to the streets of Westminster and a
Brazilian chief was presented at the Court of Henry VIII.

To celebrate the marriage of the Princess Elizabeth in 1613
— when the great Virginian venture was much in mind —
two masks were given by the Inns of Court. Bacon's Mask
of Flowers argued the merits and demerits of Virginia's
chief product, tobacco, before the anti-tobacconist James I.
Chapman's mask, a much grander affair dressed by Inigo
Jones, had the maskers attired in Indian costume 'with
high sprigged feathers on their heads, hair black and large
waving down to their shoulders'.[1] The musicians were
attired like Virginian priests — no doubt from John White's
drawing. But the serious-minded Chapman addressed himself to a searching theme, the problem posed by the diversity
of religion revealed by a new world, of which Holy Scripture,
which held the key to all human history, had no knowledge.
The orthodox poet spoke through Eunomia, representing
civilised order :

> Virginian princes, you must now renounce
> Your superstitious worship of these Suns,
> Subject to cloudy darkenings and descents,
> And of your fit devotions turn the event
> To this our British Phoebus, whose bright sky
> (Enlightened with a Christian piety)
> Is never subject to black error's night,
> And hath already offered heaven's true light
> To your dark region.

The British Phoebus had not had much success with the
Puritans at the Hampton Court Conference, and his theological mind found the questions raised by the religion of
the Indians, and even their existence, a problem.

The Elizabethans were troubled by this.[2] All human
beings, they knew from the Bible, were descended from the
sons of Noah : the Asiatics from Shem, the Africans from
Ham, Europeans from Japhet. From whom had the ab-
original inhabitants of the New World descended ? People
tried to console themselves with tales that the Indians had

---

[1] E. D. Neill, *History of the Virginia Company of London*, 61.
[2] Cf. Sir Sidney Lee, 'The American Indian in Elizabethan England',
in *Elizabethan and Other Essays*, ed. F. S. Boas.

shared the experience of the Flood. Others tried hard to
believe that they worshipped *one* god — to offset the dis-
turbing new revelations of human diversity, which offered,
after all, a more appropriate subject for anthropological
observation than theological fantasy. When they found it
no longer possible to entertain illusions on the subject, it
was concluded that it must be devils that the Indians
worshipped — all very simple in the usual human manner.
Similarly they tried hard to find assurance that the Indians
believed in immortality. A report to this effect made the
British Phoebus conclude that the gospel must previously
have been known in that benighted land and that this was
the one vestige of light that remained.

All this, of course, offered no problem to the adult mind
of a Montaigne, who well understood the relativism of
human conditions and beliefs.

There were people, even then, who speculated sensibly
whether the American Indians had not come across the
narrow divide of the Behring Strait from Asia. Some reflection of these speculations may be seen in Bacon's *jeu
d'esprit, The New Atlantis.* Naturally the influence of the
voyages and reading Hakluyt is apparent, and Bacon had
the direct interest in colonisation, by this time, of being one
of the Council for Newfoundland. Bacon's utopian island
was in the Pacific, which might still have islands and
continents not yet come to light — Australia was yet to
come out of it. But he refers to the inundation of an Atlantic
continent, and the shrinking Atlantic shelf of America.
Hence the American Indians were but remnants of a
people : 'marvel you not at the thin population of America,
nor at the rudeness and ignorance of the people; for you
must accept your inhabitants of America as a young people :
younger a thousand years, at the least, than the rest of the
world'.[1] Bacon takes pains to tell us of the inhabitants of
his New Atlantis, 'as for masculine love, they have no touch
of it'. This was very far from the case with the American
Indians, as we know from the shocked reports of the English

[1] Bacon, *Works*, ed. J. Spedding, III. 143.

voyagers and the matter-of-fact recording of the facts of life by Spanish Dominicans.

We are not concerned here with the main interest of Bacon's tract: the programme of research and discovery which mirrors his immense intellectual optimism — he looked forward to improvements in plants and fruits, vivisection for the extension of anatomical knowledge, an extended range of harmonies, the conveyance of sound through pipe-lines, means of flight and of under-water sailing, refrigeration — all of which developments have in time come to bind together the community of Atlantis. The answers to real questions were to come the way of observation and reasoned analysis on the basis of evidence.

This was not the cast of Donne's medieval mind, even though he was affected by the stimulating geographical curiosity of the time. This is reflected in his poems, in the unexpected images he reaches out for on the subject of love:

> Let sea-discoverers to new worlds have gone,
> Let maps to others worlds on worlds have shown,
> Let us possess one world, each hath one and is one.

> Where can we find two better hemispheres
> Without sharp North, without declining West?

Or in addressing his Mistress, going to bed, in somewhat unusual terms:

> O my America! my new-found-land,
> My kingdom, safeliest when with one man manned!

Or there are direct geographical references:

> We've added to the world Virginia. and sent
> Two new stars lately to the firmament.

Another poem begins:

> That unripe side of earth, that heavy clime
> That gives us man up now, like Adam's time
> Before he ate . . .

there is Donne's expression of the golden age theme.

Many were the sermons that were preached to speed

the Virginia enterprise, especially before the big venture of
1609 — Robert Gray, William Symonds, Daniel Price,
Crakenthorpe, William Crashaw.[1] John Chamberlain wrote
to his friend Carleton that sermons were becoming as
necessary as masses with Papists : one could not have a
feast without one.[2] Donne, who was interested in Virginia
all along, was given the freedom of the Virginia Company
and Council in 1622.[3] That autumn he preached a sermon
at their feast in Merchant Taylors' hall. Since we cannot
go into the sermons here, perhaps we may take Donne's
sermon as the finest specimen of the class, in which it is
elevated to literature.[4]

As we should expect, he raises the issues presented by
colonisation to a higher plane. He warned those going
against seeking independence or exemption from the laws
of England. 'If those that govern there would establish
such a government as should not depend upon this, or if
those that go thither propose to themselves an exemption
from laws to live at their liberty, this is to . . . divest
allegiance and be under no man.' It is contrary to the
Scriptural command, 'a kingdom you must not have'. His
warning that they were not to expect profit either was
much to the point. They were not to be discouraged,
'though you see not your money [he himself had none
invested in it], though you see not your men, though a
flood, a flood of blood have broken in upon them. . . .
Great creatures lie long in the womb.' 'The plantation
shall not discharge the charges, not defray itself yet, but
yet already, now at first, it shall conduce to great uses. It
shall redeem many a wretch from the laws of death, from
the hands of the executioner. . . .'[5] It shall sweep your
streets and wash your doors from idle persons and the
children of idle persons and employ them.' This was the

---

[1] For the message of these sermons *v.* Perry Miller, 'Religion and Society
in the Early Literature of Virginia', in *Errand into the Wilderness*, C. IV.

[2] *The Letters of John Chamberlain*, ed. N. E. McClure, II. 464.

[3] *Records of the Virginia Company of London*, ed. S. M. Kingsbury, II. 76.

[4] Reprinted in *Ten Sermons by John Donne*, ed. Geoffrey Keynes.

[5] The reprinted text here, p. 52, reads 'laws', not 'jaws'.

obverse side of the argument Bacon put forward in his essay 'Of Plantations', and surely a more humanitarian inflexion.

Donne had something very much to the point to say in the modern discussion about colonialism, on the central issue. The law of nations ordains that every man improve that which he hath: 'the whole world, all mankind must take care that all places be improved as far as may be to the best advantage of mankind in general'. He adjured the governors of the greatest companies to proceed with integrity and justice. Those adventurers who were old would pass out of the world 'with this great comfort that you contributed to the beginning of that commonwealth and of that church, though they live not to see the growth thereof to perfection: Apollo watered, but Paul planted; he that begun this work was the greater man'. He ended with the prayer, 'Look graciously and look powerfully upon this body which thou hast been now some years in building and compacting together, this plantation', to become in the fullness of time a famous commonwealth.

Virginia in its beginnings had a literary flavouring. George Sandys, the translator of Ovid, was a public servant of the colony for some twenty years. Unhappily married, he was able to escape from his wife into travel; he wrote no love-poetry. When Sir Edwin Sandys gained control of the Virginia Company, he was able to provide for his youngest brother by making him Treasurer. Accompanying Sir Francis Wyatt over as Governor, Sandys carried forward his translation of the *Metamorphoses*: 'yet amongst the roaring of the seas, the rustling of the shrouds and clamour of sailors, I translated two books and will, when the sweltering heat of the day confines me to my chamber, give a further assay.' [1] Anyone who knows the heat of tide-water Virginia in summer will sympathise. Drayton wrote to encourage him:

> And (worthy George) by industry and use,
> Let's see what lines Virginia will produce;

[1] R. B. Davis, *George Sandys*, 140.

Go on with Ovid as you have begun
With the first five books; let your numbers run
Glib as the former, so shall it live long
And do much honour to the English tongue:
Entice the Muses thither to repair,
Entreat them gently, train them to that air,
For they from hence may thither hap to fly . . .
If you vouchsafe rescription, stuff your quill
With natural bounties and impart your skill
In the description of the place, that I
May become learned in the soil thereby;
Of noble Wyatt's health, and let me hear,
The Governor; and how our people there
Increase and labour, what supplies are sent
Which I confess shall give me much content . . .

Drayton concedes that he would

like it well to be the first
Whose numbers hence into Virginia flew; [1]

and we may recall that the nineteenth Song of his *Polyolbion* celebrates all the Virginia voyages.   Amid distractions, like leading the first avenging column against the Indians after the Massacre — an event which was celebrated by name in a ballad, in those days when the news was sung in the streets — Sandys found time to complete the remaining eight books before returning home to publish the whole, with a dedication to King Charles I — for which he was made a gentleman of the Privy Chamber.   He seems to have been an efficient servant of the Colony, and, like John Pory,[2] was responsive to the natural beauty of the country. He corresponded with John Tradescant and may therefore be responsible for the latter's Indian collections in the Ashmolean Museum at Oxford.[3]

[1] *Poems of Michael Drayton*, ed. John Buxton, I. 143 foll.
[2] Pory might have written well about the colony.   On his appointment as Secretary in 1618, Chamberlain wrote, 'no question but he will become there a sufficient sober man, seeing there is no wine in all that climate'. *Letters of John Chamberlain*, ed. N. E. McClure, II. 190.   But, alas, we hear that he 'followed the custom of strong potations'.   q. M. C. Tyler, *History of American Literature*, I. 49.
[3] Tradescant was a shareholder in the Virginia Company.   C. C. Stopes, *The Life of Henry Third Earl of Southampton*, 422.

POWHATAN'S CLOAK

Among these the most splendid is Powhatan's ceremonial mantle, made of deerskins decorated with patterns of tiny shells, forming the figure of a man down the spine with an animal on each side, long ears and tail, in an attitude of supplication with outstretched paws. The rest has roundels of thickly encrusted shells disposed in rough symmetry around the edges and filling the spaces. The whole thing has extraordinary vivid life in it : perhaps it had magic properties to bring success in the chase? The Ashmolean tradition is that this was given to Captain Christopher Newport in 1608. There are other objects : a wallet of hide with shell-work decoration, a girdle made of wampum and a necklace, 'variety of chains, made of the teeth of serpents and wild beasts, which the Indians wear', double-ended canoe paddles and bows from Virginia. It is somehow affecting to think of these relics, treasure-trove from those shores, from all the past that has been engaging our attention, fetching up in seventeenth-century Oxford. We may think of them along with other relics from that vanished life, the Indian words like canoe, wampum, tobacco, taken over by the Elizabethans.

There is no more vivid account of that life than Captain Smith's *General History*. There has been some discussion about how much he is to be believed, but far less appreciation of how much he is to be enjoyed. His was not a Puritan inflexion, and so he has met with some disparagement, in particular from Henry Adams. (Who was it who said that vinegar, not red blood, flowed in the veins of the Adamses; and, anyway, enjoyment was not much in their line.) It is true that Smith's was an assertive personality — in that, truly Elizabethan — with himself well in the centre of action and no doubt making himself out to be more important than he was. But what is the point of an autobiographer suppressing himself? It makes for bad autobiography.[1] I am glad that he passes the test of

---

[1] The reference is, of course, to Sheridan :

'You write with ease, to show your breeding,
But easy writing's vile hard reading.'

the strict Miss E. G. R. Taylor, who has a good opinion of him as a geographer;[1] as an historian, where it is possible to test him, he seems pretty reliable. For the rest, he is a writer by nature: the very assertion of personality shows it, against dull dogs; he has an acute sense of others' personalities as well as his own, is racy and humorous, at times funny, at others indignant, but always alive, with a naïve poetry that is endearing. He can turn a good phrase, as with the sainted Pilgrims, 'whose humorous ignorances caused them for more than a year to endure a wonderful deal of misery with an infinite patience'. Or take his delightful description of the mask of Indian ladies. 'Presently they were presented with this antic: thirty young women came naked out of the woods, only covered behind and before with a few green leaves, their bodies all painted, some of one colour, some of another, but all differing. Their leader had a fair pair of buck's horns on her head and an otter's skin at her girdle, a quiver of arrows at her back, a bow and arrows in her hand. The next had in her hand a sword, another a club, another a pot-stick: all horned alike; the rest everyone with their several devices. These fiends with most hellish shouts and cries, rushing from among the trees, cast themselves in a ring about the fire, singing and dancing with most excellent ill variety, oft falling into their infernal passions, and solemnly again to sing and dance; having spent near an hour in this mascarado, as they entered in like manner they departed. Having reaccommodated themselves, they solemnly invited him to their lodgings, where he was no sooner within the house but all these nymphs more tormented him than ever, with crowding, pressing, and hanging about him, most tediously crying, "Love you not me? Love you not me?"'[2]

The Captain seems to have preserved his virtue, which,

---

[1] 'Smith has, by many besides his contemporaries, been ranked far below his worth, for his powers of observation were great, and his main arguments and forecasts have stood the test of time.' E. G. R. Taylor, *Late Tudor and Early Stuart Geography, 1583–1650*, 162.

[2] Smith, I. 140-1.

I should have thought, might have recommended him better to virtuous New England.

Geography was, in a sense, the characteristic science of the Renaissance, as astronomy had been in antiquity. With a New World being discovered, there was not only an immense extension of geographical knowledge, but a comparable impetus to improving its quality and techniques, solving problems hitherto recalcitrant. In the first half of the sixteenth century Italy was the chief centre of map-making, and most of the Atlantic coast of America was first traversed by Italians — Columbus and the Cabots, Vespucci and Verrazano.[1] But a fundamental consequence of the discovery of America was to draw the main trade-routes away from the Mediterranean, greatly to enhance the importance of the North-Western countries and ultimately make their fortune. Geographical knowledge followed: the centre passed to the Netherlands, and this was visibly expressed in the publication of the atlases of Ortelius and Mercator.

England was backward in this art, as in so much else; but now her geographers profited from their contacts with these leaders of thought, while they made use of the information gathered by the English voyagers in constructing their maps — Ortelius, of Anthony Jenkinson for Russia and Persia, Mercator, of Drake for America and the Pacific. Though English map-makers in this field were not yet comparable, they were beginning. Frobisher's and Gilbert's voyages to North America led to a considerable increase of information about the northern areas, which is reflected in the maps of Michael Lok and Thomas Best. A number of John Dee's maps of these regions remain, and illustrate, as everything about him does, his curious mixture of shrewd criticism and crazy credulity. His map of North America, for example, based on Gilbert's explorations, has a proper realisation of the width of the Continent across Canada; but theorist, *fantaisiste*, as he was, he has no compunction

[1] R. V. Tooley, *Maps and Map-Makers*, 19 foll.

in tracing a waterway right across to debouch with the Colorado into Southern California.[1] I may be rather harsh to the Celtic spirit as exemplified in John Dee: all I can say is that I should be sorry for the sailors who proceeded in accordance with his injunctions, and I have the feeling that the practical seamen at Muscovy House knew very well how to take him. Still, he gave a considerable propulsion to geographical thought, and he was early in the field; by the end of the century much more exact and useful contributions were being made to navigation and cosmography by such men as John Davis and Edward Wright.

With the marvellous 1580's, the first colonies and the defeat of the Armada, a specifically English geographical literature begins — at the same moment as the madrigals. We can read it in works that are also works of literature, written by such as Ralegh and Hariot, Hakluyt and Captain Smith, as well as the average contributors to Hakluyt and Purchas.

Hariot appears as the most complete, all-round scientist of that time, with his interest alike in mathematics and astronomy, anthropology and navigation.[2] Here again we find him at the centre of Ralegh's circle, for many years a constant associate and confidential servant.[3] The tone of this circle was unorthodox, sceptical and scientific, intellectually questing. Said Nashe in *Pierce Penniless*, 'I hear say there be mathematicians abroad that will prove men before Adam'. At Ralegh's trial Lord Chief Justice Popham described Hariot's opinions as 'devilish', and Hariot as 'that devil'. The poet Marlowe expressed the spirit of the group somewhat more carefully than the lawyer:

> Our souls whose faculties can comprehend
> The wondrous architecture of the world,
> And measure every wandering planet's course,

---

[1] Reproduced by E. G. R. Taylor, 'John Dee and the Map of North-East Asia', in *Imago Mundi*, XII. 103 foll.

[2] He wrote a book on navigation, the *Arcticon*, which is lost.

[3] After Gunpowder Plot Hariot was imprisoned for having the King's horoscope cast. Cf. S.P. 14/216, no. 122. His intimate membership of the Northumberland-Ralegh circle in the Tower made him suspect.

Still climbing after knowledge infinite,
And always moving as the restless spheres
Will us to wear ourselves and never rest.

Hariot set a model of first-class scientific method with his *Brief and true Report of the new found land of Virginia*. It is the work of a superior mind; no Elizabethan quaintness in this, no fancy, let alone fantasy; all is in due order, based on close observation, accurately brought into correlation with existing categories. It gives an account of the flora and fauna: the commodities of the country with their qualities and uses; methods of agriculture and properties of the soil, plants and fruits and roots; the beasts, fowl and fish; ending with the nature and manners of the people, for Hariot had learned enough of their language to communicate with them regarding their notions and beliefs.

This concise little work, important as it is, is only a fragment of the materials collected by Hariot and John White at Roanoke. White was similarly engaged in mapping the coasts and sounds, and rendering the life of the place in his water-colours of the plants and fishes, the characters and ways of the natives. But many of their maps and papers were lost in the sea after the hurricane that decided the colony to leave, in the hurried transfer of their goods by the sailors to Drake's ships. Others of White's papers left on Roanoke were spoiled by the Indians. But what remains is considerable. Professor Quinn sums up their work: 'between them they compiled the first detailed records to be assembled by Englishmen of the natural relations and resources of any part of North America. The high degree of objectivity and the painstaking accuracy which they brought to their tasks make their work (though much of it has been lost) a landmark in the history of English cartography and the natural sciences, as well as, almost incidentally, in the development of a native school of water-colour painting.'

If only Hariot and White had had the leisure, or perhaps the temperament, to complete their projects — what a wonderful joint work, an American masterpiece, we might have had! But circumstances were distracting: not only were precious papers lost, a war was on, we know how White was employed on subsequent fruitless attempts. Even so, in consequence of their work, 'we know the Indians of the Carolina sounds as well in some respects as we know the contemporaries of the Tudor Englishmen who drew and described them'.[1] Through their work, and the accounts of Lane and Smith, we come as near to understanding these first Indians the English met with as possibly ever again, and with all the freshness and shock of first impact. Moreover, White's cartographic work was 'incomparably the best yet done on any part of North America by any Europeans'. His depiction of Indian figures, through their reproduction in De Bry, became the regular conventional representation of the Indian to the European eye for more than a century.

The impact of America upon natural history in general, and botany in particular, was no less exciting. A wide range of new plants and animals provided continuing stimulus to the scientific curiosity, as well as the fancy, of naturalists in England as elsewhere. And this is reflected in their books. From the New World came the giant sunflower, nasturtium, Michaelmas daisy, lobelia, evening primrose and so on.[2] But by far the most important introductions were tobacco and the potato: these affected history.

In the early years sassafras was much imported, as a remedy for syphilis, one of the first bequests of the New World to the Old, which raged through Europe like a prairie fire. The Indians also used guaiacum, the bitter bark of the wood, for the same purpose. Tobacco was also thought to be of use, since its medicinal properties were considered valuable. 'Herba panacea', 'herba santa', it was called; 'divine tobacco', by Spenser, 'our holy herb nicotian', by William Lilly. Hariot reported that it 'purgeth superfluous phlegm and other gross humours, and openeth all the pores and passages of the body: by which means

---

[1] *The Roanoke Voyages, 1584–1590*, ed. D. B. Quinn, I. 316-17.
[2] W. Blunt, *The Art of Botanical Illustration*, 76.

the use thereof not only preserveth the body from obstructions, but also (if any be, so that they have not been of too long continuance) breaketh them'.[1] Hariot became a heavy smoker : frequent purchases of tobacco appear in his papers ; he died of cancer of the mouth.

The habit of smoking rapidly spread among the courtiers and in the upper class, popularised by Ralegh and those in touch with the colonies. His addiction was another of the counts in James's indictment of him: 'it seems a miracle to me how a custom springing from so vile a ground, and brought in by a father so generally hated, should be welcomed upon so slender a warrant'.[2] It was noted as a piece of arrogance on his part that 'he took a pipe of tobacco before he went to the scaffold'; it is more likely to have been to steady his nerves, or as a last pleasure on earth. Already by 1600, at Essex's trial, the peers were smoking copiously over their deliberation as to the verdict; we see thus early, and in these eminent quarters, the application of the vulgar phrase, to 'put it in your pipe and smoke it'. Even before the end of the Queen's reign, the habit was spreading to the lower orders: Hentzner tells us, 'at bull-baiting, bear-whipping and everywhere else the English are constantly smoking the Nicotian weed, which in America is called tobacco'. All this was good for Virginia : it put the colony on its feet and enabled it to survive.

The potato has had even more effect in history. Dr. Salaman writes, 'the introduction of the potato has proved to be one of the major events in man's recent history, but, at the time, it was a matter of relatively little moment and called forth no immediate public comment'.[3] Its first mention in print by this name occurs in 1596 in Gerard's Catalogue of the plants growing in his garden at Holborn. (He also had the oversight of Lord Burghley's garden in the Strand.) In his bulky *Herbal* next year he gave the potato a chapter to itself. The famous Flemish botanist

[1] Hakluyt, VI. 177.
[2] C. M. MacInnes, *The Early English Tobacco Trade*, 32.
[3] R. N. Salaman, *The History and Social Influence of the Potato*, 142.

l'Écluse, friend of Philip Sidney, kept in touch with English voyagers from whom he received specimens of American plants and he described the potato accurately.[1] It seems that Gerard got muddled between the potato and the sweet potato, and gave an inexact description; but he was not a scientist, merely a practical gardener who grew things. He says that since l'Ecluse's description, 'I have received roots hereof from Virginia, which grow and prosper in my garden as in their own native country'.[2] Apparently Hariot's 'openauks', 'growing many together one by another in ropes, as though they were fastened with a string', are not our potatoes, but sweet potatoes.[3] However, Gerard may have got hold of the real thing through ships coming back from the West Indies. To the Elizabethans the innocuous potato was not only sustaining, but stimulating to lust. We remember that when Falstaff, with the worst intentions, gets Mistress Ford and Mistress Page to come in to him, he calls on the sky to rain potatoes. Amid so much that is earthy, not to say murky, about this vegetable, Dr. Salaman thinks it quite probable that Ralegh did introduce the growing of potatoes into Ireland — one more of the many things he has to answer for. This certainly had remote and far-reaching consequences, setting in motion the cycle that ultimately led to the mass-migration of the Irish, during and after the Famine, to America.

It was from Ireland, too, not long after, that John White's drawings of American life turned up, having long disappeared from view.[4] In the end, it is through such things as these, Powhatan's mantle, a wampum girdle or a shell-necklace, the things the Elizabethans held in their hands and brought home, the flotsam and jetsam of time, that we are most directly in touch with that early American life. And perhaps through those fragments of memory that have entered into folklore, the unforgotten impression that Pocahontas made on the English people in her day — still

---

[1] John Buxton, *Sir Philip Sidney and the English Renaissance*, 142.
[2] q. Salaman, 81.   [3] Hakluyt, VI. 177.
[4] Lawrence Binyon, *English Water-Colours*, 2.

alive in the famous inn-sign, 'La Belle Sauvage'.[1] I write
these words not far from a village in Cornwall still called
after her, Indian Queens.   For it is what enters into the
unconscious life of the mind and is carried on in folklore
that expresses the truest and most intimate nature of a people.
I remember being most moved by this thought at a perform-
ance of Thornton Wilder's *Our Town* in the haggard and
heroic England of war-time.   There, to console and fortify,
were the recognisable habits and ruts trodden through the
centuries, the ways of thought, the very turns of phrase, the
same hymns sung and prayers used in America as in England.
These things and those fragments that remain of shared experience are the best evidence of the strength of common
memories, common affections and common ancestry.

[1] Her entering a tavern surprised people and may be responsible for her
elevation to inn-signs as patroness. Cf. Ben Jonson, *The Staple of News* :

> Pocahontas, as the historian calls her,
> And great King's daughter of Virginia,
> Hath been in womb of tavern.

INDEX

217

Date Due

MAY 6 '60			
SEP 29 '62			
NOV 1 2 '65			
OCT 2 1 1969			
	PRINTED	IN U. S. A.	